Vegeterranean

Vegeterranean

ITALIAN VEGETARIAN COOKING

INSIDE THE KITCHEN OF THE COUNTRY HOUSE MONTALI

Malu Simões da Cunha & Alberto Musacchio

Written with Grace Choi ❖ Photographs by David Piening

EARTH AWARE
EDITIONS

San Rafael, California

EARTH AWARE
E D I T I O N S

PO Box 3088
San Rafael, CA 94912
www.earthawareeditions.com

First published in the United States in 2012 by Earth Aware Editions.
Copyright © 2008 Malu Simões and Alberto Musacchio
Originally published by Simon & Schuster UK Ltd

Library of Congress Cataloging-in-Publication Data available.
ISBN: 978-1-60887-079-0

🌲 REPLANTED PAPER

Insight Editions, in association with Roots of Peace, will plant two trees
for each tree used in the manufacturing of this book. Roots of Peace is an
ROOTS of PEACE   internationally renowned humanitarian organization dedicated to eradicating
land mines worldwide and converting war-torn lands into productive farms and wildlife
habitats. Together, we will plant two million fruit and nut trees in Afghanistan and provide
farmers there with the skills and support necessary for sustainable land use.

Manufactured in China by Insight Editions

10 9 8 7 6 5 4 3 2 1

TABLE OF CONTENTS

ACKNOWLEDGMENTS

It has been about ten years since people asked us to write a cookbook. This, of course, sounds like an honor, but it becomes one of those things that you should do and never end up doing: a kind of memento of something you keep forgetting or postponing. Surely nothing to do with the typical Italian attitude of being precise and punctual and never postponing things! My major problem indeed was, and still is, language.

To write any book, even one on cooking, requires a perfect mastery of the language in which you write. I do speak a small number of languages apart from Italian, but none good enough to allow me to write a book—and definitely not English. A cookbook, moreover, uses very technical terminology that I was not really sure I was willing to study. When we finally decided to embark on this project, language as a concept became a big part of the game. The English reader's edition of this book, in fact, has been an amusing international mixture of British ounces and liquid ounces, checked with grams and kilos, then translated into American cups and finally rechecked to match medieval Italian culinary traditions! A new kind of language indeed.

We also extensively discussed the different accent and *parfume* that the writing should have. "Should we give it an English accent or an American one?" "Should we say courgette or zucchini?" "Bruschetta or bruscetta?" "Aubergine or eggplants?" These have often been the strange conversations we had among a Korean-American writer, a Brazilian chef, an Italian entrepreneur, a Slovakian sous-chef, and an English journalist friend who gave us hints on the "pronunciation" of the book! The major problem that even Grace could not solve, neither using her American accent nor even trying a good British version, was regarding my own writing. We all thought it would be ridiculous to "hear" an Italian speaking English. Finally we decided to let my writing stand and just apologize for the mistakes.

We also did some other food language research. Proposing mostly Italian food (even with a wider international touch) to English and American people may not be easy if you really want the reader to be able to reproduce your recipes. We decided to keep most of the Italian regional recipes as close to the old original ones as possible. Since Italian food has become so widely popular abroad, people have ended up seeing Italian pizzas being made with pineapple and ham. No Italian would ever eat a pizza with pineapple and ham! We really wanted to stick to the original source of the culinary tradition.

But the next language question was "How can I teach an American to cook something with Castelmagno cheese?" when we know Castelmagno is one of the rarest and most expensive cheeses in our country. We decided to keep the original recipes with all the original ingredients, but also give possible variations for any uncommon ingredients. The recipe will say Castelmagno, but it will also suggest what other kind of cheese might take its place. We gave quick hints for vegans as well. These were just the first stages of the main work.

To start from the beginning, in January 2005, my wife, Malu, and I were reading Grace Choi's résumé, and found her application very interesting. Grace is a young American-Korean chef who has studied at the French Culinary Institute of New York and later trained in one of the best restaurants in all the U.S. When we began reading her application to come and work at Montali as an apprentice, we both noticed her magna cum laude BA from the University of Notre Dame. She had studied a lot in her life. But what grabbed our attention even more was a sentence in her résumé in which she stated how in love she was with food writing.

This was exactly who we were looking for, someone who could be a good chef, but was also capable of

writing about food. Because we were still thinking about how to face the language problem of a book, this might be the answer to our problem. After we emailed, Grace decided to come and work here. The first few months were dedicated to her learning our recipes and working hard in the kitchen. Later she worked more and more on writing and typing the recipes and the stories of this book. Her excellent knowledge of the language, her great will power, and her natural sense of humor definitely helped a lot in drafting the book.

That is how the book started to come to life . . . with teamwork that lasted most of the summer of 2005. My wife was in charge of the recipes, of course. To keep the kitchen perfectly organized became quite a hard job, as the photography required an enormous effort—just when we needed to produce the food for the clients. Malu ran like never before in her life. Grace typed everything down and wrote some of the biographical stories. I wrote some others.

Our faithful sous-chef, Jan Bodnar, took charge of the kitchen when everyone was getting angry with the photography and plate setting. He has been with us

for five long years, the only one who never gave up, never got sick, never left the job, and never was less than perfect: a true professional in the kitchen. Daniel Sharp helped Janko and all of us in the kitchen with his incomparable sense of humor, cheering everyone up. David Piening used his excellent skill in giving life with his camera to all those splendid recipes. It is because of his expertise that the food seems to pop out of these colorful pages. Bonaria, Alena, Marketa, Sylvia, Giannina, and Giuliana helped to run the hotel, even when everyone else was busy with sauces and cameras. A deep thanks to all those splendid guys for having worked so hard.

And a deep thanks to all the wonderful clients who have always believed in the Country House Montali, who have returned and supported such a difficult business, and have also suggested this wonderful book. Special thanks to ATAL for supplying the elegant china that made these images possible and to my brother, Gianni, for the spectacular art that served as the backdrop for many of the shots.

—Alberto Musacchio

When I arrived at the Country House Montali on March 26, 2005, the stillness of the Umbrian countryside and the winding dirt roads leading to the hotel were the first to take my notice. I stood in the center of the twenty-five-acre property with a crystal-clear view of Lake Trasimeno, comparing my new surroundings with my old ones. Perfectly aligned olive trees replaced the skyscrapers of Manhattan; verdant greens spanned the mountain plateau in the same manner that yellow taxicabs flood Times Square. The hushed tranquillity was more overwhelming than the sounds of ambulances, trucks, and blaring horns that I had grown quite accustomed to. Sharp senses returned to my nose as I picked up the scent of fresh-cut grass with a flutter of rosemary and mint from the herb garden.

While the serenity of the hotel and its surroundings offers a haven to both local and international guests, the gourmet vegetarian cuisine is what leaves the greatest impression. After the kitchen has spent twenty-five years refining recipes and menu combinations in compliance with seasonal fruits and vegetables, the dishes exude not only incredible flavors and textures, but also an inimitability that arrives with the rare combination of rustic Italian cooking techniques and the exclusive use of vegetarian products.

From the beginning of my seven-month journey with Alberto Musacchio, Malu Simões, and the kitchen and waiting staff, I knew that Montali was not simply a hotel that provided rooms and hot meals. It was the home of countless stories and memories, a gathering of remarkable individuals pursuing incredible dreams, a kitchen that held years of laughter, wine, dancing, spices, and music. At the end of every day, each dish that we contributed to as a family exuded passions and new histories. In the same light, the Montali cookbook could not be a simple index of recipes and techniques. As no guest leaves Montali without experiencing something even more of the beauty of the Italian countryside and the fulfillment of a delicious four-course dinner, no reader should finish this book without having gotten to know Alberto, Malu, and the spirit of the kitchen staff.

— Grace Choi

THE COUNTRY HOUSE MONTALI

The reason why the Country House Montali has a relatively good culinary reputation is that, for a long time, it has produced an unusual gourmet vegetarian cuisine. From a fine-dining point of view, vegetarianism has never really fully developed, probably due to the difficulties of using a relatively small number of ingredients and also avoiding some particularly succulent ones, like most of the animal fats.

Starting with a restaurant in Perugia, we ended in the countryside of Umbria, where we run our resort. For more than two decades, in fact, we have been involved in trying to give vegetarian food a better interpretation and a more professional image. A bit of pride is present, I admit, as the challenge has been quite tough at times.

When they start any kind of business in India, they always begin by singing the praises of Lord Ganesha, the elephant-headed god, as he is the tutor, lord of goodwill, and helper of "starting things." He is always the first one to be worshipped. The little culinary success and gratifications we have had would never have been possible without the help of the person who first opened the fine-dining horizon to us: our first Japanese chef Akira Shishido. As he has been the embodiment of Lord Ganesha to us, we would like to start this book by referring to him.

At this time, twenty-five years ago, we were running a successful pub in the lovely city of Perugia. The town is a place crowded with young foreign students, flocking to study the Italian language in the biggest university for foreigners in the country. This pub was just an attempt to make some money and have as much fun as possible, with lots of sleepless nights and enjoying "la dolce vita" as young entrepreneurial bohemians. I was nineteen.

With no intention of producing any gourmet cuisine, we made good vegetarian food to feed the hoards of hungry young clients. Among the different ethnic groups who were populating our international pub

were quite a large number of Japanese. Surely one of the most educated groups, Japanese people have always been in love with elegant Italian cars, clothes, and, in general, any special fashion and architectural designer trend. As pub customers, they were very respectful, well educated, and most importantly, for the host, drinkers.

I remember how they introduced me, for the first time, to a trick, surely of imperial origin, that allowed them to drink more alcohol than any strong and healthy human being should have been capable of! They were not drinking glasses of wine or a few light beers but quantities of whisky. The trick that they were using consisted of literally swallowing a tablespoon of pure olive oil before starting a drinking night. The big spoon of oil lined the gastric membrane, allowing the gentlemen to consume a much larger quantity of alcohol. By the end of the evening, the alcohol was producing its consequences anyway . . . and they were generally devastating! I imagine the Emperor and his concubines originally used some horrible fish oil, but the modern Japanese "expat" had found the noble olive juice more tasty and established it as their "modern time muse."

Whisky, certainly a big source of income for our business, was always available, so that on the arrival of the Japanese, we had a large stock of scotch and spoonfuls of olive oil ready in the kitchen. In all, it was a good time because they weren't creating problems. Not the Japanese. I would imagine that anyone who started a fight after a drinking session with his Emperor would have been asked to commit hara-kiri—after first being told to clean up the mess in the restaurant!

Nevertheless we started to hide, if not the whisky then the olive oil, when one day dear Yasugi, an old client of ours, staggering with an excess of alcohol, decided to grab the long stove pipe (lit up) that ran all around the restaurant. The faces of the unfortunate customers who saw and heard thirty-nine feet of very hot, and very dirty, stove pipe falling, with the fire still lit and smoke filling up the whole restaurant, remained in our memories for a long time. From then on, we made absolutely sure that no hara-kiri knives were present (and we started to hide the olive oil as well).

And there, in the middle of this crowd of bohemian Japanese, maybe the epitome of a very sophisticated class of intellectual artists, stood the good Akira. A chef by birth, he was one of the few persons born under the sign of cooking and surely appointed to the celebrity of international fine dining. I can say now, twenty-five years later, that only some people choose the job of a chef, because it is very hard. Few keep loving the job. Very few are predestined to it. There are just some who have a karmic affinity to the kitchen itself. Akira was one.

He was the kind of chef for whom, the more he was under pressure, the more he loved to work. Working satisfaction for Akira was a busy night in which, after much work and a therefore empty kitchen, a big crowd of people would pop up from some late night theater in large numbers, all very hungry. All of us were like, "Oh shit!" Akira, on the other hand, loved to feed people without anything in the kitchen except his creativity. To work hard was not enough for him. What Akira was longing for was . . . challenge.

That was the reason that he left a nice job in a five-star restaurant to come and work for us in a less than ordinary place. He thought vegetarian food would be a big challenge because it is one of the most difficult cuisines in the world. He simply took the challenge. The night in which we offered him a job in our place, of course, we took out the olive oil spoon and a big stock of whisky to try to convince him. But he was much too clever, even under the influence of alcohol, and managed to start giving out rules to everybody in the restaurant right away, even though he had just accepted the job. Later on, we discovered that the process of hiring a great chef was not easy at all. Chefs are renowned for moodiness and temperamental attitudes . . . and Akira was a great chef!

Even for us proprietors, life became much harder. Although the big success that our place had (mostly due to having been in the right place at the right time with the right product) continued, our only interests until that moment had been partying without any particular professionality. Cooking and serving drinks were just a means to get the lifestyle.

All of a sudden things changed. I still remember the many times in which I was reproached for some small detail in serving Akira's food. One time he even refused to heat some rice because I spent a bit of time talking with a client who had asked me a question, and consequently the rice lost its temperature. "You go and heat it yourself" was his answer—and I was supposed to be the boss!!! But then came the satisfac-

tion of doing something with a lot of attention and care. More and more, we started to love what we were doing. On top of everything, Akira was joining the two best culinary and serving traditions in the world: the Japanese, with its concept of beauty and great presentation, and the Italian, with its culinary pride and flamboyance.

I do not know, in the twenty-five following years, having personally trained dozens of young men and women to cook and wait tables, how many times I have remembered my first guru in this wonderful world of fine dining, and his teachings on how to make a client feel at home and welcome in a place. And I have always remembered them with the greatest pleasure and respect.

I have realized that there is a last karmic stage that allows a cook, even from an excellent cooking school, to become a real chef. Few are, in fact, chefs who will not always repeat the same few recipes they know but will keep exploring, with willingness and pleasure, the secret world of hidden flavors. Very few will be chefs who will enjoy feeding a crowd, late at night, with an empty kitchen. But that is how a chef has to be.

This chapter is an homage to Akira Shishido, who literally kicked us in the direction of gourmet cuisine. Unfortunately, I have lost track of him, but I am sure success has smiled on him—it would be impossible for it to be any different.

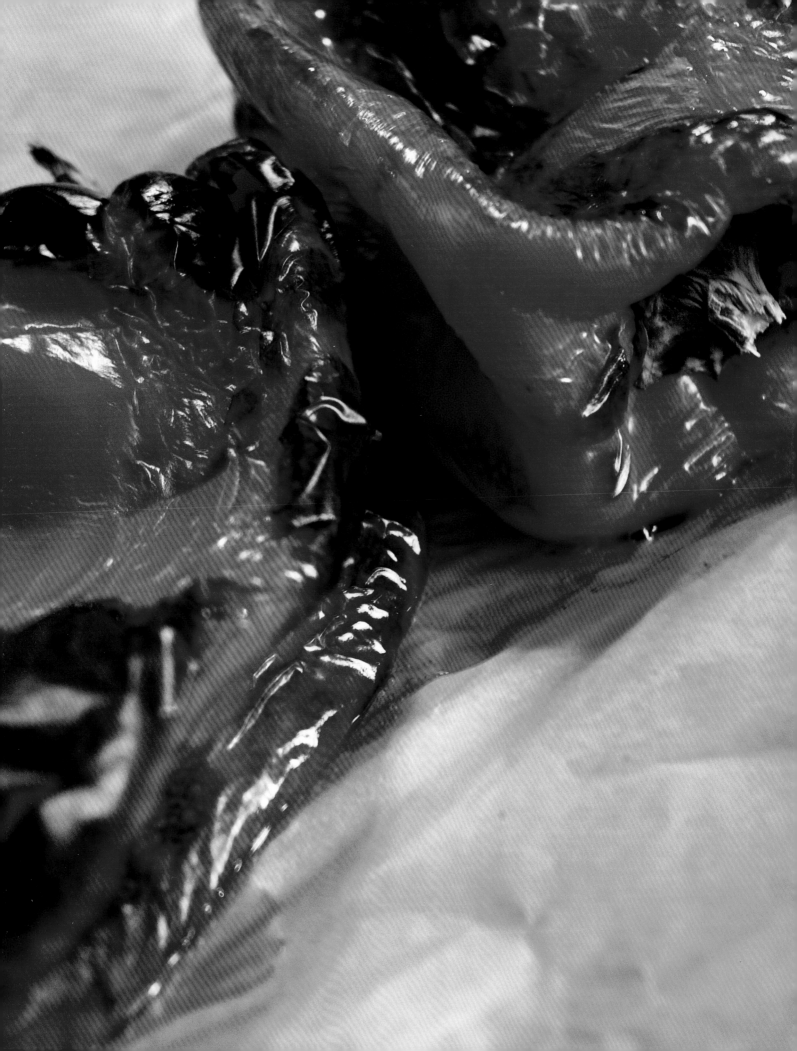

Ingredienti & Tecniche

INGREDIENTS & TECHNIQUES

A FEW THINGS TO KEEP IN MIND WHEN READING THIS BOOK

- This book has been divided into four courses in the likeness of a typical Country House Montali dinner. First are the Antipasti (starters), then the Primi (first courses), followed by the Secondi (second courses), and finally the Dolci (desserts).

- Wine has been paired with a number of recipes, specifically the Primi as is the Italian tradition.

- Vegan and gluten-free recipes are available for some recipes.

- Sauces and creams are found in the Basics section. While they are referred to within this book, they are also excellent with an array of other dishes, as so desired.

- Ingredients have been listed in the order in which they are used.

- Recipes are categorized by level of difficulty:

  E = Easy   M = Medium   D = Difficult

INGREDIENTS

Olive Oil

Extra virgin olive oil, the cold-pressed result of the first pressing of olives. At 1 percent acid, it is the highest quality of olive oil and the only variety that should be used.

Heavy Cream

Also known as whipping cream.

Milk

Always whole milk.

Butter

Always unsalted.

Cornstarch

Also known as cornflour. Not to be confused with cornmeal or polenta. Commonly used as a thickener.

Vanilla

Generally in the form of vanilla extract, unless the recipe specifies vanilla beans.

Italian '00' Flour

Used for light and airy baking. Can be replaced with all-purpose flour, if necessary.

Manitoba Flour

Unbleached, high gluten flour. Develops a high quantity of gluten during the kneading and cooking process, resulting in a chewy bread. Can be substituted with bread flour.

Grano Duro Flour

A fine semolina flour, otherwise known as durum flour or durum wheat flour.

Semolina Flour

A coarser durum wheat flour used in desserts, soups, and pastas, such as Gnocchi alla Romana.

Yeast

If the fresh variety is impossible to find, replace with a good-quality dry yeast, not fast-rising instant.

Sugar

Granulated sugar.

Confectioners' Sugar

Also known as powdered sugar.

Mosto Cotto or Saba

Grape juice reduction, also known to be the historical basis of balsamic vinegar. This syrup can be substituted with maple syrup if difficult to find. During the off-season, Malu makes her own batch out of freshly pressed grape juice. To make at home, simmer 4 cups of grape juice over low heat until it is reduced to one-tenth of the original quantity. Cool completely and keep in an airtight container for up to 1 year.

Arugula

A bitter green salad leaf, also known as rocket.

Mushrooms

Porcini, cremini, oyster, or button mushrooms. If using dry porcini, rinse them in hot water until soft.

Pumpkin

Kabocha squash or sugar pumpkin variety in the U.S.

Radicchio

A purple-colored lettuce, characteristically bitter. Great in salads as well as grilled, sautéed, or baked.

Tahini

A thick sesame seed paste originating in the Middle East.

CHEESES

Charles de Gaulle on France: "How can one rule a country that produces more than 300 varieties of cheeses?" Italy has more than 600! That's probably why Italians are so eclectically independent.

Castelmagno

A cow's milk cheese from its namesake in Piedmont, where it is famously produced thousands of feet above sea level. Aged from 2 to 6 months in natural caves. The younger variety is very crumbly in texture and delicate in flavor. The aged version is sharper and spicier in taste. Legend says that, due to the cold, the cheese is fermented under warm cow dung, thankfully with some straw in between!

Fontina

A mild cow's milk cheese produced in the Alps. The cows for this particular cheese graze on the highlands of northern Italy and the result is a strong and distinctive flavor. Used much in northern dishes like fonduta and risotto, and complements fruit and honey for a dessert.

Formaggio di Fossa

A distinct sheep's milk cheese from the Appenine of Marche region. Sometimes blended with cow's milk and goat's milk, it is left to age in underground caves due to the controlled humidity. The cheeses are kept in white cloth bags from 3 to 6 months while they lose water and fat. This fermentation process is what yields the particular flavor. Perfect by itself, alongside a Secondi, or with fruit and honey.

Mascarpone

A soft creamy cow's milk cheese and a must for the perfect Tiramisu.

Montasio

A cow's milk cheese (mild or aged varieties) commonly found in the Veneto region of northeast Italy. The younger variety is milder and slightly acidic, while the more aged types can be grated on top of pasta or served in wedges to complement the smokiness of grilled food.

Mozzarella

Most commonly made from cow's milk, produced in the southern regions of Campania, Puglia, and Lazio. This fresh, light cheese should be consumed within 3 days of buying. The buffalo variety comes from buffalo's milk and has a more distinct flavor and is very creamy. Delicious melted on top of pasta.

Parmigiano Reggiano

The "king of cheeses," this cow's milk cheese is famously produced in the city of Parma, where it is aged for 24 months. The strong flavor is perfect for final touches, grated on top of pasta and mixed in at the last minute in several dishes. To produce a 123-pound whole Parmigiano requires 700 quarts of milk!

Grana Padano Parmesan

Aged 12 months and milder than Parmigiano Reggiano. Its versatility allows it to be used in several dishes.

Pecorino di Pienza

One of the best pecorino cheeses from the small medieval town called Pienza, this sheep's milk cheese is known in Italy for its milder, soft flavor.

Pecorino Romano

A flaky, aged, salty sheep's cheese, used in pesto and sauces and grated on top of salads and pasta.

Robiola

A fresh creamy cheese made from the milk of cows, sheep, or goats, well known for its particular aroma and flavor. Wonderful spread on top of toasted bread or on a fruit and cheese platter.

Scamorza

A low-moisture, firm, dried mozzarella, also available in a smoked variety. Delicious when melted on top of your favorite foods.

Taleggio

A sweet, lightly acidic cheese from cow's milk originally from Val Taleggio in Lombardia, northern Italy. The delicate aroma resembles that of the truffle. Delicious as an accompaniment to fruit or as a base to a sauce. Buy fresh and consume within 6 days. This is one of the few cheeses that freezes well.

TECHNIQUES

Blackening Bell Peppers

Place a bell pepper on a baking sheet and cook at 350°F for 40 minutes or until the pepper has blackened. Remove from the oven, place the pepper in a plastic bag, seal, and leave for at least 30 minutes or until cooled. Remove from the bag and peel. Cut off the stem, open, and cut into desired pieces.

Boiling and Peeling Potatoes

Place scrubbed potatoes in a pot and cover with lightly salted cool water. Bring to a boil and cook until tender. Remove the potatoes with a slotted spoon one at a time. Pierce with a fork and hold with one hand while peeling with a knife in the other.

Deep-Frying

When deep-frying, pour enough vegetable oil into a heavy-bottomed pot or large pan to submerge whatever you intend to fry. Depending on the dish, there are two ways to test the proper heat of oil for deep-frying. When cooking vegetables like eggplant or dough-based dishes like Calzoni, place a small piece of bread in the hot oil, allowing the bread to sizzle. When the bread becomes still and unmoving, the oil is ready. For batter-based deep-frying, drop a small amount of batter into the hot oil. If the batter drops to the bottom and immediately rises to the top, the oil is hot enough. If the batter lingers at the bottom for even a second, the oil is not ready. When deep-frying, always place the food in the oil at a close distance to avoid splattering.

If you notice that, in either test, the bread or batter browns very quickly, turn down the heat or remove the pot to cool down the oil.

Flambéing

Toward the end of sautéing, remove the pan from the high heat but leave the flame on. Pour a fine-quality liquor like cognac or brandy into the pan and place back on the heat, holding the pan at a tilt so that the flame from the stove can ignite the alcohol. Be sure to stand back because the flames will rise rapidly and then die down after a few seconds.

Ice Bath

In order to abruptly stop the cooking of food, or rapidly cool down stocks and sauces, many recipes will call for an ice bath. Fill a large bowl with cold water and cubes of ice. For vegetables like tomatoes and asparagus, remove from the cooking water with a slotted spoon and cool completely for up to a minute in the cold water. For stocks, sauces, or creams, pour the liquid into a bowl and set over the ice bath so that the cold water surrounds the base of the bowl. Stir continuously until cool.

Peeling Tomatoes

Set a pot of water (large enough to submerge the number of tomatoes that need to be peeled) on the stove and bring to a boil. Meanwhile, make a light X incision on the skin at the bottom of each tomato. Prepare an ice bath. Place the tomatoes in the boiling water and let them cook for up to 20 seconds, depending on the size and ripeness of the tomato. (Smaller or riper tomatoes will require less time.) Remove with a slotted spoon and place in the cold water. When the tomatoes have cooled, peel, starting from the X incision where the skin will peel nicely.

Rehydrating Raisins or Dried Mushrooms

When using raisins or dried mushrooms, recipes will usually call for soaking them in a particular liquid (often water or alcohol for dry fruits) to make them moist. Place the dried items in a small saucepan and barely cover with whichever liquid is called for. Gently reheat over a low heat for 5 minutes. Drain completely and set aside for use.

Splitting a Vanilla Bean

Run the tip of a small knife along the length of a vanilla bean to halve. Separate each half and press the blade of the knife against the cut side of the vanilla bean. In one motion, scrape the flesh from the inside and reserve. Repeat with the other half. Use both the pod and scraped flesh to flavor.

Nozioni Prime

BASICS

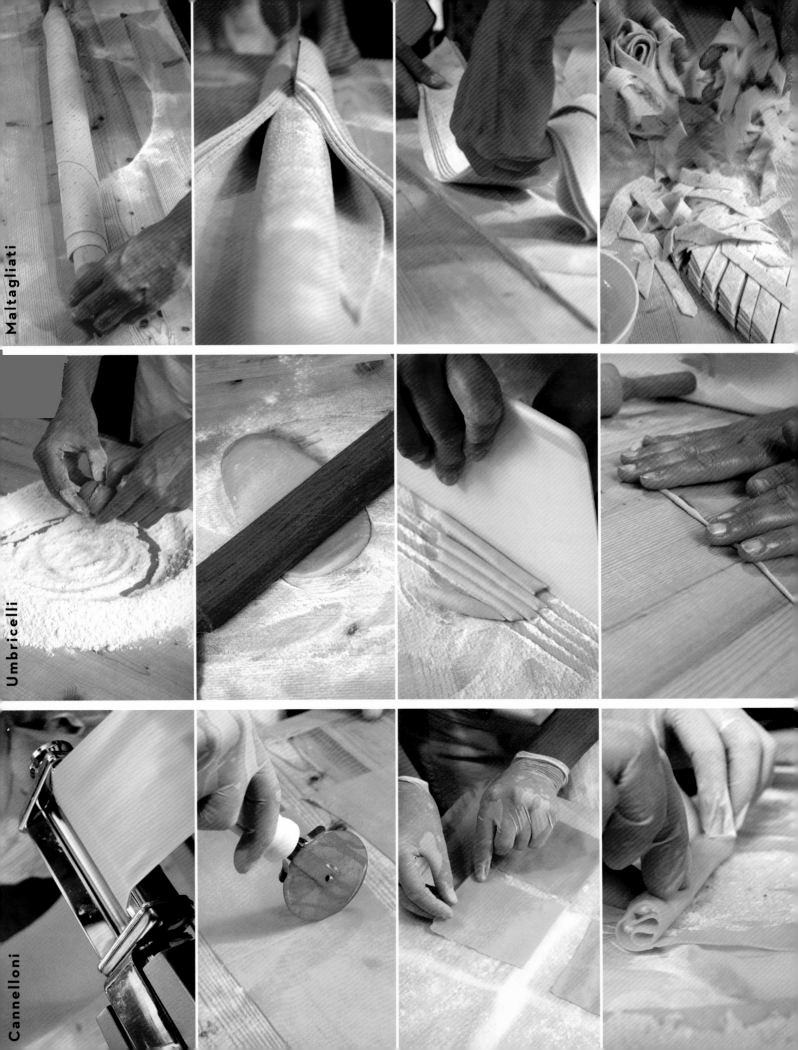

Maltagliati

Umbricelli

Cannelloni

Coxinhas

Bread

Delizia
al Limone

Balsamic Reduction Sauce
1 quantity

1 cup balsamic vinegar

½ cup red wine

½ cup port wine

4 black peppercorns

2 small shallots

1 bay leaf

2-inch strip of orange peel

———

Combine all the sauce ingredients in a small pot. Cook for 30 minutes over low heat until the balsamic vinegar is like molasses. Pass through a sieve and discard the solids. Pour into a squeeze bottle and keep in the refrigerator for up to 1 month. Reheat by running warm water over the bottle or placing the bottle in a warm water bath for 5 minutes.

Basic Béchamel
1 quantity

1 cup milk

1 tablespoon butter

1 tablespoon all-purpose flour

Salt, pepper, and nutmeg to taste

———

Heat the milk in a small saucepan until it is just warm. In the meantime, melt the butter in a small saucepan over medium heat. Add the flour to the melted butter and stir to combine with a whisk. When the roux is golden brown, add all the milk, whisking constantly so that it remains smooth. Season with salt, pepper, and nutmeg. Pour into a separate container and cover with plastic wrap, making sure that the film touches the surface of the cream so that the surface does not develop a skin. Set aside until needed.

Caper Parsley Sauce
1 quantity

2 tablespoons capers

3 tablespoons coarsely chopped parsley

Extra virgin olive oil to cover

———

Rinse the capers. Chop with the parsley and combine with the olive oil. Set aside until needed.

Cinnamon Sugar
1 quantity

¼ cup confectioners' sugar

1 tablespoon ground cinnamon

———

Combine the sugar and cinnamon together in a bowl, then pass through a sieve. Keep in a cool, dry place until needed.

Choux Pastry

1 quantity

1¼ cups water

5 tablespoons butter, cut into cubes

Pinch of salt

1¼ cups Manitoba flour (see page 16)

3 eggs

———

Heat the water, butter, and salt in a pot over medium heat, melting the butter completely. As soon as the liquid comes to a boil, remove from the heat. Add the flour all at once and whisk well until combined. Return to the heat and continue to whisk for an additional 30 seconds, or until the dough pulls away from the sides and bottom of the pot. Remove from the heat and cool slightly. Mix in the eggs one at a time with a wooden spoon, incorporating completely after each addition. After mixing in the third egg, run a line through the center of the dough. If the surrounding dough gradually fills in the line, the dough is ready.

Preheat the oven to 350°F. Transfer into a piping bag with a ½-inch tip and pipe out ½ tablespoon mounds onto a baking sheet or a baking sheet lined with a silicone mat. Lightly brush the top of each pastry with water and bake for 20 minutes. Cool completely.

Caramel Lace

1 quantity

¾ cup sugar

———

Line a baking sheet with parchment paper and spray with oil. Place the sugar in a heavy-bottomed saucepan and heat slowly so it begins to melt. When an even golden brown, remove from the heat and let stand to thicken slightly. Test the thickness by dipping a spoon into the caramel and waving the sugar back and forth over the paper. If the sugar comes out in long, fine threads that do not break easily, it is ready. Tilt the pan close to the baking sheet and, with the spoon, run crisscrossing threads of caramel repeatedly over the entire parchment paper. Freeze for half an hour, then break into rough squares to beautifully decorate a dessert.

Chocolate Sauce

1 quantity

7 ounces bittersweet chocolate, grated

⅔ cup heavy cream

———

Melt the chocolate with the cream in a double boiler, mixing well. When smooth, remove from the heat and cool to room temperature. Pour into a squeeze bottle and refrigerate for up to 1 week. To reheat, place the bottle in a bowl filled with hot water. This sauce may be drizzled over any number of desserts.

Four Cheese Sauce
1 quantity

3 ounces Taleggio (see page 20)
1½ ounces Emmenthal
1½ ounces Provolone
1½ ounces Pecorino di Pienza or other pecorino cheese
⅔ cup milk
2 tablespoons half-and-half
1 tablespoon butter

———

Grate all the cheeses and combine with the remaining ingredients in a double boiler. Melt over simmering water, gently mixing continuously with a wooden spoon. When the sauce is creamy, remove from the heat and keep covered until serving.

Ganache
1 quantity

14 ounces 70% bittersweet chocolate
1½ tablespoons water
2 tablespoons sugar
½ cup heavy cream

———

Melt the chocolate in a double boiler. In a small pan, heat the water and sugar together until the sugar dissolves. Put in a bowl. Heat the cream to a boil and immediately pour into the syrup, whisking continuously. Add the melted chocolate to the mixture of syrup and cream and whisk quickly to incorporate well. The mixture will be bubbly. Let it rest for a few minutes until it is completely smooth and bubble-free (test by coating the back of a spoon for a shiny and smooth texture).

To glaze a cake, pour the ganache evenly over the cake, covering the surface. With a spatula, spread over the top and sides and refrigerate for 2 minutes to set. Slice and serve.

Ghee
1 quantity

Ghee is essentially clarified butter. Heat 1 cup butter in a large saucepan and simmer over low heat. Skim off the milk solids as they come to the top until the butter is completely transparent and no more solids are present. Cool completely and refrigerate for up to 2 weeks.

Herb Yogurt Sauce

1 quantity

⅔ cup heavy cream

⅔ cup plain yogurt

1 small garlic clove, crushed through a press

1 tablespoon finely chopped mixed herbs (chives, thyme, rosemary, and basil)

3 tablespoons extra virgin olive oil

Salt and black pepper to taste

2 teaspoons lemon juice

_____

Lightly whip the cream and mix in the remaining ingredients. Refrigerate until needed.

Lemon Strings

1 quantity

2 lemons

1 cup plus 2 tablespoons water

1 cup sugar, plus 1 tablespoon

_____

Remove the peel from each lemon in long pieces using a vegetable peeler. Set aside the fruit for another use. Cut the peels lengthwise into thin strips (julienne) with a sharp knife. In a saucepan, boil the water with the 1 cup sugar until it melts. Set ¼ cup of this syrup aside. Bring half of the remaining syrup to a boil with the lemon strips for 30 seconds. Drain the strips in a sieve and repeat the procedure with the other half of the syrup (this process removes the bitterness). Drain the lemon strips and return to the pot with the ¼ cup syrup. Add the remaining 1 tablespoon of sugar. Bring to a boil, then reduce to a simmer and cook for 2 minutes. Remove the lemon strips from the liquid and set aside to cool until needed.

Mayonnaise

1 quantity

1 egg yolk

1 teaspoon Dijon mustard

⅔ cup vegetable oil

1 tablespoon lemon juice

Salt and pepper to taste

_____

Mix the egg yolk and mustard together and add the oil in a slow, steady stream, whisking continuously. Add the remaining ingredients and set aside.

Olive Sauce

1 quantity

1 tablespoon chopped black olives

3 tablespoons olive oil

Salt to taste

½ garlic clove, smashed

Drop of Tabasco

_____

Combine all the ingredients together and set aside until needed.

Orange Sauce

1 quantity

2 navel oranges

1 tablespoon cornstarch

3 tablespoons white wine

1 teaspoon lemon juice

1½ tablespoons butter, at room temperature

Salt and white pepper to taste

_____

Squeeze the oranges to get approximately 1 cup of juice. In a small saucepan, combine the orange juice, cornstarch, white wine, and lemon juice and cook over medium heat until thickened, approximately 3 minutes. Remove from the heat and add the butter in teaspoon increments, continuously stirring until the sauce is smooth and creamy. Season to taste and keep warm.

Paneer

1 quantity

4 cups milk

3 tablespoons lemon juice

2 teaspoons salt

_____

In a heavy-bottomed pot, heat the milk while stirring occasionally. As soon as the milk comes to a boil, add the lemon juice and stir gently to curdle the milk. Remove from the heat when the mixture has separated into liquid and solids, and the liquid appears clear. (If the liquid remains cloudy, add a little more lemon juice.)

Line a colander with a large piece of cheesecloth and pour the warm mixture into it. Draw up the sides of the cloth to close, press gently to squeeze out the liquid, and completely immerse in a bowl of water for 10 seconds. Take out, wring well, and place back in the colander. Season with salt, weigh down with a heavy pot (adding water to the pot for extra weight), and leave for 4 hours, using a bowl to catch excess liquid. Refrigerate for up to 2 days.

Pepper Sauce

1 quantity

1 red bell pepper

1 garlic clove, mashed

½ teaspoon balsamic vinegar

½ teaspoon red wine vinegar

2 tablespoons extra virgin olive oil

Salt, black pepper, and white pepper to taste

_____

Place the pepper on a baking sheet and cook at 350°F for 40 minutes or until the pepper has blackened. Remove the pepper from the oven and seal in a plastic bag until cool. Remove from the bag and peel. Cut off the stem and remove the seeds and any white flesh. Purée the pepper in a blender with the garlic, vinegars, oil, salt, and peppers. Cover the sauce and set aside.

Pesto

1 quantity

3½ cups basil leaves

2½ tablespoons pine nuts

2 garlic cloves

1 cup extra virgin olive oil

1 teaspoon salt

½ cup grated Parmesan

¼ cup grated Pecorino Romano

_____

In a food processor, combine the basil, pine nuts, garlic, olive oil, and salt and blend until fine. Pour into a small bowl and add the cheeses. Set aside until needed. If you decide to make a larger quantity to keep for the winter, leave out the cheeses and garlic until the day of use. Keep frozen for up to 6 months and thaw completely before using.

Puff Pastry

1 quantity

4 cups all-purpose flour

3/4 cup cold water

1 teaspoon salt

1 teaspoon butter, at room temperature

1 pound margarine, in flat block form*

———

On a work surface or in a large bowl, combine the flour, cold water, salt, and butter and work well with your hands. Knead until all the ingredients are fully incorporated and are very even in texture. Wrap in plastic wrap and refrigerate for 10 minutes. Dust a work surface with flour (and continue to do so if the dough sticks) and shape the dough so it is three times the width of the margarine block and 3/4 inch longer. Turn the dough so that a long side is facing you. Place the margarine in the center and fold the dough like a letter, first closing the left side, then the right. Press the borders to encase completely. Rotate the block clockwise 90 degrees and evenly pound the dough with a rolling pin to flatten. Roll out to a long strip 3/4 inch thick. Score the center of the long strip crosswise and fold in both sides of the dough so the ends meet in the center. Close like you would a book. Wrap with plastic wrap and refrigerate for 10 minutes.

Roll the dough out into a long strip 1/4 inch thick. Fold again so the ends meet in the center, then like a book. Wrap in plastic wrap and refrigerate for another 10 minutes. Repeat four more times. Finally, portion the dough into four pieces. Wrap individually in plastic wrap, and freeze until needed. Remove from the freezer and set aside until at room temperature (approximately 2 hours) before using.

*If unavailable, unwrap 4 sticks of margarine and press together to firm one solid block.

Saffron Parmesan Sauce

1 quantity

1/2 teaspoon saffron threads

3 tablespoons butter

1/2 cup milk

1/2 cup heavy cream

1 1/2 cups grated Parmesan

Black pepper to taste

Nutmeg to taste

———

Soak the saffron threads in 1 cup of warm water for 1 hour.

Melt the butter in a saucepan and add the saffron and soaking liquid. Add the milk and cream and heat until the liquid starts to boil. Add the grated cheese and mix. Transfer to a double boiler and continue to cook, stirring continuously, until the sauce is very creamy, approximately 20 minutes. Season with black pepper and nutmeg and set aside until ready to serve.

Sage Butter

1 quantity

3/4 cup butter

6 sage leaves

———

In a saucepan, melt the butter over low heat and add the sage. Keep over medium heat for 3 minutes. Cool completely.

Seitan
1 quantity (1¾ pounds)

Dough

11 cups Manitoba flour (see page 16)
3¼ cups water

Cooking Liquid

12 cups water
1 tablespoon sea salt
⅓ cup white wine
⅓ cup soy sauce
1 carrot
1 onion
3 garlic cloves
1 celery stalk
1 sprig rosemary
1 sprig parsley

Combine the flour and water in a large bowl and work very well until smooth. Place the bowl in the sink. Squeeze and rinse the dough under running water continuously until the starchiness is washed away. This will be achieved once the rinsing water runs clear and the dough feels elastic. Drain in a colander and set aside. Prepare two large pots for the cooking liquid. In one pot, combine 8 cups of the water with the sea salt and bring to a simmer. In the other pot, combine the remaining water and ingredients and bring to a simmer. Remove the dough from the colander and place on a work surface. Using your hands, roll the dough into a 4-inch-diameter log and slice into ½-inch-wide rounds. In batches, place the rounds in the pot of salted water. As soon as they come to the surface, transfer with a slotted spoon into the second pot. Cook the seitan for an additional 20 minutes. Remove from the heat and allow the seitan to cool in its liquid. Remove the seitan with a slotted spoon and delicately squeeze out the excess liquid. Refrigerate for up to 5 days.

Tartar Sauce
1 quantity

1 quantity Mayonnaise (see page 29)
2 green olives
1-inch piece of carrot
1 gherkin or cornichon
1 small shallot
1 small garlic clove
1 teaspoon chopped parsley

1-inch celery leaves
2 capers
1 teaspoon mustard
Lemon juice to taste
2 drops of vinegar
Salt and black pepper to taste
1 tablespoon plain yogurt

In a food processor, blend all the ingredients together, except the yogurt, until finely chopped. Mix in the yogurt and refrigerate.

Tomato Sauce
1 quantity (1½ cups)

1 (28 ounce) can peeled whole tomatoes

1 small carrot, peeled and halved lengthwise

1 small onion, halved

1 small celery stalk, halved

1 sprig parsley

3 basil leaves

2 garlic cloves, gently smashed

5 tablespoons extra virgin olive oil

1 teaspoon salt, or to taste

———

Pass the tomatoes through a food mill and discard the seeds. Combine the ingredients in a pot and cook over medium-high heat. As soon as the sauce comes to a boil, reduce to a simmer and continue to cook for 20 minutes, uncovered, stirring occasionally. Taste for sweetness. If the sauce is too bitter, add some olive oil and a pinch of baking soda (not sugar!) and simmer for an additional 5 minutes. Remove the aromatic vegetables with a slotted spoon and use the sauce as desired. If used solely as a sauce and not in addition to another recipe, this quantity will serve 4.

Truffle Sauce
1 quantity

3 tablespoons olive oil

1 garlic clove

1 tablespoon grated truffles

Pinch of salt

———

Heat the oil in a saucepan with the garlic. When the oil is hot and the garlic begins to brown, turn off the heat. Remove the garlic and add the truffles. Add the salt, stir, and set aside.

Vegetable Stock
4 cups

8 cups water

1 carrot, peeled and halved lengthwise

1 onion, quartered

1 celery stalk, halved

1 sprig parsley

2 basil leaves

1 potato, peeled and quartered

1 zucchini, quartered

1 garlic clove, gently smashed

Salt to taste

———

Combine all the ingredients in a large pot and bring to a boil. Reduce the heat, cover, and simmer for 45 minutes. Strain through a fine sieve, cool, and refrigerate for up to 3 days.

HISTORY

Truffles are rare and expensive, as they are found underground and the collecting season is very short. They are a hypogeal fungi that can be found in north and central Italy. The most famous places for quality and quantity are Alba, Piedmont (especially for the more requested white truffles); Norcia, Umbria; and San Miniato, Toscana (for the black ones). With their strong and inebriating perfume and unique flavor, truffles reign over all natural products. There is nothing more fascinating than truffles.

A LITTLE MORE HISTORY

Since 3000 BC, Babylonian times, there are records of the use of an ingredient similar to truffles. In the second century BC, Teofrasto di Ereso, one of the Aristotelian students studying botany, discussed truffles in his *Historia Plantarum*. According to the Greek philosopher, the fungus was reaching the peak of its taste thanks to a combination of rain and lightning.

Galen, the father of systematic medicine in the second century BC, reported its very nutritious qualities and its power to raise spirits. The mysterious fungus became an aphrodisiac believed to bestow pleasure.

In the Roman Empire, truffles were dedicated to Venus, the goddess of love. Doctors gave them to many patients for impotence, the first case of "Viagra." In the first century AD, Apicio, a famous gourmet from one of the oldest "Patrizi" families of ancient Rome, talked about the royal quality of truffles in meals, elevating the fungus to a noble status.

In medieval times, the appreciation ended. Truffles were considered to be dangerous and thought to have a demonic nature. For a time, truffles nearly disappeared completely, only to reappear during the time of the Comuni e della Signorie, a few centuries later. They were raised again to a level of high demand, and the elite made a point of having truffles on their tables. Even Francesco Petrarca, the famous poet, composed verses about the fungus.

In this period, two of the most royal types of truffles were discovered: Il Tuber Magnatum and Il Tuber Melanosporum. Until this period, people had been satisfied with poorer quality.

In the Renaissance, however, truffles reached their greatest glory, generating a kind of addiction: in any respectable banquet, truffles had to be present. In this period, the best chefs, the Masters of Cuisine (those of the nobility) were trying hard to create new recipes to offer their illustrious guests, incorporating the fungus in their dishes and even giving it as a prestigious gift.

Truffles, naturally, could not be missing among the many different products that Caterina de Medici took with her to France. She contributed to their widespread use there when she went to marry Henry II.

In the 1800s, truffles were the symbol of nobility and wealth. Many kings and emperors, Napoleon included, were excited by the taste of the fungus. Even during the final lunch of the Congress of Vienna (dated 1815), where the greatest politicians and state leaders of the world gathered, truffles were present.

TRUFFLE GROWING

Tartufaia is the area where truffles are found naturally. Unfortunately these places are becoming more scarce and/or decreasing in size because of atmospheric situations.

For many years, people have been practicing artificial cultivation, with some results. As truffles are symbiotic with the roots of oak and hazelnut, these trees are planted with truffle spores inoculated in them. Truffles get water and salts from the earth to the plants, while the plants give refined carbohydrates to the truffles.

The main competitors for man, in finding truffles, are generally wild boars, which are very common in the areas of production. They simply love the fungus, and concrete fences have been made around *tartufaie* to prevent boars digging them up.

NOTE ON SAFFRON

Originally, saffron was from Asia Minor. It has been used in dyes, medicines, and cosmetics, as well as in cooking. Well known from the Nile River region, saffron was also renowned among the Greeks, as they used it in drawings on the walls of the palace in Knossos. In Italy, since the thirteenth century, this plant has been widely used to dye linen, wool, and silk, and used as a paint. Il Perugino, Pietro Vannucci, the master of Raffael, took the flowers, extracted the color, and used it for his famous paintings and frescos. He encouraged the cultivation of the plant in the area of Lake Trasimeno in Umbria. Spanish saffron became more affordable than the local expensive Umbrian one. After the Renaissance, it almost stopped being produced commercially and nearly disappeared from this area.

In his perfectly tailored cream-colored Valentino suit and polished chocolate brown Armani loafers, forty-four-year-old Alberto Musacchio is the archetype of classic Italian style as he ambles from one table to another in his restaurant. From the dining room, one can hear the roars of laughter from guests reacting to one of his many stories while he charms them with his boyish smile.

With a slim six-foot, one-inch frame and salt-and-pepper hair, he has a sophisticated manner about him and is as strict with his own appearance as he is with the quality of food at his restaurant. To imagine the elegance of Alberto as having been any less or different than it is today is an absurd notion, as even he would allow.

Personal archive picture

In actuality, the Alberto Musacchio of 1979 would vary greatly from today's version.

During the transition between the experimental seventies and decadent eighties, Perugia became the international student capital of Italy. The city's university offered a three-month Italian language program to follow further studies in other cities like Rome, Florence,

and Milan. It was in this city that nineteen-year-old fair-skinned Alberto decided to study philosophy at the university. After traveling cross-country in the United States with only $300 in his pocket, he had long lost the naïveté of the young teenager he once was, while growing a full head of hair down to his shoulders in the process. He was eager to enjoy everything the world had to offer him, while capitalizing on his greatest strength: his business-savvy entrepreneurial foresight.

Perugia had made a quick change from a quiet medieval city to a bustling and trendy university town overnight. With young students pouring in and sharing wild antics with one another, the local establishments had hardly a fair opportunity to catch up, a detail Alberto picked up right away. His best memories from the States were of hanging out in small pubs and lounges, where anything from quiet conversations to raucous gatherings were the norm, and he found that it was exactly what Perugia was lacking. There were small cafés that served coffee and closed early, or discotheques for all-night dancing, but nowhere for people to go to hang out, listen to good music, have a few drinks, and relax.

In the historical center of the city was a small dive recognized for small-time drug laundering, macrobiotic food, and poor business. In Alberto's eyes, it was a gold mine. With the financial backing of his parents, Alberto, his older brother Gianni, and his classmate Fedele bought the bar from the eager-to-sell owners and took it upon themselves to shape the place into their dream pub.

They named their pub Califfo after a book called *Il Califfo dell'Hashish* by the French author Gerald de Nerval. The book, written in 1851, spread through the underground of the free-thinking and liberal-minded youth and rapidly gathered a cult following in the seventies. It inspired Alberto and his partners and made their pub recognizable by the crowd they wanted to attract. One of their friends created a stunning mosaic made of stained glass and copper linings for the

entrance of the pub, replicating the cover of the book. The gloriously attired sultan is a beautiful piece of artwork that still remains in the city to this day.

It was around this time that Alberto, Gianni, and Fedele decided to wear white, and only white, as a symbol of purity and cleanliness. It was an outrageous, yet distinctively cool, decision that set them apart and made them known throughout the city for several years.

From the start, Califfo was a huge success. It was the perfect place at the perfect time, attracting waves of international students from the opening day. Alberto, Gianni, and Fedele had put up flyers and posters around the city and in the halls of the university to advertise the grand opening, but it was actually a hired street performer who brought in the largest crowd. Alberto and his partners paid a musician to play a *ghironda*, or hurdy-gurdy, through the streets of the city, attracting an audi-

ence and eventually leading them to Califfo on opening night. That evening, Alberto, Gianni, and Fedele served well over two hundred people, marking the beginning of a lucrative and exciting journey.

The next seven years were dedicated to living the high life. Alberto and his partners, in their early twenties, thrived off this lifestyle, working at the pub until the early morning hours, partying with friends, and watching the sunrise after closing, then passing out until the afternoon before heading back to work. They enjoyed the throng of students who came in waves from all parts of the world, leaving after the three-month program ended to be replaced by a new group of people.

Alberto, Gianni, and Fedele all took Califfo very seriously, but no one had any aspirations of making the relaxed pub into an upmarket restaurant. Their profit came from beverage sales and various vegetarian sandwiches.

During the first year of business, one chef began to frequent the pub and seized an opportunity to work in the kitchen. He began to help at no cost to Alberto and his partners, first preparing sandwiches and later more involved vegetarian dishes.

Seeing potential, the partners hired him and began to pay him for the work that he was doing. Almost immediately, the chef began to neglect his responsibilities and started working less and less. The chef lasted six months before Alberto fired him for stealing money from the cash registers, and silently for also trying to seduce his girlfriend. It was only a few months later when Akira took over the kitchen, at which point the culinary element took off.

Students loved going to Califfo because the ambience was young and vibrant. Street artists would be given free food and lodgings in the apartment upstairs when they came to perform, so there were always musicians, magicians, and mime artists performing on a small stage in the pub. Alberto and his partners were more than the owners; they were friends and entertainers.

Under the guise of magic tricks, Alberto would flirt with the girls who came into the bar night after night. Patrons loved it when Alberto rode his unicycle over to their tables to deliver their drinks, adding to the wacky and fantastic feel of the pub. On one cool November evening in 1982, business was as usual. A group of architecture students had just arrived from Brazil and, naturally, found their way to Califfo. Alberto, with his back to the entrance, had been chatting with some people sitting at the bar when he felt and heard the front door swing open. Simultaneously, every man in the pub went wide-eyed and slack jawed, and instinct told Alberto that someone beautiful had just walked into his bar. Turning his head, he joined the throng of mesmerized men when he saw Malu, an amazon of a woman with a mane of curly golden hair, tanned skin against high cheekbones, and the longest legs he had ever seen in his life. She was wearing jeans and a colorful tank top and had an unassuming, open air about her that brought life into his pub.

When Malu approached him at the bar to order a drink, he pulled out all the stops and performed a foolproof magic trick that always, always impressed the girls. On Malu, the trick did not work, and Alberto failed miserably. Seeing that he was embarrassed, she gave him a warm smile and went back to her table with her drink. Alberto noticed that she sat down next to one particularly handsome man and, feeling his defeat, went back to work. The following day, when the same gentleman showed up at the bar with one of Perugia's most recognized homosexuals, Alberto saw his window of opportunity reopen and leapt through it.

For the next few days, he couldn't help but keep one eye out for her whenever he walked around the city. He would step into a bar and take a quick scan to see if she was there. He would sit on the steps in the main plaza with a slice of pizza and casually look around for her.

Some days he was lucky and managed to get a glimpse of her. Other days he would not. Malu began frequenting his pub and slowly began to build a relationship with her future husband. Within a few weeks, they were dating. Alberto was beside himself and Malu, on her side, was taken in by this skinny man with long hair and white clothes. He was funny and intelligent, but what captured her was his unspoken and innate desire for something inexplicably spiritual.

They had been seeing each other for nearly two weeks, when he had a day off and wanted to spend it with her. While she wanted to go to Florence for the day with a friend, he wanted her to stay in the city and spend the day with him. Both were stubborn, fiery individuals. Inadvertently attracting the attention of nearby bricklayers, they broke out into a fierce argument. The fight

was less about how they were going to spend the day and more about who was going to listen to whom. In the end, Malu went to Florence and Alberto spent his day alone. It poured the entire day and, while both felt that they were justified in some way, neither really knew what they had won.

Three months later, when Malu had finished her language program in Perugia, she headed to Rome for six months to study architectural restoration and continued to visit Alberto in Perugia. He, in turn, spent his days off in Rome with her. Their strong personalities clashed numerous times, and they fought constantly over small things, but by the time she was finished in Rome and was to leave for Brazil, she had decided to stay in Italy, in Perugia, to be with Alberto.

Aside from Masa, the Japanese sous-chef, Akira allowed no other individual in the kitchen. He was a proud man and lived for his work, and for anyone to come in and take away any of his responsibilities was an insult. Although Akira liked Malu and knew that she was dating his boss, her presence in the kitchen, as anyone else's, would not be tolerated.

On one particularly busy night, more people than usual were placing orders and, with Masa off, Akira was swamped. As the tickets piled in, dirty pans and dishes remained stacked in the sink, and Akira was up to his neck in work. Without a word, Malu appeared, washed and dried all the dishes, and left as silently as she had come in. Akira, upon noticing this act, adored her instantly. Over the next few years, he became her teacher and mentor in the kitchen. All the while, he felt and acted like a schoolboy whenever she stepped into the room.

The vigorous years of owning Califfo wore down the owners. They were exhausted from working such long hours late into the evening and were no longer the flamboyant, pleasure-seeking youths they once were. All three had grown into serious, color-wearing individuals who were anxious to embark on the next chapter in their lives. Six months after Akira left and Masa took

his place, Masa lost one leg in a serious motorcycle accident. Shortly after, Alberto and his partners decided to move on.

Seven years after the opening of Califfo, Alberto, Gianni, and Fedele sold their beloved pub to a group of wealthy footballers. Without the original owners, the pub lost its charm and appeal and, over the next twenty years, passed through several hands. Remarkably, guests continue to come to Montali and speak of this fantastic pub they frequented while studying in Perugia back in the early eighties. Their mouths open in surprise when they find out that Alberto was the original owner. Slowly, their eyes give them away as they realize that the bohemian, fair-skinned, long-haired boy behind the renowned bar is now the distinguished gentleman sitting before them.

If Giuseppe Sarti had lived to see Malu grow into a woman, his heart would have been full of pride for his granddaughter. Even more than his own children, she shared her grandfather's fierce commitment to his beliefs, his affection that he generously poured over his family, and, in particular, his passion for food and cooking.

Born and raised in Modena, he met and married a young girl from Rimini and together they immigrated to San Paolo, Brazil, at the turn of the nineteenth century. He was proud of his heritage and maintained a strong Italian-blooded household, raising his children on tales of old Italian folklore, memories of the stunning landscape and architecture, and traditional food, song and dance. He started earning money by selling food in the village and gradually expanded his business.

Eventually, he had money to build a house that was large enough for his entire extended family to come together to sing, dance, and eat.

Giuseppe died when Malu was only two years old, but her youth was full of countless stories he had passed down. From an early age, she was fascinated by the rich Italian history and culture, the pictures she had seen of historical structures and monuments, and the considerable differences between each region. She fell in love with the imagery of the rustic lifestyle and stories of festivals celebrating the fruits of the earth.

Malu was a vivacious and energetic child who loved school, music, and sports. While she enjoyed the dishes her mother expertly prepared, she drank a lot of fluids but never ate much. She was eleven years old when her height began to soar at an alarming rate, and her mother, seeing her skinny daughter stretching out, grew nervous. After seeing a doctor, Malu was no longer allowed to enjoy sports like swimming and running for fear that they encouraged her growth spurt. Nevertheless, she continued to grow well into her mid-twenties.

When she was sixteen, she was still very skinny with more arms and legs than she knew what to do with, but she also began to suffer intense migraines and stomach cramps. Slowly, she discovered that on days when she happened not to eat meat, she felt better and had more energy.

Over the course of three years, Malu slowly weaned herself off meat until she completely avoided it. A few years later, after witnessing a bucket full of live lobsters being thrown into a steaming pot and cooked to their death, she gave up seafood as well.

Malu developed her love of cooking early on from her mother, often taking her place in the kitchen to cook for her brother and sister. She followed recipes and experimented on her own. Sometimes, the outcome was incredible. Other times, it was a complete disaster. Although Malu loved tasting new and interesting flavors, she took the greatest pleasure in the purity of the simplest dishes, from roasted potatoes to pastel, a Brazilian pizzalike dough stuffed with cheese and deep-fried.

After studying architecture for a number of years, twenty-six-year-old Malu found out about a scholarship being offered by the Italian government that would send Brazilian architecture graduates to study in Italy. Following a vigorous application process, Malu was awarded one of the ten coveted scholarships. She had just started studying the Italian language and was ahead of the rest of her classmates by the time they all arrived in Perugia.

As a shock to no one, both Italians and Brazilians are meat lovers. Pork, beef, lamb, and veal are featured in most dishes, used to flavor sauces, and stuffed inside dumplings, vegetables, and even other cuts of meat. Despite the similarity in the two diets, Malu found it difficult to avoid eating meat when she first arrived in Italy. Slowly, she happened upon cafés in the center of the city that offered vegetarian entrées. She had always liked beans, nuts, and cheeses and fell in love with Italy for the wealth of all three in the cuisine. She discovered rustic dishes like lentil soups and *pasta e fagioli*, pasta with fresh beans, traditionally served all over southern Italy.

One of her friends had told her about a popular vegetarian pub called Califfo in the heart of the city by the university. There were few places for students to congregate, have drinks, and meet other international students, and the atmosphere that Califfo promised was exactly what Malu and her friends sought.

Malu stepped into Califfo with a group of students and discovered a lively pub with great music and a spirited staff. At the bar, she noticed a tall and skinny young man wearing white jeans and a white short-sleeved shirt. Later, when he made his way over to her table, she became aware of his big, sparkling eyes and long wavy hair. She was immediately taken by the fresh energy and exuberant charm that he exuded, and the two began speaking as if they were old friends. Later in the night, only Malu, an intimate group of her friends, Alberto, Gianni, and Fedele remained in the pub. They spoke together in a mixture of Italian, English, and Portuguese and somehow communicated perfectly with one another. Malu and Alberto bounced off each other the entire night, making witty comments while discovering how similar they both were. Malu was impressed by how cosmopolitan Alberto and his friends appeared to be and reveled in the open atmosphere of the late night.

She was surprised to hear that Alberto was five years younger than she was because, although he had a very young energy about him, he was mature beyond his years and already had clear ideas of what he wanted from life.

Malu and her friends spent the next three days exploring the rest of Perugia's nightlife before finally going back to Califfo. Every once in a while, she would walk with some friends in the city and see Alberto walking

up the same road, his secretive smile teasing her. They soon began dating and quickly grew close. Alberto adored her and loved being in her company, wanting to spend every waking moment with her. Malu felt the same way, but still refrained from becoming serious with anyone she would have to leave in a number of months. Malu had always been an independent person and insisted on spending time on her own to study or travel, a mind-set that spurred many of their arguments.

One fight in particular presented the first fork in the road of their relationship. She and a friend had decided to visit Florence on the same day that Alberto had his day off. He wanted her to stay with him and she insisted on going with her friend. Fuming from the argument that followed, she went back to her dorm room that she shared with other students. A few hours later, she sat on the stairwell with her face resting on her hands when she heard someone come up behind her.

"I have a present for you," Alberto said quietly. He held out an exquisite lapis lazuli necklace before her. Before placing it around her neck, he paused. "So, you'll stay?" Malu's eyes darkened and a bitter argument erupted instantly. "Do you think you can come in here and buy my time? Is that it? You show up here with expensive jewelry and expect me to do whatever you want?"

The row quickly escalated into a shouting match and drew the attention of anyone within hearing range. Malu, who was still learning Italian, found the words pouring out of her, and Alberto fought back, matching every ounce of her anger with his own.

Alberto grabbed Malu's hand, thrust the necklace into her palm, and said, "You can keep the necklace!" Malu watched as he stormed down the stairs in his white pants and white high-tops and opened the door at the base of the steps. He stepped out, threw one more look at her, and dramatically slammed the door. Malu seethed. His stubbornness was so Italian, and she was determined to stand her ground.

The next day, she went to Florence with her friend where it rained nonstop the entire time. She was wet, cold, and depressed, blaming Alberto for the miserable weather.

She and her friend, both soaked, took the bus from Florence back to the center of Perugia. They were dropped off at the bus station and headed down the main street when she saw Alberto walking toward her. He knew which bus she had taken home and wanted to meet her when she stepped off. Her heart warmed when she saw his guilty expression until the second he opened his mouth with a smirk and asked, "So, how was the weather?"

Malu opened her mouth, a quick retort on the tip of her tongue, but she had had a long day and was tired. "Let's go get coffee" was all she said, and they walked, hand in hand, to a nearby café.

After Malu's Italian language course ended, she left Perugia to complete her program studies in Rome. Despite the distance between Rome and Perugia, Malu and Alberto saw each other regularly. She remained devoted to her program and career, and she yearned to travel the world with no constraints. She was able to envision an exciting lifestyle with this young and vibrant man who shared her eagerness to experience new thrilling adventures. Over the following months their relationship continued to grow, and, although they still fought constantly, Malu and Alberto thrived in each other's company.

Time and time again, she felt torn in her feelings for him. She saw a life with him, but one in which she would have to compromise the dreams she had held onto for so many years. It was toward the end of her program, during a trip to Istanbul with Alberto, when Malu finally decided that she would hold off returning to Brazil to stay in Perugia with him.

Alberto involved Malu in Califfo's activities over the following years, and she became a faithful presence in the bar. She loved the unique characteristics that the three owners brought to the business. Alberto was always full of energy, always inventive and excited to take on new challenges. Gianni was the mystic, a sociologist turned pub owner with undoubted artistic tendencies. Fedele was the calming, grounded force that relaxed both the workers and the high-energy clientele. With Akira and Masa, the air was filled with a thick, yet delicate creative energy. After a busy night, the six of them would stay up until four in the morning to plan for the following day, share ideas and experiment with new flavors. It was a time in their lives when they were all brimming with excitement over the endless possibilities the world had to offer. Years later, Malu would recall the great meeting of minds, and much of who she became was affected by her experiences at Califfo.

Years later, Malu and Alberto married and settled in the Umbrian countryside. Stone by stone, they built the Country House Montali. They built their dream from the ground up, supported only by each other and the innate desire they shared to create something different and wonderful. Montali, they decided, would not be another piece of property with rooms and precooked, unexceptional food. It was to be a haven for guests from around the world, providing an incredible, fulfilling experience both in the serenity of the countryside and in the breaking of bread with others who shared this desire. For Malu, being the provider of a style of food that redefines vegetarianism, being able to introduce others to unexpectedly and incredibly melded flavors and ingredients, is the most rewarding element of Montali. Vegetarians come on holiday and need not worry about what they are eating, while nonvegetarians are awestruck at how delectable and satisfying meatless food can be.

Whenever guests catch her in the kitchen after an exceptional dinner and say, "Malu, that was the most wonderful meal I have ever had in my life," she always, always gets goose bumps. It is something she has heard time and time again throughout the years and yet it still affects her as if she is being told for the first time. It is her unique and humble ability to continue to take such pleasure in daily occurrences. She never ceases to amaze those around her when she sits down in the morning with her breakfast and sighs with delight while biting into a croissant, the same croissant she has had every day for so many years.

A few years ago, Malu's Brazilian aunt arrived at Montali on her first visit. While she fell in love with everything from the tranquillity of the olive grove to the delicious and fulfilling meals that Malu prepared, she was most astonished by how similar Montali was to Giuseppe Sarti's village home so many years ago. The familiarity and warmth of his house created a contented setting for all his guests to enjoy while he took pleasure in planning and preparing nourishing foods for them. So much of who he was and what he strived for had somehow remarkably been revived by a granddaughter who had never known him. For most, it is a beautiful coincidence. For Malu, it tells her she is really home.

Prima Colazione

BREAKFAST

CIAMBELLA

This traditional chocolate and yogurt swirl cake (pictured on page 46) is a favorite among children and adults alike at the Country House Montali. Enjoy with a glass of cold milk or a steaming cup of café latte.

Serves 10 ⓔ *15 minutes & 35 minutes baking & cooling time*

INGREDIENTS

3 eggs

3/4 cup sugar

Pinch of salt

1/2 cup sunflower oil

1/2 cup plain yogurt

1 3/4 cups Italian 'OO' flour (see page 16)

1 1/2 teaspoons baking powder

Grated zest of 1 lemon

1/3 cup mini semisweet chocolate chips

1 tablespoon unsweetened cocoa powder

———

Preheat the oven to 350°F. Butter and flour a 9-inch springform pan. In a bowl, beat the eggs with the sugar and salt until the mixture is pale and frothy. Slowly add the oil, stirring continuously. Add the yogurt, sift in the flour and baking powder, and then add the lemon zest, mixing well after each addition. Fold in the chocolate chips. Pour two-thirds of the batter into the pan. Sift and fold in the cocoa powder into the remaining batter and pour evenly over the light batter. Bake for 35 minutes. Remove from the oven and cool. Ciambella may be served warm or at room temperature.

MUESLI

This tasty recipe is one of the best ways to nourish your body in the morning. Rich in fiber from the cereal and full of vitamins from the fruit, it has the benefit of yogurt as well.

Serves 6 ⓔ *20 minutes*

INGREDIENTS

1 1/2 cups rolled oats

1 1/2 tablespoons sweetened flaked coconut

3 tablespoons toasted chopped almonds

1/4 cup dark raisins, soaked in hot water and drained

1 apple, peeled, cored, and cubed

1 pear, peeled, cored, and cubed

1 banana, peeled and cubed

1 1/2 teaspoons sweetened cream of coconut, such as Coco Lopez

1 1/4 cups plain yogurt

Mosto Cotto (see page 17), honey, or maple syrup for drizzling

Poppy seeds

———

In a dry, nonstick pan, toast the oats until golden brown. Add the coconut and toast for an additional 30 seconds. Remove from the heat and place in a bowl. Toss with the almonds, raisins, and fruit and add the cream of coconut. Divide into small bowls, drizzle with yogurt and Mosto Cotto, and sprinkle with poppy seeds.

TORTA di MAIS

When visiting new babies in the neighborhood, Malu's mother would bake the new mother this delightful corn and aniseed cake. The corn gives a healthy boost of energy. Aside from the health benefits, the subtle sweetness and the appealing texture of corn blend deliciously, especially when complemented by tea or a cappuccino.

Serves 12　**E**　35 minutes & 45 minutes baking & cooling time

INGREDIENTS

2 cups yellow cornmeal

2 cups sugar

2 cups milk

⅓ cup vegetable oil

1 tablespoon butter

4 eggs, separated

1 tablespoon aniseed

1 tablespoon baking powder

1 teaspoon vanilla extract

Pinch of salt

Confectioners' sugar, for dusting

———

Preheat the oven to 350°F. Butter a 15-x-10-inch jellyroll pan, flour the sides, and line the bottom with parchment paper.

Combine the cornmeal, sugar, milk, oil, and butter in a saucepan and whisk continuously over medium heat. After about 10 minutes, the mixture should start to pull away from the pan. Continue to cook for an additional 3 minutes, then remove from the heat and cool completely.

Lightly beat the egg yolks and add to the cooled batter with the aniseed. Sift in the baking powder and add the vanilla. Beat well to incorporate air.

In a separate bowl, beat the egg whites with the salt to stiff peaks. Gently fold a third of the egg whites into the batter until fully incorporated before adding the remaining egg whites.

Pour the batter into the pan and spread evenly with a spatula. Bake for 45 minutes or until a toothpick, when inserted, comes out clean. Cool in the pan before removing. Dust the surface with confectioners' sugar and serve.

ALUA

This widely known Indian dish is prepared after a religious fast. Here you'll find it with a fancy Montali variation of cream of coconut, roasted nuts, and fresh fruit.

Serves 4 to 6 Ⓜ *20 minutes*

INGREDIENTS

2 cups milk

3 cardamom pods

1 tablespoon butter

¾ cup semolina

1 tablespoon sweetened flaked coconut

8 ounces mixed fruit, such as bananas, pears, apples, and peaches, cut into ½-inch cubes

1 tablespoon sweetened cream of coconut, such as Coco Lopez

2 tablespoons dark raisins, soaked in hot water and drained

3 tablespoons toasted chopped almonds

Poppy seeds

Mosto Cotto (see page 17), honey, or maple syrup

——————

Heat the milk in a saucepan. Grind the cardamom in a mortar and pestle, removing the outer pods and crushing the tiny black seeds within. Melt the butter in a pot and add the ground cardamom to infuse for 30 seconds. Roast the semolina in the infused butter until the semolina begins to brown. Add the coconut and continue to cook for 30 seconds.

Turn off the heat and carefully add the hot milk all at once, whisking constantly. Return to the heat and continue to cook, stirring, until the mixture is no longer runny. Stir in the fruit, cream of coconut, raisins, and almonds. Top with a sprinkle of poppy seeds and a drizzle of Mosto Cotto.

FRUTTA FRITTA

Sliced fruit dipped in a light batter and delicately fried to golden perfection. Try it with various fruits other than apples, bananas, peaches, and pears.

Serves 8 (M) *15 minutes & 10 minutes for resting batter*

BATTER

2 eggs

½ cup Italian 'OO' flour (see page 16)

1½ teaspoons baking powder

2 tablespoons cornstarch

½ cup milk

¼ cup cognac

2 drops of vanilla extract

———

Mix all ingredients in a bowl until smooth and let rest for 10 minutes.

FRUIT

Vegetable oil, for deep-frying

4 bananas, peeled and halved lengthwise

2 apples, peeled, cored and sliced horizontally, about ¼ inch thick

3 peaches, pitted and sliced

3 pears, cored and cut into wedges

Cinnamon Sugar (see page 26)

———

Heat the oil in a large pot (see page 20). Dip the fruit in the batter to coat completely and deep-fry in batches. Remove the fruit individually with a slotted spoon when golden brown all around. Sprinkle the Cinnamon Sugar over the top and serve hot.

CRESPELLE FARCITE con FRUTTA e MIELE

Light, golden pancakes stuffed with fruit and honey.

Serves 4 (E) *15 minutes & 10 minutes for resting batter*

CRÊPES

7 tablespoons Italian 'OO' flour (see page 16)
½ teaspoon baking powder
5 tablespoons cognac
⅔ cup milk
2 drops of vanilla extract

———

Whisk all the ingredients together in a bowl and let the batter rest for 10 minutes. Heat and lightly butter a nonstick pan over medium-high heat. Remove the pan from the heat, ladle a spoonful of batter into the pan, and gently swirl to coat the surface. Place back on the heat and cook until one side is golden brown. Flip to cook the other side. Slide the crêpe onto a plate and repeat with the remaining batter.

FILLING

1 apple, cored and thinly sliced
1 pear, cored and thinly sliced
1 banana, peeled and thinly sliced

ASSEMBLY

Honey, for drizzling
Mosto Cotto (see page 17), honey, or maple syrup
Confectioners' sugar, for dusting

———

Cover one-quarter of each crêpe with fruit. Fold in half, then in quarters. Insert more fruit into the upper quarter. Drizzle with honey and Mosto Cotto, dust with confectioners' sugar, and serve.

"This," the wealthy miller said pleasantly while accepting Malu and Alberto's money, "is like a packet of cigarettes to me." One of the few remaining survivors of the original six owners, the miller had been trying to sell his unused mountaintop property for so many years that the buying price had dropped to, in his mind, pocket change. What was once beautiful hunting territory and cultivated soil fifty years earlier had turned into rocky jungle terrain that sat in close proximity to the medieval Castello di Montali. Contrary to the miller's view, the twenty-five-acre land held a world of dreams for young Malu and Alberto.

After years of splitting time between Califfo and various trips to India, Malu and Alberto had decided that the time had come to buy land of their own and settle down. They were tired of city life and longed for peace in the countryside where they could grow organic foods and continue self-growth. They dreamed of a place where sunlight would be unobstructed by tall buildings, trees, or even hills.

With his share of money after selling Califfo, in addition to a small sum he had inherited, Alberto began looking with Malu for their new home. For eight months, they exhausted themselves driving all over the country in their relentless search. Each potential acquisition came with numerous problems. If the price was good, the soil was ruined. If the land was nice, electricity would be next to impossible to obtain. If everything else was perfect, there was still the issue of running water being unavailable. Every place they had emotionally invested in had ultimately disappointed them.

In the most casual of circumstances, Alberto voiced his frustrations to the landlord of his small apartment, who, after hearing what they were searching for, told Alberto of a secluded and uninhabited piece of property on top of a mountain that had been on the market for fifteen years. With nothing to lose, Alberto, Malu, and their landlord drove to the top of the road-less mountain to have a look at this undesired land. What was one man's trash was another man's treasure, as they fell in love instantly. The two small buildings in the center were covered in vines and the earth had obviously been neglected, but the panorama was endless, the air was clean, and fresh running water was plentiful. It was perfect.

They immediately sought the owner, who was overjoyed at the prospect of finally selling off his land and being able to be the source of happiness to such a romantically idealistic couple. Malu and Alberto took their ownership papers and drove straight back to their new home. Looking at a view as far as Assisi, Malu was overwhelmed with joy. As she walked next to her husband, she grasped his hand and jumped in the air. "All this . . . this is our land! Can you imagine?" she said breathlessly. Alberto smiled at his wife from the corner of his mouth and replied, "No need to get so emotional. It's just land." But her excitement was infectious.

They spent the first few days giving the property a thorough assessment. Although Malu was an architect by profession, neither she nor her husband had had experience with tilling soil, cultivation, or manual construction of buildings. They discovered that the two buildings on the property were in much worse condition than they had first believed. The roof of the garage was completely caved in, as was half of the roof over the main house. The antique tiles, in great demand across the country, had been stolen from the roof years before, and the fireplace refused to function properly, emitting smoke but no flames or heat. Random plant life was growing inside the abandoned home, and plumbing was nonexistent.

A Sicilian agronomist came to inspect the soil to determine its usability. After spending hours going over every inch, he sat Alberto and Malu down. "Well, this is truly a lovely panorama you have bought here. However, it's dangerously close to desertification. Turning this land into something is going to be next to impossible, but with a lot of work, I'm sure you can plant an olive grove." It was the only thing they needed to hear before getting started.

Cleaning the soil was the first priority. At the hardware store they bought a few small ploughs and gloves to start with, but after a few hours of accomplishing nothing, they looked at each other and said, "We're going to need a bigger plough." Soon, they realized larger ploughs were not the solution. They were going to have to call in a tractor-driven plough. The soil was packed with bulky rocks that they had to carry, one by one, to a large pile for later use. What few olive trees there were, were crowded by thorny bushes and weeds. When the shrubbery was hacked away with machetes, branches sprang back unpredictably like elastic, viciously whacking the offender. Their faces and arms were soon covered in cuts and bruises.

Cultivating the soil was an arduous task that lasted years. It was not uncommon for Malu or Alberto to plop down under one of the hundreds of olive trees they were planting and weep out of frustration, exhaustion, and loss of hope. The less distressed one would assume the reassuring role, pushing the other in their belief toward accomplishing their dream. Often the only words were "Remember India? There's nothing we can't do."

Four winters in a row were spent in the brutal cold. There was no heating during those years, and as the fireplace was not functional, keeping warm on a mountaintop was impossible. The roof was the first segment of the buildings to be fixed, and Malu continuously transported cement that she had just hand-mixed to her husband and another bricklayer. Only much later did they decide to buy a machine-operated cement mixer. Both Malu and Alberto became involved in every facet of the building process. Countless mistakes significantly lengthened the building process and added to their frustration. The garage turned meditation room was rebuilt twice, while the entire plumbing system had to be placed. Alberto discovered a talent for bricklaying and, by watching carefully, learned the tricks of the old professional bricklayer who was helping them. They contracted a man to lay the road, as barely a path had existed before.

After a few years, enough of their home was built for them to open the doors to the public as a place for spiritual gathering. Malu would feed the groups that came to their home to experience music therapy or learn about meditation. Having built their home with the idea of a retreat center in mind, Malu and Alberto believed that donations would sustain their humble venture, and they had no specific billing process. It was during this time that Alberto received a letter from his mother, Wanda. She was elderly, but independent, strong, and visionary. Not only did Wanda believe in what her son and his wife were creating, but she also knew she could help them in many ways. She could have lived with her eldest son, Gigi, in his estate in Piedmont, or comfortably with Gianni in Assisi, but she chose to help Alberto and Malu. Malu was thrilled at the idea of her mother-in-law coming to live with them. An instant bond had developed between them the moment they met years earlier, and Wanda became like a second mother to Malu, whose own mother had passed away. Alberto, on the other hand, felt divided. His mother, he knew, would be an enormous help, particularly now when Malu was expecting their first child. On the other hand, his was still a harsh life that he could not ask anyone else to share, especially his own mother. Wanda assured her son that she did not mind that there was no heating, and that helping them would give her a strong sense of purpose. Despite his disinclination, Alberto welcomed his mother.

Wanda immediately became a strong source of encouragement for her son and daughter-in law. She was an elegant, well-traveled woman with a strong work ethic. With each town she visited, she collected recipes and techniques, all of which she shared with Malu. She educated her in gourmet Italian cuisine and helped her develop her already refined palate.

In the months preceding Damiano's birth, Malu and Alberto began to reevaluate the objective of their center. They were continuously spending money on the building and upkeep of their property, and survival by donations had become a withered ideal. With the impending arrival of a baby, Alberto needed to find more practical means of supporting his family. A friend working in a tourism office in Perugia introduced them to a new concept throughout Italy called *Azienda Agrituristica*, or Country House. Essentially, farmers and landowners producing agricultural products were establishing themselves as small-scale hotels. In addition, a number of grants from the *Comunita Europea* were available.

The appeal of this option was that, while they would be under a more formal umbrella, they would still

VEGETERRANEAN

Photo courtesy of Claudio "the Barber"

have the freedom to preserve the distinctiveness they had sought since the beginning. Friends and family members teased them by saying they were selling their souls to capitalism and prosperity, but Malu and Alberto knew from the beginning that would not be the case. Their goal was to provide guests with an intimate, comfortable setting and fulfilling vegetarian cuisine, never to build a luxury resort and food factory, which they could have easily done given the natural beauty and substantial acreage of the property. As a Country House, they could continue to build creatively on their core purpose with the added security that the new title gave to them. It was a marriage of reality and idealism, of keeping their feet firmly planted while daring to dream and be original and imaginative. Years later, many of the same friends who teased them saw Montali as a triumph and ventured to build their own Country Houses.

Piece by piece, Malu and Alberto continued to work and build on the Country House Montali over the following two decades. The small hotel, literally off the beaten track, steadily gained more attention and rec-

ognition across Western Europe and North America. Along with the healthy stream of newcomers, frequent guests returned year after year, seeking an experience wholly emblematic of the rustic, undisturbed Italian countryside. Because Montali is a ceaseless labor of faith and love, the atmosphere exudes a peaceful, hopeful energy that settles into any individual who passes through.

For the first time in nearly twenty years, Malu and Alberto relaxed throughout the entire winter of 2004. There were no additional walls that needed to be erected, buildings to be constructed, or pressing logistical issues to deal with. In the warmth of their stonewall home, they curled up with their son by the fireplace, now working, reading peacefully, and pushing any thought of the following season to the furthest corners of their minds. Later, there would be considerable rebuilding or expansion projects and stressful bureaucratic issues to attend to. In the interim, though, the Musacchio family indulged in a well-deserved escape.

A few pages of this book are going to be dedicated to architecture. I imagine people will think "Why should a cookbook mention architecture as a food concept?" There is a reason why. Before becoming a chef, my wife was an architect, and together we designed the restaurant, the hotel, the rooms, and the professional kitchen as well.

In a way we had to apply her architectural expertise to the cooking profession, necessitating building a working restaurant kitchen.

But why a chapter about this? The reason is quite simple. People are cooking less and less. The quality of home cooking has never been so bad. People buy cookbooks, and watch cooking shows, while sitting on the sofa eating fish and chips.

Certainly, there are some historical and sociological reasons for this: the lack of time, the rush of modern life, and . . . architecture.

Have you ever noticed how a modern European house is generally designed? With the cost increasing, houses have often turned into matchboxes, and the place that has been most sacrificed is the kitchen. Kitchens literally turn into small wardrobes, with the sink reminding one of being on a train and being about the size of a microwave. And where are they? In the darkest corners of the whole house — a kind of cooking jail. Who is going to work there? No one. That is why there is an architecture section in this book. If we want to improve our cooking skills, we should be able to do it, and we should be able to do it in an acceptable way.

Kitchens should be in a well-lit, charming part of the house, not in the greenhouse or on the balcony.

In ancient times, if you look at typical rural houses, the kitchen was the center of the community life, with a big fireplace where everybody loved sitting on long winter nights, enjoying the cooking and later on eating with all the family. Now a thirty-five-inch plasma television has taken the place of the fireplace, with the sofa in front of it, and this has pushed the cooking corner into the most hated, darkest corner of the house. No one wants to be there trapped, and families end up spending as little time as possible in those awful kitchens.

This surely means very poor quality food and, unfortunately, as little time together as possible.

The kitchen as a "memento" of unity expired, too.

This section should serve as a hint to all builders, architects, and people in the process of renovating their houses to start designing buildings in a different way. There are some splendid stoves nowadays on the market that can beautifully furnish any house.

Kitchen furniture has also become more and more elegant and sophisticated. You can now build some kitchens that look like modern art. You should never feel ashamed to invite friends to join you in your kitchen. You should always show it off with pride. And remember, a working kitchen is always the warmest place in the house — a place where you can have many lovely conversations.

What my wife, as an architect and chef, would suggest is *not* to separate the spaces of the kitchen from the living room. Especially if your house is relatively small. This is a very good secret to make any house look bigger. Do *not* isolate the kitchen, and please do not isolate the cook!

Our own house is surely not large, and our beautiful brick kitchen is definitely part of the living room. Our guests always enjoy pleasant conversations while my wife produces some of her fabulous recipes.

Mmmmmmm! All the great smells with the sound of sautéing.

Of course, then you will have to invite your guests for dinner, and rest assured, you will always have a lot of friends!

—Alberto Musacchio

Running a vegetarian business has never been an easy task. Many restaurants close after a short time. We have also gone through some difficult times, but in our case, the reasons were more bureaucratic than related to business. What follows is one of the most interesting gems of bureaucratic stupidity, which finally ended up being studied in law colleges in Brussels as a case of the "system" against the single individual.

Our hotel, being a country hotel, is categorized as *agriturismo* in our region, which means it is a farm with a hotel on its own land and, therefore, pays a little less tax, as it is set in a rural area.

To be classified this way, the law requires that we have to produce some of the agricultural products for the restaurant by ourselves. With 1,500 olive trees and a big kitchen garden, we have never had any problem accomplishing the requirements of the law. Still, some years ago, just after a famous earthquake that literally emptied the whole region of tourists (with the understandable economic consequences), we went through one of the funniest bureaucratic nightmares in the history of law.

The regional law required us to grow some agricultural products on our twenty-five-acre farm. But all of a sudden, the local agricultural department decided to tighten up this law, as there were too many *agriturismi* popping up. The new law required not only some agricultural products to be produced in situ but also a certain quantity of animals to be raised on the farm to provide the meat for the restaurant. In our case, considering the size of our restaurant, it was about 600 chickens or 200 sheep. This was what, out of the blue, the local authority expected of us.

You can imagine how pleased I was when I found out about this new law. And, of course, being a vegetarian and not being willing to kill any of those 200 sheep, I started thinking of how many thousands they would become in a short time.

The idea of raising all those chickens, which I could already imagine messing everywhere, destroying my gardens, making lots of noise, and making my life hell, was quite terrifying. The major point, of course, was that I wasn't using any meat in my restaurant, and for the law to demand that I have animals for serving as meat sounded at the very least a little strange.

The idea of training them to dance the samba on the restaurant tables to entertain the clients proved to be too complicated, so we decided to fight this injustice. I wrote to *La Repubblica,* the major Italian newspaper, reporting the matter and, of course, the journalists loved the story and published it with a comment underneath stating that it doesn't often happen that vegetarians are requested to raise animals for meat purposes in a vegetarian resort.

This was a wrong move.

The local office didn't like it at all. Within twenty days, we received an official communication telling us that our restaurant had been shut down, since we were not complying with the new regulations of meat production!

You can imagine our reactions, and this was after an earthquake that literally put the tourism economy on its knees — including our small business. Nevertheless, as the son of an army general, I never take surrender as an answer. I was born to fight! I spent the next three days locked in my office writing to everyone I could think of all over the world. After another week, a second article of mine appeared in *La Repubblica,* and, if the previous one was playful, the second was a real *j'accuse.* The funny story had intrigued many readers of the first article. To see another episode right away, and with that kind of reprisal from the local authority, made the "novella" a real success.

Two hundred faxes of protest (it was still fax times) arrived in the local office shortly thereafter. Two senators took my side and called the local bureaucrats — making quite a big mess. The President of the Republic himself wrote to them (I jealously keep a copy of the letter), asking them to "pay better attention to this case." And the icing on the cake was the Minister of Agriculture (we are under the Agricultural Department) asking for a parliamentary debate about this subject . . . wow! The little case of those vegetarian bastards made a fuss all the way up to the top political leader of the country. This was one thing that hadn't been taken into consideration by the local officer. Oops!

I got a call from the mayor of our local town a few days later, saying, "Mr. Musacchio, the law has been changed . . . but please could you tell me how you managed to do that? It generally takes two years to have a law changed." Of course, after that, the reputation of a copule of vegetarians being a real nuisance grew. Still, the politicians came to realize that it is better not to irritate the vegetarians too much.

They may not eat meat, but they can still bite!

—Alberto Musacchio

Antipasti

STARTERS

BRUSCHETTA MISTA

Olive oil makers eat only unsalted bread with their oil during the late autumn and early winter after the olives are first pressed. The bread is first baked in a wood-burning stove, then sliced and toasted over a charcoal grill. While still hot, it is rubbed with a fresh garlic clove and served drizzled with the oil maker's finest extra virgin olive oil and a sprinkle of salt. This is the original and true bruschetta, and the centuries-old method is still commonly found throughout Tuscany and Umbria. This simple, fine dish is often mispronounced. The correct pronunciation is "brusketta."

Serves 6   Ⓔ   75 minutes

MUSHROOM BRUSCHETTA

1/4 cup extra virgin olive oil

1 sprig rosemary

2 garlic cloves, smashed

1 pound mushrooms, chopped

1 tablespoon chopped parsley

Salt to taste

———

Heat the olive oil, rosemary, and garlic in a sauté pan until the garlic begins to color. Add the mushrooms and cook over high heat for 5 minutes, or until the liquid has evaporated and the mushrooms are browned and crispy. Remove from the heat, remove the garlic and rosemary, and cool completely. Add the chopped parsley and salt and set aside.

TOMATO BRUSCHETTA

1 1/2 cups cherry tomatoes, sliced

1 teaspoon chopped oregano

1 garlic clove, gently smashed

1/4 cup extra virgin olive oil

4 basil leaves, chopped

Salt and pepper to taste

———

Toss all the ingredients together in a bowl 30 minutes before serving. Set aside.

WALNUT GARLIC BRUSCHETTA

6 tablespoons coarsely chopped walnuts

1 garlic clove, minced

Salt and white pepper to taste

5 tablespoons extra virgin olive oil

———

Combine all the ingredients in a bowl. Set aside.

RADICCHIO BRUSCHETTA

1 small radicchio (about 4 ounces), ribs removed, julienned

1 tablespoon chopped walnuts

1/4 cup extra virgin olive oil

Salt, white pepper, and black pepper to taste

1/2 teaspoon balsamic vinegar

1/2 teaspoon lemon juice

————

Combine all the ingredients in a bowl right before serving to retain the freshness of the leaves.

ARUGULA PARMESAN BRUSCHETTA

4 ounces arugula, chopped

1/4 cup coarsely grated Parmesan

Salt and white pepper to taste

1/2 cup extra virgin olive oil

————

Combine all the ingredients in a bowl right before serving to retain the freshness of the leaves.

BRUSCHETTA

1 loaf Italian bread, cut into 30 slices about 1/3 inch thick

3 garlic cloves, peeled but left whole

————

Preheat the oven to 350°F. Spread the walnut garlic mixture over six slices of bread. Arrange the six slices along with the remaining slices of bread on a baking sheet and bake for 5 minutes. The bread should be crunchy on the outside and still soft and chewy in the middle. Remove from the oven and gently rub the garlic cloves over the plain toasted bread.

Lightly press one side of a piece of toasted bread in the oil of the tomato bruschetta mixture to soak. Top the same side with a portion of the tomatoes and repeat with five more slices. Follow the same pattern with the remaining bruschetta mixtures, using six slices of bread for each type.

Arrange the bruschetta on a large platter or individual plates and serve.

Caramelized figs. An adventurous sweet and sour taste, made even more interesting by the crunchy caramel.

Serves 6 (E) *15 minutes*

INGREDIENTS

4 ounces Mascarpone

1½ ounces Gorgonzola

1½ ounces Tomino di Mucca or Brie

12 fresh figs

Butter, at room temperature

Brown sugar

24 toasted walnut halves

1 quantity Orange Sauce (see page 30)

Mix the cheeses in a bowl with a fork or handheld mixer until very creamy. Scoop into a pastry bag.

Rinse and dry each fig. With a small, sharp knife, make a shallow crosslike incision through the skin, starting from the stem end of the fig and stopping right before the bottom (do not cut through the whole fig). Rub butter over the surface of each fig and roll in brown sugar. Place the figs on a heatproof surface (like the bottom of an inverted baking dish) and caramelize the outside with a kitchen blowtorch. Wait until the figs are cool enough to handle, then cut three-quarters of the way through each one, following the incisions made previously. Stuff each fig with a walnut half, fill with cheese from the pastry bag, and top with the remaining walnuts. Serve with warm Orange Sauce.

A couple of great recipes if you need something cold to serve during cocktail hour or to welcome guests before an important meal. A nice combination of colors as well.

Serves 8 Ⓜ *40 minutes & 30 minutes chilling & 1 hour for resting salads*

DOUGH

1½ cups Italian 'OO' flour (see page 16)

Pinch of salt

½ cup butter, softened

3 tablespoons cold water

_____

Combine the flour and salt on a work surface and make a well in the center. Add the butter and water to the well and gently work with your fingertips until a dough begins to form. Incorporate by cutting through the dough with a pastry blender or fork and rolling back together, three or four times, until the texture and color are even. Wrap in plastic wrap and refrigerate for 30 minutes.

POTATO SALAD

1 large potato, boiled until al dente

1 tablespoon Mayonnaise (see page 29)

1 tablespoon chopped green olives

1 tablespoon chopped red onion

1 tablespoon chopped gherkins

1 teaspoon chopped chives

1 teaspoon chopped parsley

2 teaspoons plain yogurt

1 teaspoon extra virgin olive oil

Salt, white pepper, and Tabasco to taste

_____

Peel the potato, then cut into ⅓-inch cubes and place in a bowl. Fold in the remaining ingredients gently (do not break up the potato cubes) and season to taste. Cover the bowl with plastic wrap and refrigerate for 1 hour before serving.

BEET SALAD

1 beet, boiled until just tender, peeled, and cut into ⅓-inch cubes

2 tablespoons plain yogurt

½ teaspoon lemon juice

1 teaspoon chopped parsley

1 tablespoon creamy goat cheese

Salt, black pepper, and Tabasco to taste

_____

Combine all the ingredients in a bowl and season to taste. Cover the bowl with plastic wrap and let rest for 1 hour before serving.

ASSEMBLY

Preheat the oven to 350°F. Butter twenty 3- to 4-inch pie or tart pans. Between two sheets of plastic wrap dusted with flour, roll out the dough to a large disk about ⅛ inch thick. Place the pie pans upside down on the dough and use a small knife to cut around the pans, allowing a ½-inch border. Gather the scraps and reroll dough as needed. Gently press each disk into the pans and remove excess dough from the rims. Pierce the bottom of each pie shell once with a fork and place on a large baking sheet. Bake for 12 minutes. Cool to room temperature and remove the shells from the pans. Fill half with potato salad and the other half with beet salad and serve.

CARPACCIO di RAPA ROSSA

An elegant and impressive beet carpaccio, this appetizer can be prepared within minutes. The sweetness of the beets is complemented by strong cheeses and black pepper, while the sharpness of the arugula adds to the interesting blend of flavors and textures.

Serves 6   E   *15 minutes*

INGREDIENTS

12 ounces beets, boiled until just tender

Lemon juice

1/3 cup chopped walnuts

3 tablespoons chopped parsley

Salt and pepper to taste

Extra virgin olive oil

1/2 cup creamy goat cheese

1/2 cup grated firm goat cheese

4 ounces arugula

Wearing disposable gloves, peel the beets and cut into thin slices using a mandoline. Decoratively place the slices on individual plates to form large circles. Place one slice in the center of each. Drizzle with lemon juice and sprinkle with the walnuts, parsley, salt, pepper, and olive oil.

Using a teaspoon, place small dollops of creamy goat cheese over the beets. Sprinkle with the grated cheese. Top with a small handful of arugula. Sprinkle with a little more salt and pepper, drizzle with a few drops of olive oil, and serve.

RUSTICI alla RICOTTA

A delectable pie crust filled with a lemon and ricotta cheese fusion and topped with a light choux pastry.

Serves 8 (M) *60 minutes & 35 minutes baking*

DOUGH

1 cup Italian 'OO' flour (see page 16)

1 tablespoon sugar

Grated zest of ½ lemon

4 tablespoons butter, melted and slightly cooled

3 tablespoons water

———

Sift the flour onto a work surface. Add the sugar and lemon zest and mix well. Create a small well in the center and pour in the butter and water. Using your fingertips only, slowly work the liquid into the dough until well incorporated. Gently gather the dough into a ball, wrap in plastic wrap, and refrigerate for 15 minutes.

RICOTTA FILLING

¾ cup fresh ricotta, drained

2 ounces Scamorza (see page 20), cut into ¼-inch cubes

3 tablespoons grated Parmesan

1 egg yolk, lightly beaten

Grated zest of ½ lemon

Salt and black pepper to taste

———

In a bowl, beat the ricotta with a fork until very creamy. Add the remaining ingredients, mix well, and season to taste.

BIGNE BATTER

3 tablespoons butter, cubed

½ cup water

½ cup Manitoba flour (see page 16)

Pinch of salt

1½ eggs

———

Combine the butter and water in a saucepan over medium heat. When the butter has melted and the liquid comes to a boil, remove from the heat and add the flour. Using a wooden spoon, mix the flour with the water and butter until combined. Place the saucepan back on the heat and continue stirring for 2 minutes or until the batter is shiny and begins to pull away from the sides and bottom of the pan. Remove from the heat and cool. Add the salt and then the eggs one at a time, mixing well after each addition. Cover and set aside.

ASSEMBLY

Preheat the oven to 350°F. Butter eight 3- to 4-inch pie or tart pans. Roll out the dough between two sheets of plastic wrap dusted with flour until it is a wafer-thin disk. Place the pie pans upside down on the dough and use a small knife to cut around the pans, allowing a ½-inch border. Place the disks in the pans and press lightly around the bottoms and sides. Trim the excess dough from the pans. Gather the scraps and reroll dough as needed. Fill each shell with the ricotta filling, spreading to cover the bottom. Spread the bigne batter over the ricotta to cover. It should slightly resemble a dome, covering the edges. Bake for 35 minutes. Working quickly, hold each pan with a pot holder and gently release the pastry with the tip of a knife. Serve hot.

CAPPUCCINO di ASPARAGI

Whenever this dish is presented to unsuspecting guests, it is guaranteed to be a showstopper. Be sure to serve in champagne glasses and let your guests know it needs to be stirred. Great with a chilled prosecco wine.

Serves 4 **E** *30 minutes & 40 minutes simmering*

INGREDIENTS

1 bunch asparagus (about 1 pound)
2 tablespoons butter
Salt and pepper to taste
1 shallot, finely chopped
$\frac{1}{2}$ cup heavy cream
Freshly ground nutmeg to taste

Break off the asparagus stems at the natural breaking point (each end will snap approximately 2 inches from the bottom when gently bent). Using a peeler, remove the fibrous outer layer of the stems. Leave the tips unpeeled. Reserve all the trimmings. In a pot of lightly salted boiling water, cook the asparagus for 2 to 3 minutes or until al dente. Transfer with a slotted spoon into an ice bath. Place the reserved trimmings in 2 cups of the cooking water, cover, and simmer for 40 minutes or until the stock has a full asparagus flavor. Set aside $1\frac{1}{4}$ cups of stock and keep warm.

Drain the cooled asparagus from the ice bath. Cut off the tips and set aside. Coarsely chop the stems. In a sauté pan, sauté the tips in half of the butter and season. In a separate pan, sauté the chopped stems and the shallots in the remaining butter. Season and set aside.

TO SERVE

Reheat the tips and stems in separate sauté pans. Whip the cream with a handheld mixer until soft peaks form and transfer to a piping bag. Warm the stock if necessary. Place $1\frac{1}{2}$ tablespoons of chopped asparagus stems in the bottom of each champagne flute. Fill with approximately $\frac{1}{4}$ cup warm stock. Add three asparagus tips and top with a dollop of whipped cream and another asparagus tip. Sprinkle with nutmeg and serve immediately.

Aside from the cream, the stock and asparagus should be served warm.

GAZPACHO

A cool start to a summer meal, this classic Spanish treat is a chilled tomato soup laden with garden vegetables. Serve in martini glasses for an elegant presentation.

Serves 6 (E) *10 minutes & 1 hour chilling*

INGREDIENTS

1 slice of Italian bread, without crust

1 medium red bell pepper, seeded

1 cucumber, peeled and seeded

4 tomatoes, coarsely chopped

½ garlic clove, sliced

1 tablespoon lemon juice

¼ cup extra virgin olive oil

2 teaspoons red wine vinegar

2 teaspoons balsamic vinegar

½ small onion, coarsely chopped

Salt and black pepper to taste

A few drops of Tabasco

———

Cut the bread into cubes and process in a blender until fine. Set aside.

Cube half the red pepper and half the cucumber and reserve for garnish. Coarsely chop the other half of the pepper and cucumber and mix with the remaining ingredients. Purée in a blender, in batches if necessary, and pass through a wide-mesh sieve or colander. Discard the seeds and vegetable skins. Mix in the bread crumbs, taste for seasoning, and refrigerate for at least 1 hour.

TO SERVE

Divide the soup between six martini glasses. Top with an ice cube and the reserved red pepper and cucumber, drizzle with olive oil, and serve.

CRESPELLE FANTASIA

Light pancakes stuffed with an eggplant cream and served with a velvety cheese sauce. This wonderful dish is excellent, and the strong flavor and richness of the "fonduta" goes well with a glass of vintage wine.

Serves 6 Ⓜ *95 minutes*

CRÊPES

1 tablespoon butter, plus more for pan

2/3 cup milk

1/2 cup all-purpose flour

1 egg

Salt and black pepper to taste

24 parsley leaves

6 long chives, for assembly

Melt the 1 tablespoon butter and cool to room temperature. In a bowl, whisk together the butter, milk, flour, egg, salt, and pepper. Heat an 8-inch nonstick skillet or crêpe pan over medium heat. Spread 1 teaspoon butter around the pan with a paper towel. Remove the pan from the heat and ladle 1/4 cup of the batter into the pan, swirling to spread. Arrange four parsley leaves around the center while the batter is still wet and place the pan back on the heat. Cook until one side is golden, flip, and cook the other side in the same manner. Repeat with the remaining batter (makes six crêpes).

FILLING

1 shallot, chopped

1 garlic clove, chopped

1 sprig thyme

2 tablespoons extra virgin olive oil

2 eggplants, peeled and cubed

Salt and black pepper to taste

1 tablespoon chopped parsley

1 tablespoon creamy goat cheese

In a sauté pan, gently sauté the shallot, garlic, and thyme in the olive oil over medium-low heat for 1 minute until soft. Add the eggplant and season with salt and pepper. Cook, stirring occasionally, until the eggplant is very soft, approximately 25 minutes. Remove from the heat, add the parsley, and cool to room temperature before removing the thyme sprig and mixing in the goat cheese.

FONDUTA

4 ounces Fontina cheese, cut into small cubes

1/2 cup milk

1 egg yolk

1 tablespoon butter, cut into cubes

2 teaspoons cornstarch

One hour before serving, combine the Fontina and milk in a bowl. Mix in the egg yolk, butter, and cornstarch. Cook in a double boiler with simmering water, stirring continuously, for about 20 minutes, until melted and smooth.

ASSEMBLY

Preheat the oven to 350°F. Dip the chives in a pot of simmering water for 1 second and immediately transfer to a bowl of ice water. Cool completely and pat dry. Lay out the crêpes on a work surface and spoon the filling into the center of each. Bundle each like a small bag and tie by wrapping a chive around twice and tying the ends. Transfer to a baking sheet lined with parchment paper, cover with another sheet of parchment, and bake for 10 minutes. Serve hot alongside the warm Fonduta.

CRUDITE di PERE e MELONE

A pear and melon salad served with a balsamic vinaigrette glaze and honey, topped with Fossa and Castelmagno cheeses. The unique combination of savory, sweet, and acidic tastes is as easy as it is unexpectedly delicious.

Serves 6   E   *15 minutes*

INGREDIENTS

6 small pears, peeled, cored, and thinly sliced

1 small cantaloupe, peeled, seeded, and thinly sliced

Lemon juice

Extra virgin olive oil

Honey

Balsamic Reduction Sauce (see page 26)

Salt to taste

6 slices each of Fossa and Castelmagno (see page 18), or aged sheep cheese such as Pecorino Romano

6 chives

Black pepper to taste

Decoratively place slices of pear and melon on six serving plates. Drizzle lemon juice, olive oil, honey, and balsamic sauce over the fruit. Season with salt. Top with one slice of each cheese and garnish with a single chive. Sprinkle with pepper and serve immediately.

GUACAMOLE alla MONTALI

The Montali variation remains true to the well-known Mexican dish, adding a touch of Italian flair to set it apart.

Serves 6 Ⓔ *20 minutes*

GUACAMOLE

1 ripe avocado

1 tomato, peeled, seeded, and chopped

1 tablespoon extra virgin olive oil

Juice of 1/2 lemon

1/2 teaspoon Dijon mustard

Salt and pepper to taste

———

Halve the avocado lengthwise with a small knife, cutting through the flesh and moving around the pit. Using your hands, rotate the halves in opposite directions to split. Scoop out the avocado flesh with a spoon, reserving the pit. In a bowl, mash the avocado well with a fork. Combine with the remaining ingredients and mix thoroughly. Place the reserved pit in the bowl with the guacamole, cover with plastic wrap, and refrigerate.

CORN AND BEAN SALAD

1 cup cooked corn kernels

1 cup cannellini beans, cooked

2 tablespoons chopped red bell pepper

1 small shallot, chopped

2 teaspoons lemon juice

1/4 cup extra virgin olive oil

1 teaspoon balsamic vinegar

1 garlic clove, crushed through a press

Salt, black pepper, and white pepper to taste

A few drops of Tabasco

———

Toss all the ingredients together in a bowl.

TO SERVE

1 tablespoon chopped parsley

1 tablespoon chopped chives

———

Discard the pit from the guacamole. Serve the corn and bean salad in individual glasses, topped with a dollop of guacamole and garnished with chopped parsley and chives.

TORRI di ZUCCHINE RIPIENE con CREMA di PISELLI

Zucchini towers stuffed with a pea cream and roasted almonds. A sophisticated and eye-pleasing dish, where a nearly raw zucchini shelters the soft purée, which contrasts with the crunchy almond texture.

Serves 6 (18 pieces)   (E)   *25 minutes*

INGREDIENTS

3 zucchini, each about 6 inches long
1 cup shelled peas
1 tablespoon extra virgin olive oil
Salt and white pepper to taste
½ onion, thickly sliced
1 tablespoon Mascarpone
½ teaspoon lemon juice
1 tablespoon creamy goat cheese
Sliced almonds
Confectioners' sugar

Cut off the ends of the zucchini and cut crosswise into 2-inch pieces. Halve each piece on the diagonal (see picture). Using an apple corer, remove the inside to create a tubelike cavity. Cook the zucchini in a large pot of boiling water for 1 to 2 minutes, then transfer to a bowl of ice water to cool quickly. Drain in a colander and pat dry. Grill the zucchini pieces, cavity-side down, until grill marks are visible. Turn each piece 90 degrees and continue to grill, creating a crosshatch effect. Remove from the heat and set aside.

In a small pot, cook the peas with the olive oil, salt, white pepper, onion, and just enough water to cover until tender. Drain, remove the onion and discard, and purée the peas. Pass the purée through a sieve or food mill into a bowl. Add the Mascarpone, lemon juice, and goat cheese to the peas and mix well.

Toast the almonds in a pan over low heat. When golden, lightly sprinkle with a light dusting of confectioners' sugar, just to sweeten, and toast for a few more seconds. Remove from the heat.

TO SERVE

Black pepper to taste
Extra virgin olive oil, for garnish

Fill a pastry bag with the pea purée. Arrange three zucchini towers, cavity-side up, on each of six serving plates and fill with the purée. Top each zucchini with almonds, black pepper, and a few drops of olive oil and serve.

CRUDITE di SPINACI e RUCOLA

Spinach and arugula salad dressed with a hot garlic and caper sauce, served with sun-dried tomatoes, black olives and a shaving of Parmesan cheese. This seamless combination of classic Mediterranean favorites makes for a surprisingly unique salad.

Serves 6 Ⓔ *15 minutes*

DRESSING

3/4 cup olive oil

30 capers (rinse well if packed in brine or vinegar)

6 garlic cloves, thinly sliced

———

In a saucepan, heat all ingredients over low heat. After 8 minutes, or when the garlic begins to lightly caramelize, remove from the heat. The hot oil will continue to cook the garlic and capers.

SALAD

6 cups spinach leaves

3 cups arugula

Salt to taste

Olive oil

Red wine vinegar

24 pitted black olives

6 oil-packed sun-dried tomatoes, cut into thin strips

Parmigiano Reggiano, shaved with a vegetable peeler

Black pepper to taste

———

In a bowl, toss the spinach and arugula with a sprinkling of salt, olive oil, and red wine vinegar.

Divide the dressed greens between six serving plates. Spoon the garlic chips and capers over the greens, garnish evenly with the olives and sun-dried tomatoes, top with shavings of Parmigiano Reggiano, and sprinkle with freshly ground black pepper. Serve immediately.

STUZZICHINI al FORMAGGIO e MELE VERDI

A delicate pastry teaser, with a chunky mixture of creamy cheeses and Granny Smith apples sandwiched between thin, bite-size cheesy biscuits. Serve with a crunchy mixed salad.

Serves 6 (12 pieces) (M) *25 minutes & 2 hours chilling*

DOUGH

3/4 cup Italian 'OO' flour (see page 16)

2 pinches of salt

1 tablespoon grated Parmesan

1/4 cup ricotta

4 tablespoons butter, at room temperature

1 egg yolk, for brushing

12 walnut halves

―――――

Preheat the oven to 350°F. Combine the flour, salt, and Parmesan on a work surface and make a well in the center. Add the ricotta and butter and work between your fingertips until the dough comes together. Roll into a ball and knead a few times. Wrap in plastic wrap and refrigerate for 2 hours. Roll out into a rectangle about 1/8 inch thick, large enough to cut twenty-four 2 1/2-inch squares. Place the squares 1/2 inch apart on a large baking sheet lined with parchment paper. Brush all 24 squares with egg yolk and top 12 of them with a walnut half. Bake for 12 minutes or until golden brown. Set aside.

FILLING

1 tablespoon creamy goat cheese

1/4 cup Crescenza or Mascarpone

1/4 cup ricotta

Salt and black pepper to taste

1 teaspoon extra virgin olive oil

1 teaspoon chopped chives

Pinch of paprika

1/4 Granny Smith apple, cut into 1/4-inch cubes

―――――

In a bowl, combine all the ingredients, except the apple, and mix well until creamy. Transfer to a pastry bag filled with a medium plain tip.

TO SERVE

Pipe the filling over the 12 walnut-free pastry squares, and layer the apple cubes over the filling. Top with the walnut-covered halves. Serve slightly warm.

FRITTO MISTO

A variety of vegetables dipped in tempura batter and deep-fried to crispness, this dish is typical of the Piedmont region.

Serves 6 Ⓜ *50 minutes*

INGREDIENTS

1 or 2 Japanese eggplants, cut crosswise into ¼-inch slices

1 zucchini, thinly sliced

2 medium onions, thinly sliced into rings

3 carrots, halved, then cut into ¼-inch strips

3 peaches, pitted and cut into thin wedges

Vegetable oil for deep-frying

Salt to taste

Herb Yogurt Sauce (see page 29)

1 lemon, cut into 6 wedges, for serving

SEMOLINO DOLCE

1 cup milk

1 tablespoon butter

2 tablespoons sugar

Grated zest of ½ lemon

Peel of ½ lemon

½ cup semolina flour

———

Combine the milk, butter, sugar, grated lemon zest, and rind in a saucepan and bring to a boil. Add the semolina flour and cook for 15 minutes, stirring continuously. Discard the rind and pour the mixture into a medium loaf pan lined with damp parchment paper (the semolina should come 1 inch up the sides). Cover with more parchment paper and press to remove any air pockets. Set aside to cool. When cool, invert onto a flat surface and cut into 1-inch squares about ¼ inch thick.

IMPANATURA (BREADING)

6 tablespoons Italian 'OO' flour (see page 16)

3 eggs, lightly beaten with a pinch of salt

¾ cup dry bread crumbs

———

Place each of the three ingredients in a shallow bowl.

TEMPURA BATTER

10 tablespoons Italian 'OO' flour (see page 16)

¼ cup cornstarch

1 cup beer

Pinch of salt

———

In a bowl, mix all the ingredients together until smooth. Place in the freezer for a few minutes before using.

TO SERVE

Coat the eggplant and semolino dolce squares first in flour, then egg, then bread crumbs, and place in a single layer on a baking sheet. The remaining vegetables and peach slices should be dipped into the tempura batter right before they are fried. Heat the vegetable oil in two separate pots. In one pot, deep-fry the eggplant first (see page 20), then the semolina dolce. Deep-fry the tempura-coated ingredients in the other pot, cooking the onions last. The carrots can be fried in small batches. As they are cooked, transfer the fried foods to another sheet lined with paper towels to drain and, except for the peaches and semolino dolce, season everything with salt. Serve with a dollop of Herb Yogurt Sauce and a lemon wedge.

INSALATA del BOSCO

A fresh mushroom salad prepared with arugula, walnuts, and Parmesan cheese. The rawness of this dish brings out the unique woodsy aroma and flavor of porcini mushrooms.

Serves 6   E   *10 minutes*

INGREDIENTS

6 small porcini mushrooms (others will also do)

24 walnut halves

6 large handfuls of arugula

Juice of ½ lemon

6 tablespoons extra virgin olive oil

12 generous shavings of Parmigiano Reggiano

Black pepper to taste

Thinly slice the Parmigiano Reggiano with a mandoline or vegetable peeler.

———

Wipe the mushrooms with a damp towel to clean. Slice thinly lengthwise using a mandoline, maintaining the shape of the mushroom. Split each walnut half lengthwise into 2 pieces.

Toss all the ingredients, except the Parmigiano Reggiano and pepper, in a bowl and transfer to a large serving dish.

Gently fluff up the salad with a fork, top with the Parmigiano Reggiano shavings, season with pepper, and serve.

CALZONI

This Neapolitan stuffed and fried pastry literally translates as "trousers." Best when made with buffalo mozzarella.

Serves 8 ⓜ *40 minutes & 70 minutes for resting dough*

DOUGH

2½ cups Italian 'OO' flour (see page 16)

1 teaspoon salt

1 cup warm water

1 tablespoon extra virgin olive oil

2 tablespoons compressed fresh yeast

Pinch of sugar

———

Combine the flour and salt in a large bowl. Create a well in the center and add the water and olive oil. Add the yeast and sugar to the well and mix well using your fingertips. Work around the well to incorporate the flour until the dough comes together. Knead well until soft and elastic. Gently spread a few drops of oil around the surface of the dough, cover with a towel, and let rest for 35 minutes in a warm, dry place. After the dough has rested, sprinkle the surface with flour and "turn" it by pulling small portions of the dough around the edge toward the opposite side of the bowl. Once one full turn has been made, cover again and let rest for 35 minutes longer.

FILLING

1 cup cherry tomatoes

½ teaspoon dried oregano

24 basil leaves, 12 chopped and 12 left whole

1 garlic clove, smashed and chopped

Salt and black pepper to taste

Extra virgin olive oil

4 ounces fresh mozzarella, drained

———

While the dough is resting, seed and coarsely chop the tomatoes. Drain in a colander for 30 minutes. Combine the tomatoes with the oregano, chopped basil, garlic, salt, pepper, and 2 drops of extra virgin olive oil in a bowl. Cut the mozzarella into cubes about the same size as the chopped tomatoes, pat dry, and add to the filling mixture.

ASSEMBLY

Vegetable oil, for deep-frying

———

On a clean work surface dusted with flour, roll out the dough into a disk about ⅛ inch thick. Using a 3-inch round cookie cutter or a drinking glass, cut 24 rounds from the dough. Place a full teaspoon of filling in the center of each disk. Place half of a whole basil leaf over the filling. Fold the disk in half and seal using the tines of a fork, gently pressing down so that it firmly seals the dough but does not break it. Place the calzoni on a baking sheet lined with parchment paper and dusted with Grano Duro flour (see page 17).

In a large pot, heat enough vegetable oil to cover the calzoni (see page 20). When the oil is ready, working in batches, gently place the calzoni in the pot using a slotted spoon. Allow one side to brown for about 1 minute before flipping over to cook the other side. When the calzoni are golden brown, remove with a slotted spoon and drain on a baking sheet lined with paper towels. Season with salt and serve immediately.

BIGNE con CREMA di FUNGHI

An Italian choux pastry stuffed with a mushroom cream sauce. This wonderful appetizer is complemented by port wine.

Serves 8 Ⓜ *40 minutes*

FILLING

1 pound mushrooms

2 garlic cloves, 1 minced and 1 peeled and left whole

2 tablespoons extra virgin olive oil

Salt and pepper to taste

2 tablespoons Robiola cheese (see page 20)

1 tablespoon chopped parsley

———

Wipe the mushrooms with a damp cloth and trim away the tough bottoms of the stems. Cut approximately 24 slices from the mushrooms and reserve. Chop the remaining mushrooms. In a sauté pan, sauté all the garlic in the oil until it begins to brown. Add the chopped mushrooms and cook over high heat, stirring occasionally, until any liquid has evaporated and the mushrooms are golden brown. Remove from the heat and reserve 2 tablespoons of the cooked mushrooms for garnish. Discard the whole garlic clove and purée the mushroom mixture in a blender. Season to taste with salt and pepper. Fold in the remaining ingredients and set aside.

CHOUX PASTRY

⅓ cup water

2 tablespoons butter, cut into cubes

Pinch of salt

¼ cup Manitoba flour (see page 16)

1 egg

———

Preheat the oven to 350°F. Heat the water, butter, and salt in a saucepan over medium heat, melting the butter completely. As soon as the liquid comes to a boil, remove from the heat. Add the flour all at once and whisk well until combined. Return to the heat and continue to whisk for an additional 30 seconds, or until the dough pulls away from the sides and bottom of the pot. Remove from the heat and let cool slightly. Mix in the egg with a wooden spoon, incorporating completely.

Transfer to a pastry bag fitted with a ½-inch plain tip and pipe ½ tablespoon mounds onto a baking sheet lined with a silicone mat or parchment paper. Lightly brush the top of each pastry with water and bake for 10 minutes. Cool completely.

ASSEMBLY

Preheat the oven to 350°F. Using a serrated knife, carefully slice off the top quarter of each pastry and set aside. Use a pastry bag to fill each puff with the mushroom filling. Replace the tops, dot the surface with more mushroom purée, and gently press a reserved mushroom slice onto the top of each. Place on a baking sheet, cover loosely with parchment or foil, and bake for 7 minutes. Serve hot.

CRUDITE di ZUCCHINE e SALSA allo YOGURT e ERBE

A great summer dish to refresh you or give you a lift. Light and low fat.

Serves 6   E   *10 minutes*

INGREDIENTS

6 small zucchini
Salt and white pepper to taste
Juice of ½ lemon
¼ cup extra virgin olive oil
1 quantity Herb Yogurt Sauce (recipe follows)
3 tablespoons sliced almonds, toasted

———

Trim off the ends of the zucchini and slice thinly on a mandoline. Keep refrigerated. When ready to serve, overlap the zucchini slices around a plate. Season with salt and white pepper and drizzle with the lemon juice and olive oil. Let marinate for 5 minutes.

HERB YOGURT SAUCE

⅔ cup heavy cream
⅔ cup plain yogurt
1 small garlic clove, crushed through a press
1 tablespoon finely chopped mixed herbs (chives, thyme, rosemary, and basil)
3 tablespoons extra virgin olive oil
Salt and black pepper to taste
2 teaspoons lemon juice

———

In a bowl, lightly whip the cream until soft peaks form. Fold in the remaining ingredients and refrigerate until needed.

TO SERVE

Drizzle the Herb Yogurt Sauce over the salad, sprinkle with the almonds, and serve.

PANZANELLA

A lovely summer dish with an ancient rural tradition, panzanella originates from the old Italian habit of not letting anything go to waste. It is still a great and healthy Mediterranean way to use up old bread by combining it with seasonal ingredients. Definitely a dish to be enjoyed in the summer.

Serves 6 (M) *25 minutes*

INGREDIENTS

4 slices of Italian bread, cut into ½-inch cubes

10 tablespoons extra virgin olive oil

Salt and pepper to taste

6 cherry tomatoes, cut into quarters

1 cucumber, peeled and cut into ¼-inch cubes

1 carrot, cut into ¼-inch cubes

1 zucchini, cut into ¼-inch cubes

1 celery stalk, peeled and thinly sliced on a mandoline

1 small head of romaine lettuce, cored and coarsely chopped

1 small radicchio, cored and coarsely chopped

8 ounces Pecorino di Pienza (see page 20), cut into ¼-inch cubes

1 garlic clove, crushed through a press

1 small onion, chopped

1 tablespoon chopped oregano

10 basil leaves, coarsely chopped

1 tablespoon red wine vinegar

Juice of ½ lemon

6 ounces buffalo mozzarella, cut into 6 slices

———

Preheat the oven to 350°F. In a bowl, toss the bread with 2 tablespoons of the olive oil and season with salt and pepper. Arrange on a baking sheet and briefly toast for a couple of minutes until crunchy, but not tough. Transfer to a large bowl and cool completely. Add the remaining olive oil and all the other ingredients, except for the mozzarella. Transfer to a large serving dish, top with the mozzarella, sprinkle with more pepper, and serve.

ASPARAGI con SALSA all' ARANCIA

Asparagus served with an orange sauce. A velvety acidic flavor to contrast with the predominant asparagus taste.

Serves 6   Ⓔ   *30 minutes*

INGREDIENTS

1 large bunch asparagus (at least 24 spears)

2 tablespoons chopped walnuts

2 radicchio leaves, cut into thin strips

Extra virgin olive oil

Black pepper to taste

———

Break off the asparagus stems at their natural breaking point (each end will snap approximately 2 inches from the bottom when gently bent). Using a peeler, remove the fibrous outer layer of the stems, leaving the tips unpeeled. Bring a pot of lightly salted water to a boil. Cook the asparagus for 2 minutes or until al dente. Transfer to a bowl of ice water using a slotted spoon. When cool, drain and dry on paper towels.

ORANGE SAUCE

2 or 3 navel oranges

1 tablespoon cornstarch

3 tablespoons white wine

1 teaspoon lemon juice

1½ tablespoons butter, at room temperature

Salt and white pepper to taste

———

Squeeze the oranges to get approximately 1 cup of juice. In a small saucepan, combine the orange juice, cornstarch, white wine, and lemon juice and cook over medium heat until thickened, approximately 3 minutes. Remove from the heat and add the butter in 1 teaspoon increments, continuously stirring until the sauce is smooth and creamy. Season to taste and keep warm.

TO SERVE

Lay the asparagus on individual plates, placing four stems in a row. Pour warm Orange Sauce across the center of the asparagus and sprinkle with the chopped walnuts. Garnish by placing a mound of radicchio at the base of the stems. Drizzle with olive oil and season with pepper. Serve immediately.

POLENTA TARAGNA

A variation of the typical corn recipe from the northeast of Italy. Slices of Polenta Taragna, a blend of common corn flour and buckwheat, are layered with mushrooms and a fava bean purée, with a drizzle of balsamic vinaigrette on the side.

Serves 6 Ⓜ *60 minutes*

POLENTA

1 cup milk
1 cup water
2 tablespoons butter
¾ cup Polenta Taragna*

¼ cup grated Parmesan
3 tablespoons grated Pecorino di Pienza (see page 20)
Pinch of salt

Heat the milk, water, and butter in a saucepan and bring to a boil. Immediately add the polenta and cook for 40 minutes, stirring frequently. Add the cheeses and salt and continue cooking until the cheese has melted. Line a 9-x-5-x-3-inch loaf pan with damp parchment paper covering all sides. Pour the polenta into the prepared pan and tap the bottom against the table to flatten and get rid of any air bubbles. Cover with parchment paper and press down with your hands to even. Cool to room temperature.

MUSHROOM SLICES

2 garlic cloves
3 tablespoons extra virgin olive oil
12 ounces mushrooms, sliced

Salt and black pepper to taste
1 teaspoon chopped parsley

In a sauté pan, sauté the garlic in the olive oil over high heat. When the garlic begins to color, add the mushrooms and cook until golden. Season with salt and pepper. Add the parsley last. Set aside.

FAVA BEAN PURÉE

¼ cup dried fava beans, rinsed
½ carrot, halved lengthwise
2 garlic cloves
½ medium onion, quartered
1 sprig parsley

2 tablespoons extra virgin olive oil
Salt to taste
1 cup water
1 tablespoon lemon juice
1 tablespoon tahini (see page 17)

Combine the beans, carrot, 1 garlic clove, onion, parsley, 1 tablespoon olive oil, salt, and water in a large pot and cook over low heat for 40 minutes, or until the beans are tender. Discard the vegetables, garlic, parsley, and excess liquid. Purée the beans in a blender. Purée the remaining garlic clove and add to beans along with the lemon juice, tahini, and remaining olive oil. Season to taste. Cover and set aside.

ASSEMBLY

½ cup Ghee (see page 28)
Balsamic Reduction Sauce (see page 26)

Truffle Sauce** (see page 36)

Invert the polenta onto a cutting board and cut into ¼-inch slices. In a sauté pan, brown both sides of each slice in the ghee until golden. Cool on a baking sheet lined with parchment paper. Spread ½ tablespoon of Fava Bean Purée over one polenta slice and top with mushroom slices. Cover the mushrooms with another slice of polenta and repeat the layering. Cover with a third and final slice of polenta. Repeat with the remaining slices and place on a baking sheet lined with parchment paper.

To serve, cover the Polenta Taragna with aluminium foil and reheat at 350°F for 5 minutes or until heated through. Top with ½ teaspoon of Truffle Sauce and serve with Balsamic Reduction Sauce on the side.

*If Polenta Taragna is unavailable, substitute plain polenta.
**If Truffle Sauce is unavailable, substitute Caper Parsley Sauce (see page 26).

Following strict instructions, an eleven-year-old Damiano arranged generous slices of cheese with bread around a plate and brought it out to his father on the veranda. "Thank you, Dami," Alberto said. He looked at his staff and continued, "I love my son. Always so charming and polite!" He looked down at his plate, frowned, and thundered, "Damiano! Don't ever bring out a plate without a fork! Learn to do things properly!"

Personal archive picture

Animatedly, his son bounded into the kitchen and returned with fork in hand in seconds. Alberto affectionately patted his son's cheek before turning his attention to his lunch.

Damiano, extraordinarily mature for his age, is an exact blend of both parents. Like his mother, he bounds about with verve and takes pleasure in the smallest acts of everyday life. From his father, he inherited the determination and focus to start and finish any project he tackles. He is quick to invent fantastic and hilarious stories with comic timing, eager to help in the kitchen or in the grounds, and generous with his toys and belongings. He is the joy of the Country House Montali and the marvel of those who meet him. But mostly, he is still an eleven-year-old boy with eleven-year-old interests, sensitive and protective to the needs of his parents

and resentful when his time with them is cut short. He is a young man defined by his own character and the nature in which he has been raised.

Damiano was born on February 22, 1994, after a complicated pregnancy. He was a healthy baby boy who looked exactly like Alberto. Despite warnings given by numerous doctors and specialists, Malu was determined to raise her son on a vegetarian diet. After the first few months of milk, she would incorporate vegetables into Damiano's diet, respecting his choice to accept or reject different ones. Damiano happily devoured the lentils and, later, after tasting pasta with light tomato sauce, rejected soft foods altogether for solids at the age of nine months. Doctors were amazed at the baby's growth and his alert responsiveness to stimulation. Eleven years later, he already towers over most of his classmates and continues to grow.

One November, the Musacchio family was taking their annual month-long post-season holiday, this year in Brazil. Damiano was five years old at the time and already quite perceptive. At dinner one evening, he was sitting between his parents at a table full of adults. Malu's sister-in-law, a wine aficionado, ordered a bottle of red wine. The waiter brought it to their table and poured a small amount in her glass to taste. She flamboyantly swirled her glass, sniffed deeply before sipping, swished the wine in her mouth, and nodded in approval. A few minutes later, the same waiter began pouring Damiano's soft drink into his glass. When it was partially full, Damiano took his glass, swirled it, sniffed deeply before tasting, and nodded to the waiter in approval, sending the table into howls of laughter.

Damiano's personality is based on his innate character as well as carefully observing everything he has seen. His parents decided early on that the best education they could provide their son was to open his eyes to the whole world from a very young age. Easily one of the most well-traveled children, he has been to Australia, Brazil, Lisbon, London, and five Southeast Asian countries. Staying in anywhere from

a simple village inn to a five star hotel in a major metropolitan city, he studies the rich culture and history of each town with his mother. By necessity, he assimilates easily with locals and effortlessly makes friends wherever he goes. When he is alone, he entertains himself by inventing science-fiction tales of fantastic universes. His mind is colored by the rich civilizations and experiences he has seen firsthand; his imagination is alive and vibrant.

At his age, he has an incredible work ethic. Along with witnessing the hours his parents put into the family-run business, he takes note of how various staff members work. This chef always works neatly, while the other never picks up his own mess. That girl is always happy while the other one is always depressed. He listens to his parents as they discuss what they admire and value, and he takes their work philosophy as his own.

Unfortunately, living and breathing the hospitality lifestyle wears Damiano down as well. Late one Sunday evening during dinner service, Damiano was sitting on a bench outside with his feet up and arms wrapped around his legs. He was staring sadly into space, uncharacteristically unresponsive to other people. Malu walked outside and put her arm around him and encouraged him to talk to her. He looked up at her and said simply, "Mamma, sometimes I really hate this." It was Sunday, the day his mother took off to spend with her son. Out of necessity she was downstairs working in the kitchen. His one day with her was lost.

Pressing matters and small emergencies continually interrupt the precious time that he has to spend with his parents. But rather than shut himself off, Damiano remains eager to open up and build personal relationships with nearly anyone who comes to work at Montali.

Being raised around food inevitably heightens one's awareness and understanding of it. Damiano's passions might be motorbike racing and soccer, but food is a predestined part of his life. Though he is most fond of simple foods like slabs of Parmigiano

Reggiano or *pasta e ceci*, he can also eat plate upon plate of spicy Asian-style noodles or curry-flavored couscous.

He appreciates new and uncommon flavors, but doesn't always enjoy overcomplicated smorgasbords of dishes. His ability to distinguish textures and flavors, to discriminate between different components in a dish, is beyond that of most adults. When Damiano has tomato sauce, he discerns the quality of the tomato, not always the overall flavor.

Malu and Alberto explained early on the very simple reasons why they were vegetarians. Not only was it an issue of health, but they also did not like the idea of another living creature losing its life so that others could eat. However, they stressed, that did not mean that they were any better or worse than others. Growing up as a vegetarian in a small town in Italy, Damiano has faced occasional bantering from classmates who do not understand this "odd" eating behavior.

"Eww! What is that?" one of them exclaimed one afternoon, calling everyone's attention to Damiano's lunch. Malu had made him a sandwich with several slices of seitan, his favorite. "Excuse me," Damiano quickly retorted. "Have you ever tasted this? Do you even know what it is?" The classmate shook his head sheepishly. Damiano exchanged a knowing glance with Paolo, his best friend and son of the local butcher, before returning to his lunch. While Damiano's classmates may not wholly understand his eating habits, none can deny the quality of Malu's cooking. For his February birthday, Malu always prepares a spectacular feast that all the schoolchildren look forward to for months in advance.

Should Damiano choose to stay a vegetarian for the rest of his life is a choice that Malu and Alberto have left completely to him. There may come a time when he grows curious about tasting new things, and he may want to change that aspect of his lifestyle entirely. The same is true for his career. If he wanted to take over the Country House Montali as an adult, his parents would be thrilled, but it would never be something they pushed on him. Damiano has always been encouraged to be his own person and seek his own path, and his parents have always done their best to guide him in the right direction while respecting his decisions, likes, and dislikes. They help him to distinguish between what he needs and what he wants, to work hard toward various goals, and to always use his mind as the greatest tool in life.

Malu and Alberto continue to teach him about food and hospitality at a steady pace. Already, he can make his own fresh pasta, ciabatta, and pizzas; open wine bottles; and serve with dignity. He became a star one day in Earls Court when the old chef Gennaro Contaldo called him up on stage. Since Damiano had nothing to do while his parents and staff were briefing before their cooking course for each day, he began to kindly and politely offer his help to this famous Italian chef. He was doing it for fun, but ended up becoming a real help to Gennaro, who was happy to have an extra, and excellent, helper in such busy times. On the last day of the event, at the moment when Gennaro was handing over to Alberto for the cooking classes, he called Damiano to the stage with him, in front of a big crowd of people. He signed his cookbook with best wishes and said to the big British crowd, aware of the special moment: "The reason why we have so many good chefs in Italy is that we start to train them young. Please, applause for the youngest chef of Italy and Britain!" A few eyes turned wet seeing something very similar to the "handing over of offices."

One cool August evening before dinner, Alberto was sitting on the veranda with a few guests and called out to his son. "Damiano! Three espressos!" Damiano set the tray with demitasse spoons, serving sugar and saucers before starting the espresso so that everything would be ready. He carried out the porcelain-laden tray and gently placed it on the table before his father. The service was perfect, and Alberto shared a proud, quiet smile with his son as the guests raved. Damiano, seeing that a beautiful twelve-year-old would be having dinner at the restaurant that night, left his father and raced upstairs to get ready. Fifteen minutes later, freshened with a

shower, light cologne, and hair gel, he put on his best shirt and jeans and emerged downstairs to help his mother with dinner. The kitchen staff grinned and Malu sighed wistfully. "Amore di mamma. Now it begins. Oh, my son is growing up so fast!"

FIRST COURSES

BIPARMENTIER

A velvety combination of two classic soups. At the end of the nineteenth century, a disease destroyed potato crops all over Europe, resulting in thousands of casualties. A French scientist, Monsieur Parmentier, discovered that potato plants near copper mines had not been affected. Parmentier found that treating potato crops with copper sulphate protected them from the disease. This delicious potato and leek soup is named after that scientist. Here it is served with a pumpkin soup. Great with a mild red wine.

Serves 6   **E**   *45 minutes*

PARMENTIER (POTATO AND LEEK SOUP)

1 leek, white and light green parts only

1 tablespoon extra virgin olive oil

1 tablespoon butter

12 ounces potatoes, peeled and thinly sliced

¼ cup coarsely chopped green olives

1 tablespoon coarsely chopped parsley

3½ cups Vegetable Stock (see page 36)

1 tablespoon heavy cream

Salt and black pepper to taste

Clean the leek well and chop coarsely. Cook in the oil and butter in a large pot over medium heat for 2 minutes. When soft, but not colored, add the potatoes, olives, parsley, and stock and simmer until the potatoes are tender and thoroughly cooked.

Remove from the heat. Purée in batches in a blender until the soup is completely smooth. Pour through a sieve to strain out any remaining chunks, then pour into a clean pot. Stir in the heavy cream and season with salt and black pepper. Cover and set aside until ready to serve.

ZUCCA (PUMPKIN SOUP)

1 leek, white and light green parts only

1 small shallot, finely chopped

1 tablespoon extra virgin olive oil

1 tablespoon butter

8 ounces pumpkin, peeled and cut into ½-inch cubes

1 potato, peeled and thinly sliced

3 sage leaves

2 teaspoons chopped parsley

Nutmeg

3¼ cups Vegetable Stock (see page 36)

1 tablespoon heavy cream

Salt and black pepper to taste

Clean the leek well and chop coarsely. In a large pot, cook the shallot in the oil and butter over medium heat until nearly transparent. Add the leek and continue to cook slowly until tender but not browned. Add the remaining vegetables, herbs, nutmeg, and stock and simmer until the potato and pumpkin are tender and thoroughly cooked. Remove the sage.

Remove from the heat. Purée in batches in a blender until the soup is completely smooth. Pour through a sieve into a clean pot. Stir in the heavy cream. Season with salt and pepper. Cover and set aside until ready to serve.

CROÛTONS

6 slices day-old bread

2 tablespoons olive oil

Salt and pepper

1 tablespoon mixed chopped herbs (parsley, sage, thyme, rosemary)

————

Preheat the oven to 350°F. Cut the bread into ½-inch cubes. Place in a bowl and toss with the olive oil, salt, pepper, and herbs. Toast on a baking sheet for 5 minutes or until golden brown and crispy on the outside and still soft in the middle.

ASSEMBLY

Heavy cream for drizzling (optional)

————

When ready to serve, cook the soups until heated through and check the consistency of each. If one is too thick, add a small amount of stock until equal consistency is achieved. Scoop ½ cup of each into two equal-sized ladles. Holding one ladle in each hand, slowly pour out both soups at the same time, starting at the center of the bowl. Move the ladles up and down for a straight line down the center or play around with different designs. Drizzle with cream, if desired. Serve immediately with croûtons on the side or on top of the soup. These soups are also delicious served chilled in the summertime.

ZUPPA REALE

This "royal soup" is deliciously light and made from mixed vegetables and crispy egg-dough fritters.

Serves 6 Ⓜ *35 minutes & 1 hour simmering*

STOCK

2 medium tomatoes

1 medium onion

2 medium zucchini

2 carrots

2 medium potatoes

2 celery stalks

4 ounces spinach leaves

2 garlic cloves

8 cups hot water

1 sprig parsley

1 teaspoon extra virgin olive oil

1½ teaspoons sea salt

———

Quarter the tomatoes and onion. Halve the zucchini, carrots, potatoes, and celery and cut into large chunks. Combine all the ingredients in a pot. Cover and simmer for 1 hour. Strain and discard the vegetables. Return to the pot.

FRITTATINE

4 eggs

6 tablespoons semolina flour

2 pinches of salt

¼ cup grated Parmesan

Black pepper to taste

———

In a bowl, lightly beat all the ingredients together. Ladle 3 tablespoons of the egg mixture onto a buttered nonstick pan over medium heat. Let the mixture spread to approximately 5½ inches in diameter. When the bottom is cooked, gently flip with a spatula. Repeat with the remaining egg mixture. Cut each fritter into ¼-inch squares.

ESCAROLE

2 heads escarole, cored and coarsely chopped

2 garlic cloves

2 tablespoons extra virgin olive oil

Salt and pepper to taste

———

Bring a large pot of lightly salted water to a boil. Blanch the escarole in the water for 1 minute, then drain in a colander. In a large skillet, sauté the garlic in the olive oil until golden brown. Add the escarole and cook for 1 minute. Season with salt and pepper.

ASSEMBLY

5 ounces Scamorza (see page 20), or other soft mild cheese, cubed

Extra virgin olive oil, for drizzling

———

Heat the vegetable stock, add the escarole and Fritattine, and simmer for 5 minutes. Divide the Scamorza between six bowls and ladle the soup over the cheese. Drizzle a few drops of olive oil on top and serve immediately.

PASTA e FAGIOLI

In the heat of the summer, fresh borlotti beans and tomatoes are harvested at their peak. Best when made in July and August, this creamy and comforting stew with slightly under-ripe green bell pepper exudes the essence and flavors of an Italian kitchen garden. Serve with a smooth red wine, such as a dolcetto or merlot.

Serves 8 Ⓜ *55 minutes & 1 hour simmering*

STEW

12 ounces fresh borlotti beans or 6 ounces dried beans soaked in water for 8 hours

6 basil leaves

2 sprigs parsley

4 garlic cloves

1/2 medium onion, sliced

1 celery stalk

1 small green bell pepper, halved and seeded

1/3 cup extra virgin olive oil

3 1/2 cups water

1 teaspoon salt

3 tomatoes, peeled, seeded, and coarsely chopped

———

In a large saucepan, combine the beans with 3 basil leaves, 1 sprig of parsley, 2 cloves of garlic, and half of the vegetables, except the tomatoes. Add 3 tablespoons of the olive oil, the water, and salt. Cover and cook slowly over low heat until the beans are al dente, approximately 1 hour. Remove the vegetables with a slotted spoon, leaving only the beans and cooking liquid. In a separate saucepan, combine the tomatoes with the remaining herbs and vegetables. Cook over low heat for 20 minutes until the liquid from the tomatoes has evaporated. Season with salt. Add the tomato mixture to the beans and continue to cook over low heat for 10 minutes. Remove the aromatic vegetables.

MALTAGLIATI

1 1/2 cups Italian '00' flour (see page 16)

1 1/2 cups Grano Duro flour (see page 17)

1 tablespoon finely chopped herbs (thyme, sage, and rosemary)

1 teaspoon extra virgin olive oil

Pinch of salt

1 cup water

———

Sift the flours together over a work surface, add the herbs and make a well in the center. Add the remaining ingredients and work into the flour with your fingers until a dough forms. Gather the dough into a ball and knead for 8 minutes until the texture is soft and elastic to the touch. Wrap in plastic wrap and let rest for 15 minutes. Divide the dough in half and roll each portion into a long strip. Pass each long strip through a pasta machine from the widest setting to number 6. Dry out for 10 minutes on a work surface. Dust the pasta strips with Grano Duro flour and halve each strip lengthwise. Stack the four strips on top of each other and cut in half horizontally. Stack the eight strips on top of each other and, starting from one end, cut the dough on a bias into 1/2-inch pieces. Toss the pasta between your fingers to separate the pieces and lay them on a baking sheet dusted with Grano Duro flour.

TO SERVE

Reheat the bean stew. Bring a large pot of water to a boil. Season with salt and reduce to a simmer. Gently gather the pasta with your hands, shake off excess flour, and cook in the boiling water. As soon as the pasta comes to the surface (approximately 1 minute), use a slotted spoon to transfer the pasta to the stew with beans. Gently stir the stew, taste for seasoning, and serve immediately with a sprinkling of chopped basil and a drizzle of extra virgin olive oil over each portion.

ROTOLO di CRESPELLE

A roulade of crêpes stuffed with crunchy mixed vegetables. As delicious as it is beautiful, this dish is a huge success at any gathering. Great with a crisp white wine like a Müller Thurgau.

Serves 6 to 8   Ⓜ   *55 minutes*

CRÊPES

1 cup all-purpose flour
Salt and black pepper to taste
1 cup milk

3 eggs
1 tablespoon butter, melted, plus extra for the pan

———

Combine the flour, a pinch of salt, and a pinch of black pepper in a bowl. Whisk the milk, eggs, and 1 tablespoon butter gently in another bowl. Add the liquid to the flour, whisking until even and lump-free. Set aside for 30 minutes. Heat a 9-inch skillet or crêpe pan and brush lightly with butter. Remove the pan from the heat, ladle ¼ cup of the batter into the pan, and swirl slowly to cover the bottom. Place back on the heat. When one side is golden brown, gently flip and cook the other side in the same manner. Repeat with the remaining batter. Set the crêpes aside.

FILLING

3 garlic cloves
3 tablespoons chopped onion
3 sage leaves
3 mint leaves
1 tablespoon chopped parsley
2 tablespoons butter
2 tablespoons extra virgin olive oil

1½ pounds mixed vegetables (zucchini, carrots, and cabbage), cut into thin strips
Salt and pepper to taste
2 egg yolks
6 oil-packed sun-dried tomatoes, chopped
¼ cup grated Parmesan
1½ cups ricotta
Nutmeg to taste

———

In a sauté pan, sauté the garlic, onion, sage, mint, and parsley in the butter and olive oil over medium heat until the onion is slightly transparent. Add the mixed vegetables. Increase the heat to high and cook for 5 minutes, tossing occasionally. Season with salt and pepper. Remove from the heat, discard the garlic, sage, and mint, and cool completely. Mix in the egg yolks, tomatoes, cheeses, and nutmeg.

ASSEMBLY

1½ teaspoons dry bread crumbs mixed with 1 tablespoon grated Parmesan
3 tablespoons melted butter

———

Preheat the oven to 350°F. Place three crêpes side by side on a work surface. Spread 2½ table-spoons of the vegetable mixture over each crêpe. Stack them on top of each other. From one side, gently roll the stack to create a large cannelloni shape. Set aside and repeat with the remaining crêpes.

Cut the roulade into 1½-inch-thick slices. Place the slices in a buttered casserole dish cut-side up. Sprinkle the bread crumbs over the surface and drizzle with the melted butter. Bake for 15 minutes or until the top is golden brown. Serve immediately.

This dish can be served with a variety of fillings. Feel free to experiment with your favorites.

A ravioli from the south Tyrol, on the Italian border with Austria. The spinach and potato dough is stuffed with two mushroom varieties and topped with juniper cream and shallot sauces, transforming a classic ravioli into the divine. Enjoy with a full-bodied wine, such as an amarone.

Serves 4 to 6   **D**   *80 minutes*

FILLING

1 ounce dried porcini mushrooms	Salt and pepper to taste
1 garlic clove, gently smashed	1 tablespoon chopped parsley
2 tablespoons extra virgin olive oil	1 tablespoon grated Parmesan
4 ounces fresh mushrooms, coarsely chopped	

Soak the dried porcini in a small saucepan of hot water for 30 minutes. Drain in a colander and chop coarsely. In a sauté pan, sauté the garlic in the oil over high heat. When it begins to color, add the rehydrated and fresh mushrooms and cook until golden brown and the liquid has evaporated. Season with salt and pepper and cool before adding the parsley and Parmesan. Set aside.

SHALLOT SAUCE

3 shallots	5 tablespoons olive oil

With a mandoline, slice the shallots crosswise into thin rings. In a saucepan, cook the shallots in the oil over low heat, stirring occasionally, for 30 minutes or until dark and tender. Cover and set aside.

JUNIPER CREAM SAUCE

1⅓ cups Vegetable Stock (see page 36)	1 tablespoon cornstarch
5 juniper berries, crushed	1 cup half-and-half

In a saucepan, bring ½ cup of the stock and the juniper berries to a boil and let infuse for 5 minutes. Pass through a sieve, discard the berries, and add the infused stock to the regular stock. In a saucepan, heat the stock to a simmer. Mix the cornstarch with the half-and-half and pour into the hot stock, whisking constantly. Continue whisking until the sauce comes to a simmer, then cook for 1 minute longer. Cover and set aside.

DOUGH

2 yellow potatoes	1 egg, lightly beaten
1 tablespoon butter	Dash of nutmeg
2½ cups spinach leaves, cooked, drained well, and finely chopped	Salt and pepper to taste
	⅔ cup Grano Duro flour (see page 17)

In a saucepan, boil the potatoes in water to cover until tender. Let cool slightly, then peel. In a bowl, mash the potatoes with the butter while still warm. Cover and cool to room temperature. Place on a floured work surface, add the spinach, and incorporate well. Add the egg, nutmeg, salt, and pepper. Work the dough with a spatula to combine. Add the flour in three batches, incorporating well after each addition. Add more flour if the dough is still too sticky. Sprinkle the work surface with Grano

Duro flour and roll a third of the dough into a large disk about ⅛ inch thick. Cut out as many circles as possible using a 2-inch cutter. Place ½ teaspoon of the filling in the center of each disk and gently fold in half into a crescent shape. Seal by pressing lightly with your fingertips. Repeat with the remaining dough, using the scraps as well, until either the dough or the filling runs out. Place the ravioli, not touching, on a floured baking sheet.

TO SERVE

Reheat the shallot and the cream sauces. Bring a pot of lightly salted water to a boil and reduce to a simmer. Gently add half of the ravioli. When the ravioli rise to the surface, use a slotted spoon to transfer about six pieces to each plate. Ladle the cream sauce over the top. Dot with shallots and shallot-infused oil. Repeat with the remaining ravioli. Sprinkle with freshly ground white pepper and serve.

A famous hand-rolled Umbrian pasta served with a tomato, caper, and olive sauce. The texture and feel of the pasta can only be achieved by the use of hands, and the "puttanesca"-like sauce demands the accompaniment of a merlot. Similar pasta is called Pici in Tuscany.

Serves 4 to 6   (M)   *50 minutes*

DOUGH

1¼ cups Italian 'OO' flour (see page 16)

1 cup Grano Duro flour (see page 17)

1 egg

½ cup water, at room temperature

½ teaspoon extra virgin olive oil

Pinch of salt

———

Sift both flours onto a work surface and make a well in the center. Add the remaining ingredients to the well and work with your fingertips until a dough forms. Gather the dough and knead for 8 minutes. Wrap in plastic wrap and let rest for 15 minutes.

Using a knife or pastry cutter, portion off a quarter of the dough, leaving the rest in the plastic wrap. With a rolling pin, roll it into a long rectangle ¼ inch thick. Cut into ¼-inch-wide strips starting from the short end. Roll each piece into a long, thin rope approximately ⅛ inch in diameter. Gently toss with flour and transfer to a floured baking sheet. Repeat with the remaining dough.

SAUCE

2 garlic cloves

2 tablespoons capers, coarsely chopped

12 black olives, pitted and coarsely chopped

¼ cup extra virgin olive oil

1½ quantities Tomato Sauce (see page 36)

———

In a sauté pan, sauté the garlic, capers, and olives in the olive oil until the garlic is golden brown. Remove the garlic, add the Tomato Sauce, and heat.

TO SERVE

1 handful grated Parmesan

———

Bring a large pot of lightly salted water to a boil and reduce to a simmer. Slide the pasta into the simmering water. Refrain from stirring the delicate noodles; if pieces stick together as they come to the surface, gently separate with a fork. Cook for an additional minute after the pasta comes to the surface and check for doneness. When the pasta is al dente, drain off the water, reserving 1 cup of cooking liquid, and add the pasta and Parmesan to the sauce. Toss together, adding the reserved cooking liquid, a few tablespoons at a time, if the sauce is too dry. Serve immediately.

RISOTTO allo ZAFFERANO

The comforting texture and sophisticated flavor of this saffron risotto make it one of the most praised dishes at the Country House Montali. Pair with a mild white wine, like regaleali or sauvignon blanc, to avoid competing with the saffron.

Serves 4 to 6 Ⓔ *20 minutes & 1 hour soaking*

INGREDIENTS

1 teaspoons saffron threads

1¼ cups Carnaroli or Arborio rice

3 cups Vegetable Stock (see page 36)

1 tablespoon extra virgin olive oil

2 tablespoons butter

1 small garlic clove, minced

½ medium onion, finely chopped

⅓ cup white wine

4 ounces Fontina or Taleggio, cut into ½-inch cubes

6 tablespoons grated Parmigiano Reggiano

Salt and white pepper to taste

———

In a small bowl, soak the saffron in 3 tablespoons of hot water for 1 hour. Rinse the rice thoroughly and drain in a sieve. Heat the stock in a saucepan until it just comes to a boil and turn off the heat.

In another saucepan, heat the olive oil and half of the butter over medium-low heat. When the butter has melted, add the garlic and onion and cook slowly, stirring. When the onion is translucent, add the rice and stir. When the rice becomes slightly translucent, add the white wine and stir until evaporated. Add 2 ladlefuls of the hot stock and stir gently until the liquid nearly evaporates. Add the remaining stock, two ladlefuls at a time, and stir until each addition is nearly evaporated before adding more. Add the saffron and its soaking water and stir to combine. If the rice is still undercooked, add a small amount of hot water. When the rice is al dente (about 15 minutes from the start of cooking), turn off the heat and stir in the cheeses and remaining butter. Season to taste with salt and white pepper and serve immediately.

When using the parboiled variety, rice will usually take 12 to 15 minutes to cook. For best results, check the instructions for the brand of rice you are using.

FRANCOBOLLI di GORGONZOLA al PESTO

Rich, decorative francobolli, or "stamps," are stuffed with rich Gorgonzola cheese and served with a classic pesto sauce. Pair with a strong red wine. Pesto is surely one of the greatest achievements of the city of Genoa.

Serves 8 **D** *35 minutes*

DOUGH

1 cup Italian 'OO' flour (see page 16)
3/4 cup Grano Duro flour (see page 17)
2 whole eggs
   olive oil

3 egg yolks
Pinch of salt
1/2 teaspoon extra virgin

Sift the flours onto a work surface and create a well in the center. Add the remaining ingredients to the well and work with your fingertips until the dough comes together. Gather into a ball and knead for 3 minutes. If the dough feels dry, moisten your hands with water and continue to work. Wrap with plastic wrap and refrigerate for 15 minutes.

FILLING

2 ounces Crescenza or creamy goat cheese

3 ounces Gorgonzola

In a bowl, beat both cheeses together with a fork until very creamy and transfer to a pastry bag fitted with a 1/2-inch tip. Refrigerate for at least 15 minutes.

SAUCE

1/2 quantity Pesto (see page 31)
1 teaspoon butter

In a medium sauté pan, heat the Pesto with the butter until warm.

ASSEMBLY

1 egg white, lightly beaten, for brushing
Grated Parmesan
Black pepper to taste

Roll the dough to number 7 through a pasta machine into a long sheet approximately 5 1/2 inches wide. Brush half of the sheet with the egg white. Leaving a 1/2-inch border around the edges, pipe out approximately 1/3 teaspoonfuls of cheese filling 3/4 inch apart over the brushed half (see picture). Carefully cover with the unbrushed half of the sheet and press gently between the mounds of filling with your fingertips to push out excess air and seal. Trim the outside borders with a fluted pastry wheel, then run the wheel between the rows of filling to separate each piece. Place the pieces of pasta, not touching, on a lightly floured baking sheet.

Bring a pot of lightly salted water to a boil and reduce to a simmer. Slide the pasta into the simmering water. As soon as the pasta comes to the surface, transfer with a slotted spoon directly into the sauce. Add 1/2 ladleful of the pasta cooking liquid. Toss the pasta three or four times so that each piece is coated with sauce. Transfer to a large serving dish. Sprinkle with grated Parmesan and black pepper and serve immediately.

STROGANOFF

A meatless version of a popular Russian recipe, this dish loses none of the famous texture or flavor with the addition of seitan. Savor o n a cold winter night with a glass of hearty barbaresco wine.

Serves 6   Ⓜ   *50 minutes*

SAUCE

3 garlic cloves, 2 whole and 1 minced

5 tablespoons extra virgin olive oil

1 pound porcini or button mushrooms, sliced

½ quantity Seitan (see page 35)

1 shallot, finely chopped

2 tablespoons butter

3 tablespoons brandy or cognac

1½ quantities Tomato Sauce (see page 36)

⅔ cup half-and-half

———

In a sauté pan, sauté 2 whole garlic cloves in 3 tablespoons of the olive oil over high heat. When the garlic begins to color, add the mushrooms and cook until they are browned and the liquid has evaporated. Discard the garlic and set aside the mushrooms. Slice the seitan into ½-x-1½-inch pieces. Sauté the minced garlic and shallot in the remaining olive oil and the butter for 1 minute over medium heat. Add the seitan and cook for 5 minutes or until nicely browned. Flambé with the alcohol (see page 21). Add the mushrooms to the seitan and cook for an additional minute. In a saucepan, heat the Tomato Sauce to a simmer. Mix in the half-and-half and add the seitan-mushroom mixture. Stir well to combine the ingredients. Cover and set aside.

RICE

2¼ cups Vegetable Stock (see page 36), or as much as rice package directs

1 small garlic clove, minced

1 small shallot, finely chopped

1 tablespoon extra virgin olive oil

1 tablespoon butter

1½ cups converted white rice, rinsed

Salt and pepper to taste

———

In a saucepan, bring the stock to a simmer. In a large heavy-bottomed pot, gently sauté the garlic and shallot in the olive oil and butter until translucent. Stir in the rice and cook for 1 minute. Add the stock, cover, and cook over low heat for 12 minutes (or for as long as the rice package directs), or until the rice has absorbed all the liquid and is tender. Reheat the sauce, adjust the seasoning, and serve surrounding the rice on individual plates.

CANNELLONI di RICOTTA con SUGO di POMODORO

Ricotta cheese cannelloni with tomato sauce. An Italian family favorite for Sunday lunch, this classic cannelloni needs only a simple tomato sauce and a glass of mild red wine.

Serves 6   M   *45 minutes*

DOUGH

1¼ cups Italian '00' flour (see page 16)
⅔ cup Grano Duro flour (see page 17)
2 whole eggs

3 egg yolks
Pinch of salt
1 teaspoon extra virgin olive oil, plus more for ice bath

———

Sift the flours together on a work surface and make a well in the center. In a separate bowl, lightly beat the remaining ingredients together and add to the well. Work with your fingertips until a dough forms. Gather the dough and knead well for 5 minutes until the texture is smooth and elastic. Wrap in plastic wrap and let rest for 15 minutes. Cut the dough in thirds, roll each portion to number 6 through a pasta machine, and lay out on a floured surface. Cut into 5-inch squares and layer between parchment paper dusted with Grano Duro flour. Bring a large pot of lightly salted water to a boil and reduce to a simmer. Prepare a large bowl of ice water and add 1 tablespoon oil. Cook the pasta in batches of eight squares, adding them to the water one at a time. As soon as each square comes to the surface, transfer to the ice bath with a slotted spoon to cool quickly. Transfer the squares one by one to clean, dry towels on a work surface. Do not overlap the squares.

FILLING

1½ cups fresh ricotta, well drained
1 egg
Black pepper to taste
Nutmeg

1 tablespoon grated Pecorino Romano
1 tablespoon grated Parmigiano Reggiano
1 tablespoon grated Pecorino di Pienza (see page 20)
Grated zest of ½ lemon

———

In a bowl, beat the ricotta with a fork until creamy. Add the remaining ingredients and mix until smooth. Set aside.

SUGO DI POMODORO

2 garlic cloves, peeled
3 tablespoons extra virgin olive oil
1½ teaspoons chopped parsley

1½ teaspoons chopped basil
1½ quantities Tomato Sauce (see page 36), warmed

———

In a sauté pan, sauté the garlic in the olive oil until colored, then discard. Then add the herbs to the oil and stir to infuse. Add to the warm Tomato Sauce. Set aside.

ASSEMBLY

¼ cup grated Parmigiano Reggiano

8 ounces mozzarella, cut into ¼-inch cubes

———

Preheat the oven to 350°F. Using a pastry bag or spoon, place 2 tablespoons filling along one edge of each pasta square and roll up evenly so that each cannelloni is ¾ inch thick. Ladle half of the sauce onto the bottom of a medium gratin dish, spreading evenly. Arrange the cannelloni over the sauce. Sprinkle with Parmigiano Reggiano, cover with the remaining of the sauce, then top with the mozzarella. (Alternatively, prepare individual servings in small gratin dishes.) Bake for 13 minutes. Serve immediately.

SPAGHETTI alla CHITARRA con SALSA ai QUATTRO FORMAGGI e TARTUFO

This famous guitar-string spaghetti is for all rock 'n' roll aficionados! Cut from a guitarlike pasta cutter, this dish features three different kinds of pasta and is served with Four Cheese and Truffle sauces.

Serves 4 **D** *75 minutes*

SAFFRON DOUGH

½ cup Italian '00' flour (see page 16)

½ cup Grano Duro flour (see page 17)

1 whole egg and 2 egg yolks

Pinch of salt

½ teaspoon extra virgin olive oil

½ teaspoon saffron powder*

*If using saffron threads, soak in 2 tablespoons of hot water for one hour. Add an additional tablespoon of Italian '00' flour to the dough when mixing.

SPINACH DOUGH

⅓ cup Italian '00' flour (see page 16)

⅓ cup Grano Duro flour (see page 17), plus more for dusting

2 tablespoons cooked spinach, squeezed dry and puréed

1 whole egg and 1 egg yolk

Pinch of salt

½ teaspoon extra virgin olive oil

BEET DOUGH

⅓ cup Italian '00' flour (see page 16)

⅓ cup Grano Duro flour (see page 17)

2 tablespoons finely chopped cooked beet, puréed and well drained

1 whole yolk and 1 egg yolk

Pinch of salt

½ teaspoon extra virgin olive oil

Starting with the Saffron Dough, sift the flours onto a work surface and make a well in the center. Add the remaining dough ingredients to the well and work with your fingertips until a dough forms. Knead for 3 minutes. Roll into a ball, cover with plastic wrap, and set aside. Repeat this process for the Spinach and Beet doughs.

Start with one ball of dough. Roll out half the dough into an 8-x-2-inch rectangle, ⅛ inch thick, on a work surface dusted with Grano Duro flour. Repeat with the other doughs and dry on a floured baking sheet for 10 minutes. Cut with either a pasta guitar, pressing the dough through the strings with a rolling pin, or with a long knife. If using a knife, flour each strip and wrap around a rolling pin, starting from the short end. Carefully slide out the rolling pin and cut the coil of dough crosswise into ⅛-inch-wide strips. Toss with Grano Duro flour and set, in nests, on a floured baking sheet.

SAUCE

1 quantity Four Cheese Sauce (see page 28)

1 quantity Sage Butter (see page 32)

1 quantity Truffle Sauce (see page 36)

Heat the Four Cheese Sauce in a double boiler. Bring a pot of salted water to a boil and reduce to a simmer. Cook the pastas together in the boiling water. As soon as they come to the surface, remove from the heat and drain in a colander. In a large nonstick sauté pan, melt the Sage Butter, add the pasta, and toss together. Pour the Cheese Sauce onto individual plates and add the pasta. Drizzle with more Cheese Sauce and dot with Truffle Sauce.

MACCHERONI LADUS

Of Sardinian origin, this "stretched maccheroni" is a handmade pasta served with a medley of earthy vegetables in a tomato sauce. Wonderful with a Sardinian "cannonau" or a pinot noir.

Serves 6 Ⓜ *60 minutes*

MACCHERONI DOUGH

1 cup Italian '00' flour (see page 16)

1 cup Grano Duro flour (see page 17)

1 egg

⅓ cup water, at room temperature

½ teaspoon extra virgin olive oil

Pinch of salt

———

Sift both flours onto a work surface and make a well in the center. Add the remaining ingredients to the well and work with your fingertips until a dough forms. Gather the dough and knead for 8 minutes. Wrap in plastic wrap and let rest for 15 minutes.

Using a knife or pastry cutter, portion off a quarter of the dough, leaving the rest in the plastic wrap. Roll out into a long rope ⅓ inch thick on a work surface dusted with Grano Duro flour. Cut the rope into ⅓-inch pieces. Roll each piece into a ball, press the middle with your thumb, and gently push forward to pull the dough. With your fingertips, gently stretch each piece into a 2-x-¾-inch rectangle. Transfer the pasta to a floured baking sheet and repeat with the remaining dough.

STEW

1 small red bell pepper

1 eggplant, peeled and cubed

3 zucchini, cubed

Vegetable oil, for deep-frying

1 tablespoon chopped parsley

2 garlic cloves, minced

3 tablespoons extra virgin olive oil

5 tomatoes, peeled, seeded, and cubed

1 cup Vegetable Stock, heated (see page 36)

———

Blacken and peel the bell pepper (see page 20) and cut into 1½-x-½-inch pieces. In batches, deep-fry the eggplant and zucchini cubes in the vegetable oil until brown (see page 20). Transfer from the hot oil onto a baking sheet lined with paper towels. Season and let cool to room temperature. In a saucepan, cook the parsley and garlic in the olive oil for 1 minute. Stir in the tomatoes and cook for 10 minutes. Add the eggplant, zucchini, and red pepper and cook for 3 minutes. Add the hot stock and cook for an additional minute.

TO SERVE

Grated Pecorino Pienza (see page 20)

———

Bring a pot of salted water to a boil. Reduce to a simmer, and slide in the pasta from the baking sheet. Cook until al dente (approximately 5 minutes), drain off the cooking liquid, and transfer the pasta to the stew. Add a handful of grated cheese and serve immediately.

LASAGNE alla MONTALI

There is no comparison to fresh lasagne layered with roasted cherry tomatoes, pesto, and a creamy velouté sauce minutes before serving. Topped with arugula, pine nuts, and black olives, this special dish may be paired with a good white wine, like a chardonnay or a greco di tufo.

Serves 8 **D** *75 minutes*

SHEET PASTA DOUGH

1¼ cups Italian 'OO' flour (see page 16)

⅔ cup Grano Duro flour (see page 17)

2 whole eggs

3 egg yolks

Pinch of salt

1 teaspoons extra virgin olive oil

———

Sift the flours together on a work surface and make a well in the center. In a separate bowl, lightly beat the remaining ingredients together and add to the well. Work with your fingertips until a dough forms. Gather the dough and knead well for 5 minutes until the texture is smooth and elastic. Wrap in plastic wrap and let rest for 15 minutes. Cut the dough into thirds, roll each portion to number 6 through a pasta machine, and lay out on a floured surface. Using a 4-inch round cookie cutter or drinking glass, cut out disks and lay out on floured parchment paper.

CHERRY TOMATO SAUCE

1 cup extra virgin olive oil

32 cherry tomatoes, halved horizontally

5 tablespoons dry bread crumbs

1 tablespoon chopped basil

1 tablespoon chopped parsley

1 garlic clove, crushed through a press

Salt and pepper to taste

———

Preheat the oven to 350°F. Drizzle ¼ cup of the olive oil onto a 13-x-9-inch baking pan. Cover with the tomatoes, cut-side up. Combine the remaining ingredients, except 3 tablespoons of the olive oil, in a bowl and season. Top the tomatoes with the bread crumb mixture, pressing gently with your fingertips. Drizzle with the remaining olive oil and bake for 30 minutes or until golden brown.

VELOUTÉ

1½ cups Vegetable Stock (see page 36)

2 tablespoons butter

5 tablespoons all-purpose flour

2 tablespoons half-and-half

6 tablespoons grated Parmesan

6 tablespoons grated Pecorino Romano

6 tablespoons grated Emmenthal

———

In a saucepan, bring the stock to a boil and reduce to a simmer. Melt the butter in a separate pot over medium-low heat. Add the flour, stirring constantly until the roux is golden brown. Add the stock, whisking to combine. Stir until creamy, about 5 minutes. Stir in the half-and-half and cheeses. Cover and set aside.

ASSEMBLY

½ cup grated Parmigiano Reggiano

½ quantity Pesto (see page 31)

3 tablespoons pine nuts, toasted

¼ cup black olives, pitted, chopped, and covered in oil

10 ounces arugula

Extra virgin olive oil

Salt and pepper to taste

Bring a pot of lightly salted water to a boil and reduce to a simmer. Reheat the velouté and spread 2 tablespoons onto each serving plate. Cook the pasta in two batches in the simmering water. As soon as the pasta comes to the surface, place one disk on each plate over the sauce. Top with more sauce, a sprinkle of Parmigiano Reggiano, a teaspoon of Pesto, and four tomato halves. Cover with one more disk and repeat the filling. Cover with a final disk and top with a sprinkling of cheese, Pesto, and pine nuts. Dot with olives and a small handful of fresh arugula. Drizzle with olive oil and season with salt and pepper to taste.

GNOCCHI di PATATE

The soft, mouth-watering texture of this famous potato pasta makes gnocchi one of the most frequently demanded dishes in Italy. The quick flick of the fingers in the preparation of the pasta adds to the enjoyment of making gnocchi at home. Choose a strong red wine to accompany the Four Cheese Sauce.

Serves 4   Ⓜ   *35 minutes*

DOUGH

4 medium potatoes, yellow or red
¾ teaspoon butter
Pinch of salt
Pinch of nutmeg
2 egg yolks
½ cup Italian '00' flour (see page 16)
½ cup Grano Duro flour (see page 17)

———

In a saucepan, cook and peel the potatoes in water to cover until tender. Peel the potatoes and push through a potato ricer onto a lightly floured work surface. Add the butter and salt. Work well with a spatula until evenly incorporated. Cover and cool completely. Add the nutmeg and egg yolks and work them into the potato with your hands until the dough is even in color and texture. In batches, incorporate the two flours into the dough with the help of a dough scraper. When the dough begins to come together, knead quickly and gently until even, adding more Grano Duro flour if it is too sticky.

Using a dough scraper or knife, portion off 2 tablespoons of dough. Roll out on a lightly floured surface into a long ½-inch-thick rope. Cut crosswise into ½-inch pieces. Gently press your index and middle fingers into the center of one piece and slowly roll your fingers back toward you, allowing the dough to follow and form a shell shape. Repeat with the remaining dough, gently tossing batches with Grano Duro flour to avoid sticking. Set aside on a floured baking sheet, making sure the pieces do not touch.

SAUCE/GARNISH

1 handful red or green grapes, preferably seedless
Confectioners' sugar, for sprinkling
½ handful chopped walnuts

1 quantity Four Cheese Sauce
   (see page 28)

———

Preheat the oven to 350°F. Peel and halve the grapes. Gently remove the seeds, if needed, and lay the halves, cut-side down, on a baking sheet lined with parchment paper. Sprinkle very lightly with confectioners' sugar and bake for 10 minutes. Heat the Four Cheese Sauce in a double boiler and transfer to a sauté pan.

ASSEMBLY

Bring a pot of lightly salted water to a simmer and slide in the gnocchi from the baking sheet. As soon as the pieces come to the surface (approximately 1 minute), remove with a slotted spoon and place immediately into the sauce. Toss together and transfer to a large serving platter or individual plates. Garnish with chopped walnuts and baked grape halves and serve immediately.

RISO alla ORIENTALE

An aromatic basmati rice served with a lively tomato sauce laden with peas, Asian spices, and Paneer, a homemade cheese. Enjoy this interesting combination of flavors with a crisp gewürztraminer wine.

Serves 4 to 6 Ⓜ *70 minutes*

PANEER

1 quantity Paneer (see page 30)

2 tablespoons Ghee (see page 28)

Salt and black pepper to taste

———

Cut the Paneer into ½-x-½-inch pieces. In a sauté pan, sauté the pieces in the ghee until golden brown. Season to taste.

SAUCE

1½ cups shelled fresh or frozen peas

¼ cup extra virgin olive oil

½ small onion, sliced

Salt and black pepper to taste

1 teaspoon cumin seeds

1 shallot, chopped

1 small garlic clove, minced

2 tablespoons Ghee (see page 28)

1 tablespoon grated fresh ginger

1 small green bell pepper, seeded
  and chopped

10 tomatoes, peeled, seeded, and chopped

1 teaspoon ground coriander

1 teaspoon curry powder

1 teaspoon ground fennel seeds

1 tablespoon brown sugar

1 tablespoon chopped mint

2 tablespoons chopped parsley

⅔ cup plain yogurt, at room temperature

———

In a saucepan, combine the peas with 1 tablespoon of the olive oil, the onion, salt, black pepper, and enough water to cover. Cook until the peas are tender. Drain off the liquid and discard the onion. In a saucepan, heat the cumin seeds, shallot, and garlic in 2 tablespoons olive oil and the ghee until the cumin seeds color. Add the ginger and green pepper and cook for 1 minute. Add the tomatoes, coriander, curry powder, fennel, sugar, and half of the fresh herbs. Cook for 15 minutes, partially covered, stirring occasionally. Purée in a blender, transfer back to the heat, add the peas, and cook for 5 minutes. Remove from the heat, cool for 10 minutes, and slowly mix in the yogurt until fully combined. Add the Paneer and remaining herbs and taste for seasoning. Keep warm.

RICE

3 tablespoons sesame seeds

Salt

1½ cups Vegetable Stock (see page 36)

1 small garlic clove

2 shallots, finely chopped

2 tablespoons olive oil

2 tablespoons butter

1¼ cups basmati or long-grain rice

2 tablespoons Ghee (see page 28), melted

2 tablespoons chopped parsley

———

Toast the sesame seeds in a small dry skillet with ½ teaspoon of salt and set aside. In a saucepan, heat the stock and keep at a simmer. In a heavy-bottomed pot, gently sauté the garlic and shallots in the olive oil and butter until the shallots are translucent. Stir in the rice and cook for 1 minute. Add the stock, partially cover, and cook over low heat for 10 minutes, or until the rice has absorbed all the liquid and is cooked. Divide the rice between serving plates, drizzle with the ghee, and sprinkle with the parsley and sesame seeds. Serve alongside the sauce.

GNOCCHETTI SARDI

These small Sardinian gnocchi are made from durum wheat flour. The shape of this pasta is similar to that of the Gnocchi di Patate. The texture and sauce of this spectacular Mediterranean dish capture the essence of a refreshing Italian summer.

Serves 6 Ⓜ *40 minutes & 1 hour resting*

TOMATO OLIVE SAUCE

1¼ pounds cherry tomatoes, seeded and cut into eighths

½ cup black olives, coarsely chopped

½ cup green olives, coarsely chopped

1 tablespoon capers

5 basil leaves

1 garlic clove, crushed through a press

1 teaspoon chopped oregano

1 tablespoon chopped parsley

Salt and black pepper to taste

1 teaspoon soy sauce

6 tablespoons extra virgin olive oil

1 small zucchini, grated

Combine all ingredients in a large bowl and squeeze with your hands to mix together and break up the tomatoes. Cover and set aside for 1 hour to allow the flavors to blend.

DOUGH

1 cup Italian 'OO' flour (see page 16)

1 cup Grano Duro flour (see page 17)

1 egg

½ cup water, at room temperature

½ teaspoon extra virgin olive oil

Pinch of salt

Sift both flours onto a work surface and make a well in the center. Add the remaining ingredients to the well and work with your fingertips until a dough forms. Gather the dough and knead for 8 minutes. Wrap in plastic wrap and let rest for 15 minutes.

Using a knife or pastry cutter, portion off a quarter of the dough, leaving the rest in the plastic wrap. Roll out into a long ½-inch-thick rope on a floured surface. Cut the rope crosswise into ½-inch pieces. Press each piece in the middle with the tip of a thumb and gently roll forward, creating a shell-like shape. Repeat with the remaining dough and transfer the pasta to a floured baking sheet.

TO SERVE

2 ounces Pecorino di Pienza (see page 20), cut into small cubes

10 ounces buffalo mozzarella, cut into small pieces

5 basil leaves, chopped

Chili oil (optional)

Add the Pecorino di Pienza to the Tomato Olive Sauce. Bring a large pot of lightly salted water to a boil and reduce to a simmer. Shake the gnocchetti in a sieve or colander to remove excess flour and add the pasta to the cooking water. When the pasta comes to the surface, cook for an additional minute or until al dente. Drain off the water and add the hot pasta to the sauce. Toss to combine and serve immediately, topped with the mozzarella, basil, and a drizzle of chili oil, if desired.

GNOCCHI alla ROMANA

This variety of gnocchi originates from Rome, where the semolina pasta is cut into disks, layered, then baked with a topping of juniper sauce and grated cheese. Take pleasure in this hearty winter dish with a good sangiovese wine.

Serves 6      50 minutes

GNOCCHI

4 cups milk

5 tablespoons butter

1½ cups semolina flour

Pinch of nutmeg

Salt and black pepper to taste

¼ cup grated Pecorino Romano

½ cup grated Parmesan

1 egg yolk, beaten

————

Combine the milk and butter in a saucepan and bring to a boil. Add the semolina and cook for 20 minutes, stirring continuously. Mix in the nutmeg, salt, pepper, Pecorino Romano, and half of the grated Parmesan. Remove from the heat and stir for 1 minute to cool slightly before adding the egg yolk. Pour the dough onto a buttered marble or granite surface* and, using wet hands, flatten it into a large rectangle. Dampen a rolling pin and roll the dough out into a 17-x-10-inch rectangle that is ¼ inch thick. Wet the rim of a 2-inch round cookie cutter or drinking glass and cut out as many disks from the dough as possible. Butter an 11-x-8-inch baking dish and line the bottom with the dough trimmings. Overlap the disks over the trimmings, sprinkle the surface with the remaining grated Parmesan, and dot with butter.

A large cutting board covered with buttered parchment paper may replace a marble or granite surface.

SAUCE

2 cups Vegetable Stock (see page 36)

5 juniper berries, crushed or finely chopped

1 tablespoon cornstarch

1¼ cups half-and-half

1 handful grated Parmesan

White pepper

————

Combine all of the ingredients, except the Parmesan and pepper, in a saucepan, mix well, and bring to a boil. Add the Parmesan and cook, stirring until the cheese has melted. Set aside.

TO SERVE

Bake the gnocchi at 350°F for 15 minutes or until golden brown. Heat the sauce, ladle over the gnocchi, and serve hot with a sprinkle of white pepper.

CAPPELLETTI al POMODORO

This unique ravioli stuffing of roasted pepper, sheep's milk cheese, and spinach makes for a delectable and impressive pasta dish worth every bit of the effort.

Serves 4 to 6   Ⓜ   *50 minutes*

DOUGH

1 cup Italian 'OO' flour (see page 16)

1/3 cup Grano Duro flour (see page 17)

3 egg yolks

1 whole egg

Pinch of salt

1/2 teaspoon extra virgin olive oil

2 teaspoons tomato paste

———

Sift the flours onto a work surface and create a well in the center. Add the remaining ingredients to the well and work with your fingertips until the dough comes together. Knead for 3 minutes. If the dough feels very dry, wet your hands and continue to work. Wrap in plastic wrap and refrigerate for 30 minutes.

FILLING

1/2 small red bell pepper

2 cloves garlic, 1 whole and 1 thinly sliced

1 1/2 teaspoons finely chopped celery

Salt and black pepper to taste

Extra virgin olive oil

1/4 cup cooked spinach, chopped and squeezed dry

1/4 cup grated pecorino cheese

1 egg white, lightly beaten

2 ounces brie, cut into 1/4-inch cubes

———

Blacken the bell pepper (see page 20) and cut into 1/2-inch squares. In a bowl, toss the squares with the sliced garlic, celery, salt, pepper, and olive oil to coat. Meanwhile, in a sauté pan, sauté the whole garlic clove in olive oil until golden brown. Discard the garlic. Add the spinach and cook for 2 minutes, seasoning to taste. Remove from the heat and cool. Mix the grated cheese with 1 tablespoon of the egg white to form a paste. Reserve the remaining egg white for brushing.

ASSEMBLY AND TO SERVE

2 quantities Tomato Sauce (see page 36)

1 handful basil leaves, coarsely chopped

Parmigiano Reggiano, for topping

———

Roll out the dough to number 7 through a pasta machine and, on a work surface dusted with Grano Duro flour, cut into circles using a 4-inch round cutter or drinking glass rim. Brush half of each disk with egg white. Place a pinch of spinach slightly off the center of each disk. Top with one piece of brie, pepper, and a pinch of the grated cheese paste. Close the unbrushed side over the filling into a crescent shape and seal by gently pushing out the air from the center. Wrap the opposite ends of the crescent around and pinch together. Arrange the cappelletti on a baking sheet dusted with Grano Duro flour.

Heat the Tomato Sauce in a large sauté pan with the basil. Bring a pot of lightly salted water to a boil and reduce to a simmer. Slide the cappelletti into the water and cook until the pasta rises to the surface and floats for about 3 minutes. Transfer with a slotted spoon to the sauce and toss briefly to combine. Serve with a drizzle of olive oil and shavings of Parmigiano Reggiano to taste.

PIZZOCCHERI

A speciality of Valtellina in the Italian Alps, this pasta is made partly with buckwheat flour, creating a highly unusual texture. Match the beautifully blended flavors of cabbage and spinach with a full-bodied wine like an amarone or cabernet sauvignon.

Serves 8 (M) *45 minutes*

DOUGH

2¾ cups Grano Duro flour (see page 17)

1½ cups buckwheat flour

4 eggs, lightly beaten

2 tablespoons grappa liquor

6 tablespoons beer

Pinch of salt

———

Combine both flours on a work surface and make a well in the center. Add the remaining ingredients to the well and work with your fingers until a dough forms. Gather into a ball and knead well for 8 minutes. Wrap in plastic wrap and refrigerate for 30 minutes. Then roll out to number 6 in a pasta machine into a long strip, or by hand into a large wafer-thin disk. Let air-dry, uncovered, for 10 minutes.

If rolling out through a pasta machine, halve the dough vertically and then horizontally, flour the surface, and stack the quarters. Slice into ½-inch strips. If rolling out by hand, dust the surface with Grano Duro flour and roll the dough over a rolling pin from the bottom up until all the dough is wrapped around the pin. Take a sharp knife and cut lengthwise across the top of the pin in a straight line and let the dough fall away. Remove the pin and cut again lengthwise across the middle. Dust the surface of one stack with flour and place the two stacks on top of each other. Cut crosswise into ½-inch strips. Gently toss with more flour and set aside on a floured baking sheet.

SAUCE

3 garlic cloves, gently smashed

3 sage leaves

¾ cup butter

2 medium potatoes, peeled and cut into ½-inch cubes

12 ounces savoy cabbage, spinach, or black cabbage, coarsely sliced into strips

8 ounces mildly aged cheese like Fontina or Gouda, cut into small cubes

½ cup grated Parmesan

White pepper

———

Preheat the oven to 350°F. Heat the garlic and sage with the butter in a small sauté pan. When the garlic begins to color, press the cloves down with the back of a spoon to extract the juices, then discard the cloves. Set the sage butter aside. Cook the potatoes and greens in a saucepan with 8 cups of lightly salted simmering water for 10 minutes. Slide in the pasta from the baking sheet and cook for an additional 5 minutes (the pasta should be slightly undercooked). Drain the pasta and vegetables well in a colander. Spread half of the pasta mixture and half of the sage butter over the bottom of a 13-x-9-inch baking dish. Top with half of the cubed cheese and half of the grated Parmesan. Repeat the layers. Bake for 10 to 15 minutes. Top with a sprinkling of white pepper and serve directly from the baking dish.

TIMBALLO alla TERAMANA

Originally from the town of Teramo in central Italy, this timballo is constructed of five layers of crespelle (thin crêpes) and four succulently prepared vegetables. Serve this impressive dish on special occasions with a sauvignon blanc or a vermentino di sardegna.

Serves 6   Ⓓ   90 minutes

CRÊPES

1 cup milk

⅔ cup all-purpose flour

2 tablespoons melted butter, plus more for cooking

1 egg

Salt and pepper to taste

———

In a bowl, whisk all of the ingredients together. Heat a nonstick 8-inch skillet or crêpe pan over medium-high heat. Spread 1 teaspoon butter around the pan and wipe with a paper towel. Remove the pan from the heat. Ladle ¼ cup batter into the pan and swirl to spread. Place the pan back on the heat and cook until one side is golden. Flip and cook the other side. Repeat with the remaining batter to make a total of 12 crêpes.

FILLING

3 garlic cloves

1 sprig rosemary

7 tablespoons extra virgin olive oil

8 ounces mushrooms, coarsely chopped

Salt, black pepper, and white pepper to taste

1½ cups shelled fresh or frozen peas

2 shallots, chopped

10 ounces zucchini, cut into
   ½-inch cubes

1¼ cups cooked spinach, squeezed dry

1½ teaspoons butter, cut into bits

½ cup grated Parmesan

¼ cup grated Pecorino Romano

8 ounces mozzarella, cut into
   ½-inch cubes

———

Mushrooms: In a sauté pan, sauté 2 cloves of the garlic and the rosemary in 2 tablespoons of the olive oil until brown. Add the mushrooms and sauté over high heat until the liquid has evaporated. Remove from the heat, discard the garlic and rosemary, and season to taste. Set aside.

Peas: In a saucepan, cook the peas, half of the chopped shallots, 1½ tablespoons of the olive oil, white pepper, and enough water to just cover. When the peas are tender, remove the vegetables, strain off the liquid, season to taste, and set aside.

Zucchini: In a sauté pan, sauté the zucchini with the remaining shallots in 1½ tablespoons of the olive oil until the liquid has evaporated. Season to taste. Remove from the heat and set aside.

Spinach: In a sauté pan, sauté the spinach in the butter, remaining 2 tablespoons oil, and remaining garlic. Season to taste. Remove from the heat and discard the garlic. Chop well and set aside.

ASSEMBLY

Preheat the oven to 350°F. Grease an 8-inch square baking dish. Line the bottom with two crêpes. Sprinkle with a quarter of each grated cheese. Spread the chopped spinach over the bottom. Add a quarter of the mozzarella cubes over the spinach. Line with two more crêpes. Repeat the layering of crêpes, grated cheese, vegetables, and mozzarella with the mushrooms, peas, and then zucchini. Top the final layer with the remaining two crêpes. Dot with butter. Cover with aluminium foil and bake for 20 minutes. Cut into six equal portions. Serve immediately.

This ginger and lemon risotto is, as some put it, mystifyingly good. One of the most celebrated risottos in Montali. Pair with a flowery white wine like a gewürtztraminer, never with a red.

Serves 4   E   20 minutes

INGREDIENTS

½ small onion, finely chopped

1 shallot, finely chopped

1 small garlic clove, minced

1 sage leaf

3 tablespoons extra virgin olive oil

8 ounces pumpkin, peeled and cut into 1-inch pieces

½ cup hot water

Salt and white pepper to taste

1¼ cups Carnaroli or Arborio rice

2¼ cups Vegetable Stock (see page 36)

¼ cup white wine

1½ teaspoons grated fresh ginger

1 tablespoon finely chopped parsley

1 tablespoon butter

¼ cup grated Parmigiano Reggiano

2 tablespoons lemon juice

In a large pot, cook half of the onion, shallot, and garlic and the sage in 2 tablespoons of the olive oil over medium-low heat. When the vegetables are translucent, add the pumpkin and water. Cover and cook until the pumpkin is tender. Discard the sage and mash the pumpkin mixture with a fork. Season to taste with salt and white pepper. Cover and set aside.

Rinse and drain the rice. In a small pot, bring the stock to a boil, then turn off the heat. In a separate pot, heat the remaining 1 tablespoon oil over medium heat with the remaining onion, shallot, and garlic and cook until the onion and shallot are translucent. Add the rice and cook until white spots appear in the center of each grain. Add the white wine and stir gently for 30 seconds. Add two ladlefuls of the stock and stir in a gentle wavelike motion until the rice absorbs the stock. Continue adding stock, two ladlefuls at a time, and stir until each addition evaporates before adding more, until the rice is half-cooked (about 7 minutes after the start of cooking). Mix in the ginger, pumpkin, and half of the parsley. Continue to add the stock until the rice is al dente (about 7 additional minutes). Take off the heat and add the butter, 2 tablespoons of the Parmigiano Reggiano, and the lemon juice, mixing well. Season to taste and serve with a sprinkle of the remaining grated cheese and parsley.

This has never been an easy business.

Nevertheless it seems that, in the last fifteen years, very few other investments have expanded more than hotel and restaurant ones. I reckon for hotels, the reason is a bit easier to understand because the building that is manufactured for the hotel represents quite a big and important investment on its own, meaning, in many ways, a further guarantee on the investment. If the hotel, for instance, doesn't do particularly well later on, the company can always sell or rent the building and make a gain anyway. The building structure is the first and most important part of a hotel investment.

This means a relatively easy way to use extra cash for big multinational companies that do not often know where to invest their capital. They spend money to establish a hotel somewhere popular, and that is already an investment. Then they will try to manage it themselves, but, eventually, will rent the entire complex to any hotel group interested in working in that region and not willing to pay for building. That is how hotel business works in a simple way, on a big scale, and that is why it has developed so much in the last ten years.

The restaurant business is much more complex. I still wonder why it is developing so much, when it is such a hard and complicated job. Few people, for example, know that statistically less than 50 percent (yes, 50 percent!) of the restaurants open in London will survive two years. Yes, quite a number of restaurants do not live long enough to see two winters. How many times have you gone to eat in a recommended restaurant, or even in a place where you had already eaten before, and found that it was closed or under new management with a totally different quality? You ask, "Are they making so much money, so quickly and so shortly, that they can retire?" No, that is definitely not the answer. The obvious reason is that they have not managed to survive the enormous competition.

I'll bet that anyone can guess the reasons for a restaurant business failing. They are easily identifiable with the acronym: NGF BS HP (no good food, bad service, high prices)! These are the usual components of a restaurant's breakdown.

But let's see, instead, what the components of a successful restaurant business should be. What have people missed while attempting to enter the food industry? What are the few rules that unfortunately not all people observe or even know about?

Let us say generally a good restaurant will develop well if it has:

1) Location. Of course, a restaurant in the center of London has more visibility than one in the coun-tryside of France. But even in London, there is a big difference between being in Soho or in Shepherd's Bush. The rent of the place will prove it. A good entrepreneur has to foresee which particular geographical area is going to be developed sooner in order to have a great location for the minimum price. On the protected beach of Jericoacoara in Brazil, for example, the prices of a restaurant-sized piece of land have increased 2,500 percent in ten years. If you don't foresee which location will be valuable and pay a cheaper price for it, you have already made a small mistake.

2) Quality, of course. That is what always makes, and luckily will always make, the difference. A great chef will always be well accepted anywhere in the world.

3) Ideas. Any French chef can create a good French restaurant in France. Maybe a bit better or worse, but . . . it is a French person making French cuisine in France. That's quite obvious. The fun is making an English restaurant in Rome, or a fish restaurant in the desert — doing something that has not been done before, in an individual way. Or at least trying to give your own personal interpretation of the cuisine you prefer. That's part of the fabulous process of creation. So, you have to come out with an idea, trying your best to develop something as absolutely yours.

Look for it as long as you want, but get it. Get your idea and believe in it. Fight for it and, eventually, you will achieve it. Then you will start considering the costs of it, but get it anyway. The "idea" as a concept doesn't particularly mean anything difficult. It is better to have just a good simple *pizzaiolo* in a good pizzeria, than a mediocre so-called chef in a so-called posh and expensive restaurant.

Again our acronym: NGF BS HP.

You like French fries? Do a place specializing in French fries, with the best quality and variety of potato from all over the world and twenty different kinds of batters and salts as well, and you may be full all the time! (At least as long as your kidneys and liver allow you.) As they say: be yourself!

4) Trend. This is a very important concept, as "trends" nowadays have the power to move hundreds of people, or even millions, when properly piloted by media and general press coverage. A few years ago, for example, the sushi bar was *the* trend. If you had a business meeting or a professional date, a sushi bar was the place to be and be seen. Before that were the fashion cafés. And still before that were celebrity restaurants. These are the official trends, which are often launched and followed by people like Armani or highly cre-

ative geniuses working with hundreds of the best architects and stylists. And that is how we end up having restaurants often looking like jewelry and costing as much. Those are great moments for the industry, as a new place, if started well, can become a real economy boost for many, not only for a few chefs and some waiters. A small town can double its income, for example, if just a little tourism starts to develop in the region. Of course, many people will try anything to obtain some kind of press coverage from the media when they launch a new place.

That is usually the secret to being seen and having more people come. It is funny to realize that statistically, in an unexpected large number of cases, a big media review for a new opening creates more havoc then help. So many small places have started with a couple of guys with a good new idea that developed into a new place. But, they didn't know they had launched a new trend. They opened their new place, then a journalist from a famous media group fell in love with the character or the idea, and the next day there are 1,200 people wanting to enter the place for the night. And two months later, the couple of guys have gone broke, as it was too hard a job, and they had not yet planned for it that way!! It works only if you manage to literally catch the new trend, and be the first to ride it (in the sense that you will become the launcher of a new trend), and then . . . well, then you will be running!

It's best, of course, to launch the idea and to be able to ride it without falling down!

5) Conclusions. Trends and ideas will help you about 80 percent of the time in running a successful business but, unfortunately, just for some time.

The same famous journalist who launched and pushed your idea will crucify you two years later. Even if you have managed to control the pressure of an explosive beginning, he will become your nemesis. It is a cruel game, but so it goes. There is always new space for new faces! Only quality goes beyond all those points. A good chef will do well selling fish in the desert or ice cream to the Eskimos. The trend has the power to give you the energy to do so much with so little. But, of course, after two years people will be tired of spending, for example, $20 instead of $2 for a burger, just to be eating it under a picture of Sylvester Stallone in his restaurant in Hollywood, when they can have it on the next block for a tenth of the price. Those are the trends — if you happen to be a celebrity at the time of celebrity restaurants. But only the quality of a good chef will manage to keep going

when the trend enthusiasts vanish. And this always happens relatively quickly. The bigger the city, the more quickly it will happen.

If you don't work in a big city, you are less involved with all the trend madness and its consequences. But you will be less visible. You will need to rely on your quality even more as there will not be any kind of "kicks" by other people's trends.

We have chosen to run a vegetarian restaurant, for example, in one of the most meat-oriented places in the world and in the middle of nowhere.

And somehow it is working.

You can also go against all the marketing strategies in the world, and it may work if you like what you do. At any rate, everything always has a price in life.

I said at the beginning that I did not understand why so many people enter such a difficult life as a restaurateurs'. It is such a tough life . . . The only thing that can keep you going, if you manage to be successful enough not to be in the 50 percent losing bracket, is the love for this work. Only that will help you to run the sixteen-hour shifts that are required daily from a good chef. You need enormous discipline to be able to always be there, always at top quality, even when life struggles with you.

I still remember when my mother died on a day in which both the hotel and the restaurant were fully booked. No one, of course, was expecting it and no one was ready for it. Still, we had to manage it. But Schumacher raced on the same day that his mother died. And surely he earns more money than me! Meaning that you would expect that money could buy you a substitute for such a day. But Schumacher is a champion, and life is hard. There is no way that you can cry for yourself. That is why Schumacher is a champion, because he trains a lot and has great discipline. You need discipline in this life because in this job you are always on stage somehow.

I still remember my first big lesson in discipline, when I assisted in my own kitchen more then twenty years ago. I already mentioned my best chef, Akira Shishido from Japan. He worked hard for us for two full years alone in the kitchen. After two years, we decided to hire another Japanese chef to help him.

Of course, it didn't work: Akira was the Schumacher of the situation, and he was simply, constantly, training himself to be better in the kitchen. The young sous-chef was just a cook without the love and self-denial required for this job, even though he was a nice chap.

And they were both Japanese — so different from us Italians!

One afternoon I arrived in my restaurant at about 5:00 P.M. The chefs usually arrived at 4:00 P.M. and started to prepare the food for the restaurant, which would open at 8:00 P.M. Of course, I was expecting to find Masa (the sous-chef) working in the kitchen with Akira. But my major surprise was that I found him standing on the doorstep of the kitchen. Seeing his face, I immediately understood that he had not gone out to smoke a cigarette or to relax a minute. His eyes were watching his shoes, with the typical guilty face that the Japanese put on when their boss is ready to ask them to commit suicide on the spot. I wasn't particularly keen on entering a situation that wasn't promising to be either friendly or easy.

Unfortunately, I was the boss, and this was my restaurant. So, with politeness, I had to try to understand what had just happened. It was the usual situation in which the executive chef (Akira) had not liked one of the mistakes the sous-chef Masa had just made, for the sixth time that day! God's heaven, Akira got mad, and, as he didn't manage to obtain an instant hara-kiri from Masa (in Italy, it would have been inappropriate), he imposed on the young one the punishment of having to stand on the doorstep without moving for the whole night!

That was for him the minimum punishment for someone who had just burnt the risotto for the third time. In my imagination, I caught just a quick glimpse of the headlines in the Italian newspapers if I ever dared to do something like this to any of my employees! The unions would have surely deep-fried me on the burner with lots of boiling olive oil and rosemary.

Different cultures. Still, that was how the situation was at that moment. Nevertheless, my mediating Italian attitude pushed me, after some time, to ask the executive chef, "Hey, what if he does the dishes?" as I was also watching the time passing and thinking of the up-coming meals to be served with 50 percent of my workforce missing.

Akira looked at me horrified, of course conscious that the penalty of being kicked out of the kitchen was surely not enough for the high crime of inefficiency, and still missing a good suicide commitment. I don't know if he was right, but Masa, finally, went to wash dishes and we managed to serve dinner that night. They didn't work for long together.

Still, I learned my first lesson that day, of professional efficiency and how a kitchen has to be properly directed. I remember so many times in which we worked in a kitchen with fewer staff than the previous day, but managed to do so much more and so much better. Better one person in a kitchen who loves his job than three who are there just to make some money. And discipline is the only rule for doing this work for more than the mentioned two years. Discipline and kitchen organization.

—Alberto Musacchio

"Wake up! Wake up! It's three o'clock!" Agnes shook her roommate awake. It was three o'clock! "What are you talking about?" Ursula replied groggily.

"It's three o'clock! Let's go!" Agnes's green eyes were wide in panic. Her roommate checked her watch and saw that it was, in fact, three o'clock in the afternoon.

"So what? It's three o'clock. What's wrong with you?" Agnes blinked, slowly realizing there was no significance to "three o'clock." Siesta had begun at two and the Montali staff was not expected to return to work for another hour. In her sleepy haze, she had awoken with a start and, after looking at her clock, believed that three o'clock was late for something.

To the young men and women of the Country House Montali staff, work is everything. All in their early to mid-twenties, they travel from different parts of the world, sever themselves from the lives they have grown comfortable in, and work anywhere from fourteen to seventeen hours a day, six days a week, for seven months. This, in combination with being fifteen minutes away from the nearest town by car, results in being completely consumed by the hotel and restaurant life. For many, the amount of work or the distance from home is too much and they leave. For the rest, it is a personal commitment that they are determined to make the most of. There is an innate fear in each of them of being late. Even if, like Agnes, they are not.

The opportunity to live and work in Italy is a dream that many do not have the time or reason to pursue.

To a young chef, the chance to immerse oneself in the study of Italian cuisine, in a real Italian kitchen, is amazing. They know there will be hardships and ordeals, as there are in any workplace, but any shortcomings or inconveniences are quickly overshadowed because, "Guess what? I'm going to Italy, baby!" No matter how much one emotionally gears up for any difficulties, no one can be fully prepared for the baptism-by-fire that is the first month.

Depending on the individual, the adjustment period is challenging for a number of reasons. The idea of living in the Italian countryside may be a bucolic fantasy to some. For a city person, learning to cohabit with insects and strange mountain creatures can become a shocking and inescapable reality.

Later on you learn that when you live in the country, you will more frequently come across wild boar while driving at night and pheasant during the day than cars on the road. You just have to get used to it.

The Country House Montali is packed with peculiarities. It is a gourmet vegetarian restaurant in the heart of Italy with a Brazilian head chef. The food is prepared and served by Slovakians, Mexicans, Asians, Poles, Swedes, and Americans. In such a diverse staff, miscommunication is bound to occur regularly. At times it can cause needless drama, and at others can serve as much needed comic relief in a tense situation.

One evening, the restaurant was packed with people and the last of the primi had been served.

The stress level had been mounting in the kitchen since the afternoon, and the extreme heat only added to everyone's irritability. Janko turned to Marta and said, "Marta, isn't it you washed pans?" At Marta's confused look, Marketa intervened and said, "Marta, have you already washed the pans?" After Marta nodded, Marketa turned to Janko and joked in her accented English, "Janko, you really must work on your grammar." "What are you talking about? My grandma is eighty-seven years old!" Janko responded, sending everyone rolling on the floor.

To many, the workload is the easiest aspect of Montali life to adjust to. By the third or fourth month, a comfortable routine is in place. The chefs begin seeing the rotation of dishes come back around, familiarizing themselves with Malu's cooking style, and the waiting staff have a clear idea of their daily responsibilities in addition to serving dinner at night. However, while speed and efficiency improve noticeably, there is also the visible wear and tear of nerves. As one member of the team put it, "You can feel so lonely in a huge city like Los Angeles with millions of people surrounding you, but claustrophobic at the top of a mountain with only eight other people." Inevitably, people lose it.

Nobody knows better than Malu and Alberto that working at Montali is difficult. To them, their restaurant and hotel is their life, a choice and passion. If every member of their staff puts as much love into their work as they did, life could not be better. On their part, Malu and Alberto make an effort to make sure every one of their employees feels as settled or comfortable as possible.

In the same light, there is a common thread among those who stay and work for the entire season. Not only do they possess an incredible work ethic, but they feel committed to both the restaurant and the decisions that they have made. Malu and Alberto see these individuals as gold. They are people who come in every day, leaving all of their worries behind, and work as if Montali is their own.

Sustaining this level of work, this level of professionalism, is not without reward. Many of the young men and women who come do so to learn about themselves, the kinds of people they want to become, and the limits that they can excel beyond. It is a sabbatical for those in their mid-twenties and a chance to study a unique cuisine with various people from all over the world. In return for imparting such an enormous amount of time, chefs feel real ownership of their efforts, contributions, and creativity. They learn to delegate their time and maximize physical efficiency, to clear the mind and only focus on the task at hand. It is an incredible period of self-discovery and growth.

Toward the end of the season, the weather cools down significantly and staff members slowly trickle home one by one. The warmth of the kitchen compared to the chilly weather creates a cozy environment and Malu, Alberto, and the Montali staff enjoy everyone's company more than ever. The end of the season looms, and the family will soon be dispersed around the globe.

When the staff passes through the front gates, they don't know if they will ever see the hotel, Malu, Alberto, or each other again. They leave with both a sense of pride for having fulfilled their commitment, and a devotion to the people they have come to love.

They dwell on how far they have come as individuals rather than how much catching up there is to do in their lives back home. They will remember learning how to drive the manual old Fiat Uno with over 160,000 miles on the clock, passing the shepherd and his grazing sheep every morning, and the suicidal bunny that chose the exact moment they drove by to race across the road. They realize they've become accustomed to the insects in their bathtub, the spiders in their sink, and the leg cramps that recurrently shocked them awake at three in the morning. They remember small traditions they've created for each other, the unparalleled view of Lake Trasimeno from their medieval castle's apartment window, and the countless "a la salutes" at Happy Hour.

Nobody knows if they will ever become good chefs, but surely in Montali they have built the foundation for it.

APPRENTICES

In our long restaurateurs' life, we have worked with a lot of different chefs. Chefs can be very difficult people: temperamental, moody, prima donna types, and they have always been quite complicated characters to work with.

Luckily the executive chef in the hotel is my own wife, so we can depend much less on others. Still, we have always needed some good help for a relatively complicated cuisine. We often found that young chefs who already had cooking-school training and were also willing to do some professional apprentice work were the best people to use. They were the ones ready to put in a real effort and research to master the profession. Relatively young, they were also a bit easier to handle than older chefs, and they were generally very motivated to learn new skills. And I personally love motivation.

There are no cooking schools that give specific courses on vegetarian cuisine, even though there is a greater demand for low-fat and good-tasting diets, making our courses even more interesting from a professional standpoint. The idea also that our unique cuisine could be spread around the world through these happy young people was, and still is, a source of special satisfaction for us. I still remember the very excited email from one of our previous chefs, happily writing how the band Black Sabbath had gone to a restaurant where he was working in Kansas and asked for twelve vegetarian meals. The terrified owner, who didn't have any special recipes for vegetarians or know that Matthew had been trained at Montali, was scared to death by the appalling looking group and ran to the kitchen seeking any help from his chef.

Great was the general satisfaction when our previous cook announced he had no problems with that specific request, but even greater when Black Sabbath loved the food and went back for dinner on three consecutive days.

This is a pleasure to us as well, sharing Matthew's pride in showing a widely developed culinary skill to his boss and to his clients as well. But, of course, it isn't always like that. Life may be more of a struggle than pleasure and people reflect life — life that is not easy in Montali. We run a seasonal business and everybody used to this work knows how hard it is to make your annual income while officially being open to the public only half the year. You literally have to do one year's work in half that time. The working hours are so hard, starting at eight in the morning and ending at midnight sometimes, that it makes the days long, and not everyone is capable of working so many hours. The hotel life looks more like a type of retreat where you are expected to run most of the time and keep going.

It is generally more a question of rhythm and working attitude, because, otherwise, my wife and I would already be dead. Many people simply don't manage. But the ones who do will gain a fantastic experience and will be able to work in the future under any circumstances and conditions. This is quite common for any successful restaurant or hotel nowadays. The tough ones will be the ones who make it. The others will run away through the season.

That is how a seasonal tourist job is. Lots of fun because you are located in a paradise, but lots of work as well. A bit like working on a cruise! It is quite hard to make a choice when, at the beginning of the season, we collect résumés of the new applicants. How do you choose a chef from a small picture and a one-page résumé that may not mean anything? I remember one chef sending a great picture of himself in an impeccable white chef's uniform and a gold medal, looking like Jean Paul Bocuse. Very impressive. But then it was a surprise to discover later that he had been a drug addict for many years, ended up in jail four times, and was living on antidepressants to keep going! Not a person who would manage fifteen hours a day. He did, in fact, only work two weeks and then, there I was, without one chef in the middle of the season.

Researchers have also proven that 70 percent of résumés are false or exaggerated. A guy wrote to me once claiming he had been working for Celine Dion at her personal house. I found out later he had just worked as a waiter in a Canadian fast-food chain that seemed to be owned by the famous singer.

Another had been "head of garcons" in the Hilton in Prague . . . pity he was there only carrying suitcases as a porter! That's how recruitment goes sometimes. You must follow your gut, making a choice and hoping it was a good one. In all cases, the seven months' long season will inevitably be full of those special moments in which workers burst into tears or get frustrated because of work.

It is impossible to make any rules. Sometimes men are easier to handle than women, because they are less emotive. Sometimes it is just the opposite, because women can be milder. Sometimes Americans can be easier than British, sometimes not. We had one Korean male chef who was boring and stubborn. We have a Korean female chef who is writing this book with me, and she is the embodiment of energy, cleverness, and good humor. It is so difficult to make a choice at recruitment time.

Running a seasonal business makes it more complicated, as we have to restart and train most of the staff every year, which is such an endless job and sometimes tiring. Mostly, it depends on the person you end up dealing with. It is so nice when you find someone willing to learn and ready to dedicate their energy to the job. It is such a pain when you have someone who doesn't give a dime and isn't willing to learn. A big problem is that some young people having to work as waiters think, "I'm not a servant." This is a very common mentality for the current generation, diminishing a job that anybody should be proud of! Aren't we all servants anyway? Everybody in life serves someone else. But pride has gone, unfortunately, for the majority.

It is such a great pleasure instead to see a slow chef ending his season "running" in the kitchen, or watching how a bakery chef has learned desserts and starters, or seeing a "not so sophisticated" waitress ending the season behaving finally with dignity. Those are some of the satisfactions in our work, at least to balance the times when you really get mad.

I remember one time when, after a lovely dinner, I was enjoying the company of some of my guests while sipping some wine on the outer veranda. A girl from the staff came to ask the gentlemen if he would like another drink.

After that she also kindly asked me if I wanted one. I ordered a glass of Grecale, a chilled sweet after-dinner wine that I am pretty fond of. The attractive young girl went to get the drinks and some of my clients commented on how my life could seem like a dream to many. The pergola where we were sitting was covered with fully blossoming jasmine and honeysuckle flowers and the wonderful aroma spread through the romantic night on that isolated hill. Montali is a gorgeous spot and the views of the valley were breathtaking on that full moon night. One of the gentleman said to me, "Hey Alberto, you really live like a king here." He said this exactly when the young girl, just having returned with the drinks, (very elegantly) stumbled across the veranda giving me the sweetest bath of all my life. Of course, the life of King Alberto didn't last long, and people had a glimpse of how animated a hotelier's life can be.

Naturally, as a boss you also know that you are often simply hated by many of your employees, regardless of how much fun they can be having. Montali for instance can be a lot of fun: the staff spending nights drinking different drinks on the house, afternoon siesta hours sunbathing by the pool, every day eating top gourmet food, sightseeing with the hotel car in all the fabulous medieval towns in Umbria and beyond. Tough life! But all this is forgotten when the boss shouts. He is just a jerk, of course, even if such a place would not exist without a jerk keeping it going. Still, in the long run I know my staff loves me, even when I shout, and everybody admits that some shouting makes work progress much better.

—Alberto Musacchio

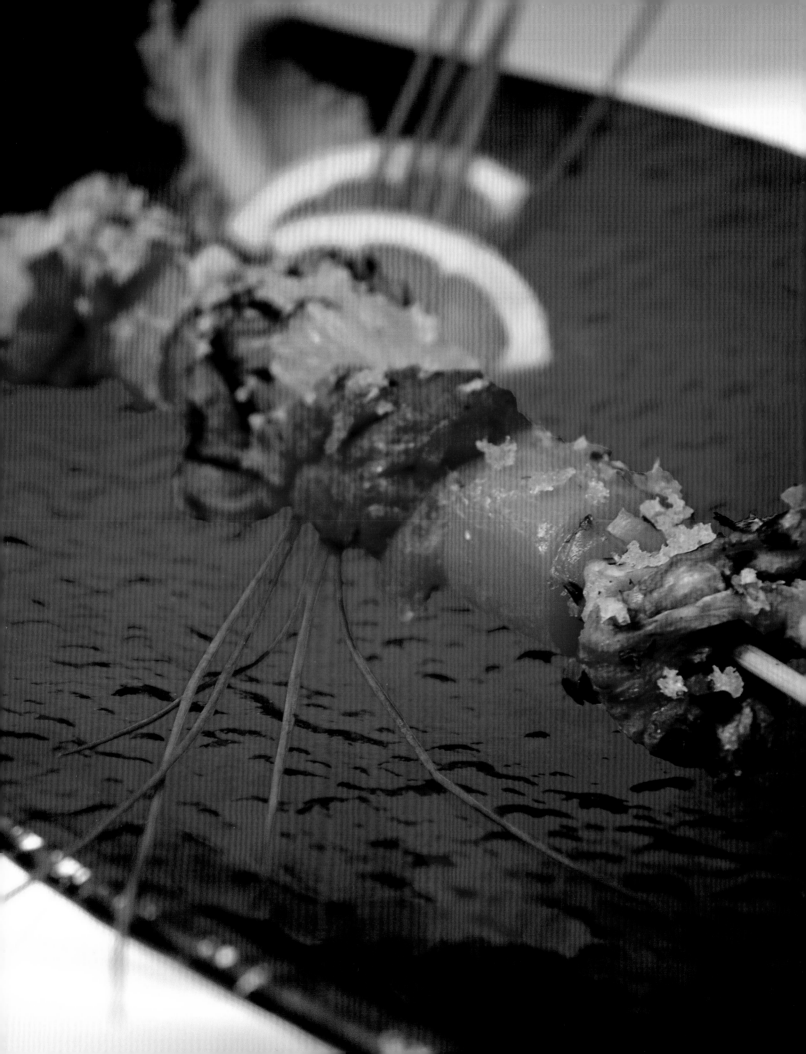

Secondi

SECOND COURSES

Spring vegetable skewers. An intriguing combination of grilled vegetables and seitan with an herb topping. This colorful dish is great for a buffet.

Serves 6 Ⓜ *95 minutes*

INGREDIENTS

1 eggplant, thinly sliced lengthwise

¼ cup extra virgin olive oil, plus more for drizzling

Salt and pepper to taste

3 tablespoons chopped parsley, plus 1 whole sprig

4 garlic cloves, thinly sliced

2 zucchini, thinly sliced lengthwise

1 red bell pepper

1 tablespoon chopped celery leaves

1 orange

6 small Belgian endives, halved lengthwise

3½ carrots, peeled

1 teaspoon white wine vinegar

1 shallot, finely chopped

1½ tablespoons chopped celery

½ quantity Seitan, cut into 1-inch squares (see page 35)

1 tablespoon all-purpose flour

2 tablespoons white wine

Two 1-inch-thick slices pineapple

———

Eggplant: Grill the slices, turning once, until tender. Transfer to a bowl. Drizzle with oil and season with salt, pepper, 1 tablespoon of the chopped parsley, and a bit of the sliced garlic. Set aside.

Zucchini: Follow the same procedure as the eggplant.

Bell pepper: Blacken and peel the pepper (see page 20), cut into 1-inch squares, and fold in the celery leaves, a bit of the sliced garlic, a little oil, and salt.

Orange: Use a serrated knife to remove the peel and pith, leaving the pulp exposed. Slice into ½-inch pieces and quarter into wedges. Remove any seeds, if needed.

Endives: Grill the halves and season with oil, salt, and pepper. Cut crosswise into thick slices.

Carrots: Cut three into ½-inch-wide pieces. Steam until al dente, transfer to a bowl, and season with salt, pepper, the remaining 2 tablespoons chopped parsley, a bit of the sliced garlic, olive oil, and the white wine vinegar.

Seitan: Sauté the shallot, remaining garlic, celery, and ½ carrot in the ¼ cup extra virgin olive oil for 2 minutes. Add the seitan and parsley sprig and cook over high heat until the seitan begins to brown. Sprinkle with the flour and cook for 1 minute. Add the wine and cook until evaporated. Taste for seasoning.

Pineapple: Peel, core, and cut each slice into eight wedges.

TOPPING

3 tablespoons dry bread crumbs

1½ teaspoons chopped parsley

1½ teaspoons chopped basil

1 small garlic clove, crushed through a press

1 teaspoon extra virgin olive oil

Salt to taste

———

Combine all the ingredients together in a bowl.

ASSEMBLY

Preheat the oven to 350°F. On 12 skewers, arrange one piece of each component in this order: zucchini*, eggplant*, endive, carrot, pepper, seitan, orange, zucchini, eggplant, carrot, pepper, seitan, and pineapple. Arrange the skewers on a baking sheet, sprinkle with the Topping, and bake for 10 minutes. Serve hot.

Thread the zucchini and eggplant slices onto the skewers by pleating them, to resemble ribbon candy.

QUICHE di PORRI

A buttery-crusted leek quiche, fit for a dinner party or a Sunday brunch.

Serves 8 Ⓜ *45 minutes & 30 minutes chilling & 20 minutes baking*

DOUGH

2 cups Italian 'OO' flour (see page 16)
Pinch of salt
9 tablespoons butter, melted and slightly cooled to room temperature
1 egg, lightly beaten
3 tablespoons water, if needed

———

Combine the flour and salt on a work surface and make a well in the center. Add the butter and egg to the well and gently work with your fingertips until a dough begins to form. Incorporate by cutting through the dough with a pastry blender and rolling back together, three or four times, until the texture and color are even, adding the water if the dough is too dry. Wrap in plastic wrap and refrigerate for 30 minutes.

FILLING

1 pound leeks, white and light green parts only
2¼ cups milk
⅔ cup heavy cream
Salt to taste

———

Clean the leeks well. Thinly slice on a mandoline and combine with the milk in a large sauté pan. Cook over low heat until the consistency is creamy, like that of a beaten egg. Let cool slightly. Transfer to a blender or food processor and pulse on and off several times to blend coarsely, leaving some large pieces of leek; then pulse in the cream. Taste, adding salt as needed. Cool to room temperature.

ASSEMBLY

Preheat the oven to 350°F. Roll the dough between two sheets of floured parchment paper into a disk 13 inches in diameter. Remove the top layer of parchment paper and invert eight 3-inch pie or tart pans onto the dough. With a small knife, cut disks ½ inch larger than the pans. Gently press the dough into the bottom, edges, and sides of the pans. Pierce the bottoms with a fork a few times and fill with the leek mixture. Run the tines of the fork evenly over the surface of each tart in concentric circles. Bake for 20 minutes. Serve hot.

RULLO di SPINACI e RICOTTA

Spinach and ricotta cheese roulade. An Italian classic where spinach accompanies ricotta in a soft creamy dream. All enveloped by a crunchy light pastry.

Serves 4 **D** *45 minutes & 30 minutes baking*

FILLING

4 cups spinach, cooked and squeezed dry

½ tablespoon butter

Salt and black pepper to taste

⅔ cup fresh ricotta, drained of excess liquid

¼ cup grated Parmesan

Pinch of nutmeg

———

Finely chop the spinach and sauté in a medium sauté pan with the butter. Season to taste and cool completely. In a bowl, work the ricotta with a fork until creamy. Mix the Parmesan and nutmeg into the ricotta. Fold in the cooled spinach and mix. Season to taste, cover, and set aside.

DOUGH

1 cup Italian 'OO' flour (see page 16)

Pinch of salt

4 tablespoons butter, softened and cut into chunks

1 egg, lightly beaten

½ teaspoon water

———

Sift the flour and salt into a bowl and make a well in the center. Add the butter to the well and work into the flour with your fingertips until the dough resembles a coarse meal. Scoop handfuls of the dough into your hands and gently rub between your palms. Repeat until the dough reaches a sandlike consistency and all the ingredients are well incorporated. Add the egg and, using a pinching motion, work into the dough until a ball begins to form. Knead for 1 minute until smooth. Pick up the dough and forcefully throw it down onto the work surface 20 times. Cover with plastic wrap and refrigerate for 15 minutes. Roll out the dough on a floured work surface into an 13-x-11-inch rectangle, with a short side facing you. Loosely roll dough around the rolling pin, then unroll onto a large sheet of parchment paper. Use a pizza cutter to even the edges.

ASSEMBLY

2 tablespoons half-and-half

1 tablespoon milk

———

Preheat the oven to 350°F. Mix the half-and-half and milk in a small cup and brush the entire surface of the dough. Spread the filling over the surface, leaving a 1-inch border on a short side uncovered. Gently roll in the long sides. Using the parchment paper as a guide, start from the short side opposite the 1-inch border and roll the dough, creating a log shape. Brush the surface with the milk mixture. Transfer, using the paper as the base, to a baking sheet and bake for 30 minutes. Cool for a few minutes before slicing and serving.

This dish can be prepared and baked 1 day in advance. Reheat at 300°F for 10 minutes, then increase the temperature to 350°F and bake for an additional 5 minutes.

COXINHAS ENCANTADAS

An incomparable version of the Brazilian teardrop-shaped fried pastry, stuffed with a creamy eggplant filling. As lovely as it is delicious, this dish is a definite crowd-pleaser.

Serves 6 (M) *55 minutes*

FILLING

1 small garlic clove, minced

1 teaspoon thyme leaves

1 tablespoon chopped onion

2 tablespoons extra virgin olive oil

1 eggplant, peeled and cubed

Salt and pepper to taste

1 tablespoon grated Parmesan

1 tablespoon grated Pecorino Romano

————

In a sauté pan, sauté the garlic, thyme, and onion in the olive oil for 1 minute. Add the eggplant and season with salt and pepper. Cook, stirring often, until the eggplant is soft and dry, about 20 minutes. Purée in a blender and cool completely before mixing in the cheeses.

DOUGH

1 small potato, boiled until tender

½ cup Vegetable Stock (see page 36)

½ cup milk

1 tablespoon butter

½ teaspoon salt

1 cup all-purpose flour

————

Peel and mash the potato and set it aside. In a saucepan, bring the stock, milk, butter, and salt to a boil. Add the flour all at once and stir immediately. Continue to stir for 5 minutes or until the dough begins to dry and pull away from the bottom of the pan. Remove from the heat and mix in the potato. On a work surface, knead the dough for 2 minutes.

ASSEMBLY

2 tablespoons all-purpose flour

¼ cup dry bread crumbs

2 eggs, beaten and lightly salted

Vegetable oil, for deep-frying

Salt to taste

Herb sprigs and leaves, for decorating (optional)

————

Roll 1 rounded tablespoon of dough into a ball and flatten into a 2½-inch disk. Place 1 teaspoon of eggplant mixture in the center and close the dough around it, taking care not to break the dough. Seal gently and form into a pear shape. Repeat with the remaining dough.

Place the flour, bread crumbs, and eggs in separate bowls. One by one, neatly coat each coxinha with flour, then egg, and lastly bread crumbs. Set aside on a plate. Heat the vegetable oil in a saucepan and fry the coxinhas in batches to a golden brown (see page 20). Transfer to a baking sheet lined with paper towels and season with salt. If desired, push an herb sprig or leaf into the top of each coxinhas to resemble a stem. Serve hot.

PASTICCIO di MELANZANE

An eggplant tart, served with a Caper Parsley Sauce. A great dish for any special occasion. The tart blends with the salty caper sauce in a fusion of pure pleasure. A favorite of many of our clients.

Serves 8 (M) *30 minutes & 25 minutes baking*

PASTICCIO

3 eggplants, peeled and cut into ¼-inch cubes

8 ounces Scamorza cheese (see page 20), cut into ¼-inch cubes

2 eggs, lightly beaten

⅓ cup grated Parmesan

2 garlic cloves, mashed

1 tablespoon chopped oregano

Salt and pepper to taste

———

Soak the eggplant cubes in cool water for 10 minutes. Drain, squeeze, and place in a large heavy-bottomed pot over high heat. Cook the eggplant by itself, in batches if needed, stirring occasionally, until softened and nearly dry. Cool to room temperature and place in a bowl. Fold in the Scamorza, eggs, grated Parmesan, garlic, and oregano and mix well. Season with salt and black pepper. Line the bottom of a 9-inch springform pan with parchment paper and grease lightly. Spoon the mixture into the pan and, using a fork, spread evenly. Set aside.

CAPER PARSLEY SAUCE

1 tablespoon capers

2 tablespoons coarsely chopped parsley

½ cup extra virgin olive oil

———

Rinse the capers under cold running water and drain well. Chop with the parsley, then combine the capers with the olive oil in a small bowl. Set aside.

TO SERVE

Preheat the oven to 350°F. Bake the pasticcio for 25 minutes or until heated through. Remove the pan sides and cut into wedges. Serve immediately, topped with the Caper Parsley Sauce.

Enhance this dish further with servings of Carrot Purée (see page 212), Beet Salad (see page 213), and a drizzle of Pepper Sauce (see page 31).

VEGETERRANEAN SECONDI

SFORMATINI di ZUCCHINE

Soft, creamy ricotta cheese and zucchini flans with hint of marjoram. A dish of true refinement with the addition of Parmesan cheese shells.

Serves 6 Ⓜ *25 minutes & 20 minutes baking*

INGREDIENTS

2 tablespoons extra virgin olive oil

1 shallot, finely chopped

2 zucchini, coarsely grated

1 teaspoon dried marjoram

White pepper and salt to taste

⅔ cup ricotta

1 tablespoon grated Parmesan

1 whole egg

2 egg whites

Heat the oil and shallot together in a sauté pan for 30 seconds. Add the zucchini, marjoram, and white pepper. Cook, stirring occasionally, until the zucchini are soft and dry, about 15 minutes. Remove from the heat and cool. In a bowl, work the ricotta and Parmesan with a fork until very creamy. Beat the egg yolk and whites together, and mix into the ricotta until the mixture is smooth. Add the cooked zucchini and season to taste.

Preheat the oven to 350°F. Bring a kettle of water to a boil. Butter six ramekins or six standard muffin cups. Line the bottoms with small rounds of parchment paper. Divide the zucchini mixture evenly among the ramekins and place in a baking dish. Carefully pour hot water into the baking dish until it reaches halfway up the sides of the ramekins. Cover with aluminium foil and bake for 20 minutes.

PARMESAN SHELL

Butter

12 tablespoons grated Parmesan cheese

Melt some butter in a nonstick pan over medium-high heat. Sprinkle 2 tablespoons of the grated Parmesan into the pan, forming a 5-inch round. When the cheese is melted, use a spatula to carefully transfer the cheese wafer from the pan to an inverted and greased ramekin. Press gently with your fingers to give the wafer a shell-like shape. Cool for 1 minute, then transfer, flat-side down, to a sheet of parchment paper. Repeat with the remaining cheese.

TO SERVE

One quantity Truffle Sauce (see page 36)

Transfer the Parmesan shells to individual plates. Place a flan inside each one, garnish with Truffle Sauce, and serve.

Olive Sauce (see page 30) may be used in place of the Truffle Sauce.

Eggplant spring rolls. A delightful Mediterranean taste with cherry tomatoes contrasting with the fried eggplant. Lovely with a filling of buffalo mozzarella.

Serves 6   (M)   *35 minutes & 15 minutes baking*

EGGPLANT

4 medium eggplants, peeled and cut lengthwise into ¼-inch slices

3 cups Italian 'OO' flour (see page 16)

Sunflower oil, for frying

Salt to taste

3 fresh mozzarella balls, preferably buffalo, about 4 ounces each, well drained

24 basil leaves

———

Fill a bowl with water and stir in 1 tablespoon of the flour. Soak the eggplant in the water for 15 minutes. Meanwhile, heat oil in a sauté pan. Drain the eggplant from the water, pressing two slices at a time between your palms, and arrange in a colander to dry. Put the remaining flour in a bowl. Dredge the slices in the flour to coat all sides. Fry in the hot oil until golden brown and transfer to a baking sheet lined with paper towels. Cool for 2 minutes, then gently press each slice between clean paper towels to get rid of any excess oil. Season with salt. Slice the mozzarella into rounds about ⅓ inch thick, and cut again into ⅓-inch-wide strips to make 24 pieces. Place one piece of mozzarella and one basil leaf across the lower third of each eggplant slice and gently roll up (makes 24 rolls).

ASSEMBLY

18 cherry tomatoes, quartered

3 garlic cloves, thinly sliced

Salt and pepper to taste

5 basil leaves, coarsely chopped

Extra virgin olive oil

———

Preheat the oven to 350°F. In a bowl, toss the tomatoes with the garlic, salt, pepper, and basil and drizzle with olive oil until well combined. Layer half the seasoned tomatoes over the bottom of an 8-x-8-inch baking dish. Arrange the eggplant rolls in a single layer and top with the remaining tomatoes. Bake, uncovered, for 15 minutes or until heated through. Serve hot.

RULLO di SCAROLA

Escarole roulade. The slightly bitter taste of this escarole fuses perfectly with the fresh Crescenza cheese. The texture of the pine nuts and bread crumbs makes each bite a symphony of delight.

Serves 8 Ⓜ *20 minutes & 15 minutes proofing & 35 minutes baking*

INGREDIENTS

½ cup dark raisins

3 garlic cloves, 2 whole and 1 crushed through a press

6 tablespoons pitted and chopped black olives

3 tablespoons extra virgin olive oil

4 heads escarole, cored and coarsely chopped

Salt to taste

¼ cup pine nuts, lightly toasted

¼ cup dry bread crumbs

1 tablespoon butter

1½ tablespoons chopped mixed herbs
  (basil, sage, and chives)

———

Soak the raisins in a small bowl of hot water until plump and tender, about 15 minutes. Drain well. In a large pot, sauté the whole garlic cloves with the black olives in the olive oil until golden. Add the escarole and toss to cook until any liquid is evaporated. Season with salt and fold in the pine nuts and raisins. In a sauté pan, toast the bread crumbs in the butter until golden brown. Transfer to a bowl and mix in the herbs and pressed garlic. Set aside.

DOUGH

2 cups Italian 'OO' flour (see page 16)

½ cup water

3 tablespoons butter, at room temperature

Pinch of salt

———

Sift the flour onto a work surface. Make a well in the center, add the water, butter, and salt, and work with your fingers until a dough begins to form. Knead for 30 seconds, then forcefully throw the dough onto the work surface 100 times. Cover with a warm glass bowl for 15 minutes (the glass bowl can be heated for 1 minute in a warm oven). Flour a clean towel. Shape the dough into a disk and slowly roll over your wrists to stretch it. When the dough begins to thin (but not break), place on the cloth and gently pull into a rectangle, maintaining the thickness, approximately 18 x 10 inches. The dough should be slightly transparent. Trim the edges with a pizza cutter.

ASSEMBLY

Half-and-half for brushing

4 tablespoons Crescenza or soft creamy cheese

———

Preheat an oven to 350°F. Brush half-and-half over the dough and sprinkle with the bread crumb mixture. Dot the escarole filling and the cheese evenly over the crumbs, leaving a ½-inch margin along one short side uncovered. Using the towel as a guide, fold in the long sides. Pull the towel up from the bottom corners and gently roll up the roulade working toward the ½-inch margin. Continue to roll onto a sheet of parchment paper until the seam side is down. Brush with more half-and-half. Transfer, with the parchment paper, to a baking sheet. Bake for 35 minutes or until golden. Slice and serve warm.

A dish made to impress all the senses. This zucchini and ricotta cheese mélange is served over a Beet Sauce and garnished with fried carrots.

Serves 6 Ⓜ *45 minutes & 25 minutes baking*

OUTSIDE

3 zucchini, thinly sliced and grilled until tender

1 garlic clove, sliced

1 tablespoon chopped parsley

Salt and pepper to taste

2 tablespoons extra virgin olive oil

———

Marinate the grilled zucchini with the remaining ingredients and set aside for 30 minutes.

FILLING

1 cup ricotta

6 tablespoons Pecorino di Pienza (see page 20), cut into small cubes

2 tablespoons grated Parmesan

1 egg, lightly beaten

Salt and pepper to taste

———

Beat the ricotta with a fork until very creamy. Add the remaining ingredients, mix well, and set aside.

BEET SAUCE

1 medium beet, steamed until tender and puréed

3 tablespoons plain yogurt

2 tablespoons Vegetable Stock (see page 36)

1 tablespoon chopped parsley

1 tablespoon extra virgin olive oil

1 teaspoon lemon juice

Salt and white pepper to taste

———

Pass the beet purée through a sieve to remove any lumps and mix well with remaining ingredients.

FRIED CARROTS

3 carrots, peeled and shaved into thin strips with a vegetable peeler

Vegetable oil, for deep-frying

Salt to taste

———

Working in batches, deep-fry the carrot shavings in hot oil until crispy (see page 20). Drain on paper towels and season with salt.

ASSEMBLY

Preheat the oven to 350°F. Line the bottom of six standard muffin cups or ramekins with rounds of parchment paper. Line with slices of zucchini, allowing them to overhang. Spoon the filling into the cups, and fold the zucchini ends over the top to enclose the filling. Place the muffin pan in a 2-inch-deep roasting pan and fill with boiling water to reach halfway up the sides of the muffin cups. Cover with a sheet of parchment paper and bake for 25 minutes. Remove the muffin pan from the water and carefully invert onto a work surface. Use a blunt knife or spatula to release the stuffed zucchini from the pan. Coat the bottom of each serving plate with warm Beet Sauce. Gently place the filled zucchini in the center of the sauce and top with the fried carrots. Serve immediately.

PARMIGIANA alla CASERTANA

A variation of Parmigiana di Melanzane. A classic southern Italian dish from the town of Caserta, this is a favorite, especially among vegan guests.

Serves 6 Ⓜ *50 minutes*

INGREDIENTS

2 tablespoons raisins

1 tablespoon Italian 'OO' flour (see page 16), plus more for coating

1½ pounds eggplant, peeled and sliced crosswise into ¼-inch rounds

Vegetable oil, for deep-frying

3 medium onions, thinly sliced into rounds on a mandoline

2 tablespoons extra virgin olive oil

2 tablespoons capers, rinsed and drained if packed in brine, and chopped

2 tablespoons pitted and chopped black olives

2 tablespoons pitted and chopped green olives

1 tablespoon toasted pine nuts

5 tomatoes, peeled, seeded, and coarsely chopped

5 basil leaves, coarsely chopped

1 tablespoon red wine vinegar

Salt and pepper to taste

———

Soak the raisins in a small bowl of hot water until plump and tender, about 15 minutes. Drain well. Fill a bowl with water and stir in the 1 tablespoon flour. Soak the eggplant in the water for 15 minutes. Drain and press each round between your palms to squeeze out any excess water. Put enough flour in a bowl to coat the eggplant. Coat each round in the flour and place on a large baking sheet. Deep-fry the rounds in vegetable oil until golden brown (see page 20). Transfer to another baking sheet lined with paper towels and pat dry with more paper towels to soak up the excess oil. Cool.

Meanwhile, in a large pan, slowly cook the onion rounds in the olive oil over low heat, stirring occasionally, for 30 minutes or until golden brown and dry. Mix in the raisins, capers, olives, pine nuts, tomatoes, and basil and cook for 1 minute before adding the vinegar. Season with salt and pepper and cook for 1 minute or until the vinegar has evaporated.

ASSEMBLY

Preheat the oven to 350°F. Spread a third of the onion mixture over the bottom of a 13-x-9-inch baking dish. Overlap half the eggplant slices over the onion mixture and sprinkle with salt. Add another third of the onion mixture, layer the remaining eggplants on top, and sprinkle with salt. Top with the final third of the onion mixture and press the surface gently with the back of a spoon. Bake, uncovered, for 5 minutes or until heated through. Cut serving portions with clean kitchen scissors and serve hot.

Radicchio, pear, and smoked cheese rolls. A very sophisticated recipe, with a unique blend of tastes. It's surprising how the sweetness of the pear matches the bitterness of the radicchio and works with the smoked cheese. A winning taste.

Serves 4 ⓜ *35 minutes & 20 minutes baking*

FILLING

1 radicchio, cut into 8 wedges (do not remove the core)

2 tablespoons extra virgin olive oil, plus more for drizzling

Salt and pepper to taste

1 pear, peeled and cored

2 garlic cloves

1 shallot, finely chopped

1 tablespoon chopped walnuts

2 tablespoons white wine

2 teaspoons red wine vinegar

————

Drizzle the radicchio wedges with olive oil and season with salt and pepper. Grill all sides on a grill pan. Cool, chop coarsely, and place in a bowl. Cut the pear into $1/4$-inch-wide slices and grill in the same manner. Cool briefly before cutting into $1/4$-inch cubes and tossing with the radicchio. Sauté the garlic and shallot in the 2 tablespoons olive oil until the garlic is golden and the shallot is translucent. Discard the garlic and add the radicchio and pear. Cook for an additional 2 minutes, then add the walnuts, wine, and vinegar. Cook until the liquid has evaporated, about 10 minutes. Season with salt and pepper and drain in a colander. Cool completely.

ASSEMBLY

$8 1/2$ ounces Puff Pastry (see page 32) or purchased frozen puff pastry, thawed

1 ounce Taleggio (see page 20), cut into $1/2$-inch cubes

1 ounce smoked Scamorza (see page 20), cut into $1/2$-inch cubes

1 egg yolk, for brushing

————

Preheat the oven to 350°F. Roll out the puff pastry on a lightly floured work surface into a large rectangle $1/8$ inch thick. With a pizza cutter or sharp knife, cut it into $3 1/2$-inch squares. Spread 2 tablespoons of filling over one side of each square, leaving a $1/4$-inch border around the edges, and top the filling with a few cubes of the cheeses. Brush the borders with egg yolk. Loosely roll the uncovered side over the filling to create a cylinder and gently press the edges to seal. Brush the entire surface with egg yolk. Arrange on a parchment-lined baking sheet. Bake for 20 minutes, or until puffed and golden. Serve hot.

PARMIGIANA di ZUCCHINE

Traditionally made with eggplant, this recipe calls for zucchini. The light crispy batter that surrounds the zucchini melts with the béchamel and tomato sauce in a delicious way. A real Italian treat.

Serves 6 (M) *60 minutes*

INGREDIENTS

³⁄₄ cup cornstarch

²⁄₃ cup all-purpose flour

Salt to taste

1 cup beer

Vegetable oil, for deep-frying

4 zucchini, thinly sliced lengthwise on a mandoline

1 quantity Tomato Sauce (see page 36)

1 quantity Basic Béchamel (see page 26)

6 tablespoons grated Parmesan

2 ounces Pecorino di Pienza (see page 20), cut into small cubes

3 ounces mozzarella, cut into small cubes

———

In a bowl, combine the cornstarch, flour, a pinch of salt, and the beer and whisk until smooth. Heat the vegetable oil in a large, heavy-bottomed pot (see page 20). When the oil is hot, dip the zucchini into the batter and deep-fry in batches until golden brown and crispy. Remove with a slotted spoon and set on paper towels to drain. Season with a sprinkle of salt. Set aside to cool.

ASSEMBLY

Preheat the oven to 350°F. Drizzle a third of the Tomato Sauce over the bottom of a 12-x-8-inch baking dish or gratin dish and add a few drops of Basic Béchamel. Layer the zucchini slices side by side. Sprinkle with half of the grated Parmesan and cubed Pecorino di Pienza. Pour over another third of the Tomato Sauce and more Basic Béchamel and repeat the layering, ending with a topping of mozzarella. Bake for 20 minutes, or until golden brown and bubbly. Serve hot.

GATEAU di PATATE

Individual potato delights with the distinct earthy flavor of smoked Provolone cheese.

Serves 6 (M) *15 minutes & 30 minutes baking*

INGREDIENTS

3 large potatoes

3 tablespoons butter, plus more, out into bits, for topping

2 eggs, lightly beaten

2 tablespoons extra virgin olive oil

2 tablespoons grated Parmesan

1 tablespoon grated Pecorino Romano

Salt, black pepper, and white pepper to taste

Dry bread crumbs

1 ounce smoked Provolone cheese, cut into small cubes

———

Cook the potatoes in a saucepan of water to cover until tender. Peel the potatoes, and mash well with the 3 tablespoons butter in a bowl. Let cool to room temperature. Mix in the eggs, olive oil, and grated cheeses, and season to taste. Grease six 2-inch-diameter ramekins with olive oil and dust with bread crumbs. Line the bottom of each ramekin with a small round of parchment paper.

ASSEMBLY

Preheat the oven to 350°F. Divide half of the potato mixture among the ramekins. Top with the smoked cheese cubes and then with the remaining potato mixture. Use the tines of a fork to draw concentric circles over the top. Dot with butter and bake for 30 minutes. Unmold and serve hot.

If smoked Provolone is not available, use a different mild smoked cheese.

PIZZA e MINESTRA

A crunchy cornmeal "pizza" is combined with dandelion greens and minestra (vegetable broth) for a hearty stew. Of humble origins, this dish comes from the region of Molise in central Italy and is enjoyed by both poor and rich alike.

Serves 8 (E) *25 minutes & 30 minutes baking*

BAKED POLENTA

2 tablespoons extra virgin olive oil, plus more for drizzling

2 tablespoons bread crumbs

1½ cups instant polenta or yellow cornmeal

⅔ cup water

⅔ cup milk

1 teaspoon salt

_____

Preheat the oven to 325°F. Line the bottom of a nonstick 10- to 11-inch springform pan with parchment paper. Drizzle a generous amount of olive oil over the bottom and sprinkle the bread crumbs over the oil. Toast the polenta in a dry sauté pan over medium heat until barely colored and transfer to a bowl. Mix in the 2 tablespoons of olive oil and the remaining ingredients and pour into the prepared pan. Press gently to spread out and create indentations all over the surface with your fingertips. Drizzle more oil over the top and bake for 30 minutes or until golden brown and crunchy on top. Cool for a few minutes, and invert onto a work surface. Peel off the parchment, cut into ½-inch cubes, and set aside.

DANDELION GREENS

2 pounds dandelion greens

4 garlic cloves

1 small cayenne or other chile, sliced

¼ cup extra virgin olive oil

Salt to taste

1 cup Vegetable Stock (see page 36)

_____

Bring a pot of lightly salted water to a boil and cook the greens for a few seconds to wilt. With a slotted spoon, transfer to a plate. In a sauté pan, sauté the garlic and chile in the olive oil until brown. Add the greens and sauté for an additional minute, seasoning to taste with salt. Add the polenta cubes and stock and continue to cook for 3 minutes. Taste for seasoning and serve hot.

STRUDEL di ZUCCHINE

The rich addition of toasted pine nuts and basil leaves gives this zucchini and Taleggio strudel a very special touch. Enjoy for a formal dinner or a nice casual lunch.

Serves 8 Ⓓ *45 minutes & cooling time & 35 minutes baking*

FILLING

2 garlic cloves

3 tablespoons extra virgin olive oil

1 tablespoon pine nuts

4 zucchini, coarsely grated

Salt and white pepper to taste

1 cup ricotta

2 tablespoons grated Parmesan

Pinch of nutmeg

———

In a sauté pan, sauté the garlic cloves in the olive oil until they begin to brown. Toss in the pine nuts and toast. Add the grated zucchini and cook until all the water released has evaporated and the zucchini begin to color. Season with salt and white pepper and remove the garlic cloves. Set aside in a bowl and cool completely. In another bowl, mix the ricotta, Parmesan, and nutmeg together and then add to the cold zucchini mixture. Set aside.

DOUGH

3/4 cup Italian '00' flour (see page 16)

3/4 cup Grano Duro flour (see page 17)

2 tablespoons extra virgin olive oil

1 egg white

1/3 cup water

Pinch of salt

———

Sift both flours onto a work surface. Make a well in the center and add the remaining ingredients. Work with your fingers to incorporate until a dough forms. Gather the dough and knead until the consistency is even throughout. Throw the ball of dough down onto the work surface 50 times, then cover with a warm glass bowl (the glass bowl can be heated for 1 minute in a warm oven) and let dough rest for 15 minutes.

ASSEMBLY

2 tablespoons half-and-half, for brushing

3 ounces Taleggio (see page 20), coarsely cut into pieces

4 basil leaves, coarsely chopped

———

Preheat the oven to 350°F. Place a clean towel on a dry work surface and dust with flour. When the dough has rested, shape into a disk and slowly roll over your wrists to stretch it. When it begins to thin (but not break), place on the towel and gently pull the dough into a rectangle shape with your fingers, maintaining the thickness. The dough should be thin and slightly transparent. Trim the edges with a pizza cutter. Brush the surface with half-and-half.

Dot the zucchini filling evenly over the dough, leaving a 3/4-inch margin on one short side uncovered. Repeat with the ricotta mixture and the Taleggio and sprinkle with basil. Using the towel as a guide, gently fold in the long sides of the pastry. Pull up the towel from the bottom corners and gently roll up the dough toward the 3/4-inch margin until the seam side is down. Place on a baking sheet lined with parchment paper, brush the surface with half-and-half, then bake for 35 minutes or until golden brown. Cool for a few minutes before slicing and serving.

Stuffed eggplant. A succulent traditional dish. Thyme and marjoram enhance the great taste of the ingredients. It's even better if cooked in a terra-cotta casserole. You will see the difference.

Serves 4   Ⓜ   *25 minutes & 1 hour cooking*

INGREDIENTS

5 medium-size long Italian or Asian eggplants

Sea salt

1 medium shallot, finely chopped

1 garlic clove, chopped

1 teaspoon marjoram leaves

1 teaspoon thyme leaves

3 tablespoons extra virgin olive oil

Salt and black pepper to taste

1 tablespoon chopped parsley

3 crustless bread slices, soaked in milk

1 tablespoon grated Parmesan

1 tablespoon grated Pecorino Romano

1 tablespoon grated Fossa cheese

———

Rinse the eggplants and trim the ends. Cut four eggplants into eight 2½-inch-long pieces. Using a melon baller, scoop out the inside of the pieces, leaving ¼ inch of flesh around the rim and at the bottom. Reserve the scooped-out portion. Lightly sprinkle sea salt on the inside of the cylinders and place, upright, in a colander for 10 minutes. Rinse off the excess salt and place the cylinders upside down on a towel to dry. Peel the fifth eggplant and chop with the reserved flesh.

In a sauté pan, sauté the shallot, garlic, marjoram, and thyme in the olive oil for 1 minute, then add the chopped eggplant. Season with a pinch of salt and black pepper and continue to cook for 20 minutes more, stirring occasionally. Cook until the eggplant mixture is soft and any excess water has evaporated. Remove from the heat and add the chopped parsley. Cool completely. Squeeze any excess milk from the bread and add the bread to the mixture. Add the grated cheeses and mix.

SAUCE

1 pound cherry tomatoes, halved

2 garlic cloves, sliced

4 basil leaves, coarsely chopped

¼ cup extra virgin olive oil

Salt and black pepper to taste

———

Mix all the ingredients in a bowl and season to taste.

ASSEMBLY

8 basil leaves

5 ounces mozzarella, sliced into 8 pieces

———

Spread the sauce in a heavy-bottomed 10-inch flameproof casserole or baking dish at least 3 inches deep. Fill each eggplant cylinder with the eggplant filling and insert a basil leaf. Place each piece upright on the sauce. Cover the casserole with parchment paper and a lid. Cook over low heat for 1 hour. Turn off the heat and place one slice of mozzarella over each cylinder. Serve hot.

POLPETTONE di SEITAN VESTITO

Polpettone translates to "meat loaf." In the Montali version, meat is replaced by seitan and encased in puff pastry. Delicious with Tartar Sauce (see page 35).

Serves 4 **D** *65 minutes*

SEITAN FILLING

1 small shallot, finely chopped

1 small garlic clove, minced

1/2 carrot, sliced crosswise

1/2 celery stalk, sliced crosswise

1 bunch parsley, plus 1 tablespoon chopped

1 tablespoon butter

2 tablespoons extra virgin olive oil

12 ounces Seitan, cut into 1/2-inch
    cubes (see page 35)

1 1/2 teaspoons all-purpose flour

2 tablespoons white wine

Salt, pepper, and nutmeg to taste

Finely grated zest of 1/2 lemon

1/4 cup ricotta

2 tablespoons grated Parmesan

1 tablespoon grated Pecorino Romano

1 whole egg plus 1 yolk

1 slice of crustless bread, cut into cubes and soaked
    in milk for 3 minutes, then squeezed to drain

In a sauté pan, sauté the vegetables and parsley sprigs in the butter and oil for 30 seconds. Add the seitan, cook for 2 minutes, then sprinkle with the flour and continue to cook. Add the wine to break down the flour and cook until the liquid has evaporated. Cool completely. Remove the parsley and purée the seitan in a blender. Mix in the chopped parsley, salt, pepper, nutmeg, lemon zest, cheeses, egg, egg yolk, and soaked bread cubes. Set aside.

PUMPKIN

2 ounces pumpkin

Carefully peel the pumpkin and keep the piece whole. In a saucepan with a steaming rack, steam the pumpkin over simmering water until al dente. Let cool. Cut into long sticks about 1/2 inch thick.

ASSEMBLY

8 ounces Puff Pastry (see page 32), or 1 sheet purchased frozen puff pastry, thawed

1 egg yolk, for brushing

1 tablespoon sesame seeds

Preheat the oven to 350°F. Soak a 13-x-13-inch sheet of parchment paper in water. Gently wring out the excess moisture and lay out on a work surface. Spread the seitan mixture in a 9-x-9-inch square on the paper, aligned with the bottom center of the sheet. Line the pumpkin sticks 8 inches across horizontally, 2 inches from the bottom. Lift the bottom of the paper and tightly roll the seitan around the pumpkin into a long log shape. Twist the ends of the paper like a candy wrapper to close and place in a 9-x-5-x-3-inch loaf pan. Bake for 40 minutes. Cool completely.

Open the puff pastry sheet and roll, if necessary, into an 11-x-9-inch rectangle. Brush the edges with egg yolk. Unwrap the seitan from the paper and place toward the bottom of the pastry. Roll gently, as before. Brush the whole surface with egg yolk and sprinkle with the sesame seeds. Place on a baking sheet and bake for 20 minutes. Cool for a few minutes before slicing and serving.

PORRI al MONTASIO

The delicate sweetness of leeks combines well with the pleasantly sour taste of Montasio cheese (see page 18). This is great to eat with disks of fried puffy bread.

Serves 4 ● Ⓔ *20 minutes & 70 minutes resting*

INGREDIENTS

1½ pounds leeks, white and light green parts only
2 tablespoons butter
2½ tablespoons all-purpose flour
2 cups milk
5 ounces Montasio or Cheddar cheese, cut into ½-inch cubes
Salt, pepper, and nutmeg to taste

———

Clean the leeks and cut each into three equal pieces; then halve each piece crosswise on the diagonal. Cook in a saucepan of lightly salted boiling water for 3 minutes and set aside. In a separate saucepan, melt the butter and add the flour. Stir until the roux is golden brown and add a quarter of the milk, stirring until smooth. Add the remaining milk and cook until thickened, approximately 3 minutes. Stir two-thirds of the cheese into the sauce until melted. Season with salt, pepper, and nutmeg.

ASSEMBLY

Preheat the oven to 350°F. Butter the bottom of a shallow 8-x-8-inch baking dish. Stand the leeks diagonal end up and drizzle with the sauce. Top with the remaining cheese and bake for 10 minutes or until the cheese is bubbly and golden brown. Serve hot with the Bread Disks.

BREAD DISKS

1 cup Italian 'OO' flour (see page 16)
1 teaspoon compressed fresh yeast
⅔ cup warm water
2 teaspoons extra virgin olive oil
¼ teaspoon salt
Vegetable oil, for deep-frying

———

Sift the flour into a large bowl and make a well in the center. In a separate bowl, mix the remaining ingredients together, then pour into the well. Work the dough in a wavelike motion to incorporate air. When the color and texture are smooth, cover with plastic wrap and let rest in a warm, dry place for 35 minutes. Sprinkle the surface of the dough with flour and "turn" it by pulling small portions of the dough around one edge of the bowl toward the opposite side. Once one full turn has been made, repeat twice, starting by sprinkling with more flour. Let rest for 35 minutes longer.

Dust a work surface with flour and roll the dough into a ⅛-inch-thick disk. Cut out rounds with a 2¼-inch cookie cutter. Working in batches, deep-fry in vegetable oil until puffed and golden on the outside and cooked through (see page 20). Drain on paper towels and season with salt. Serve hot.

Escarole and leek tart. The crunchy pastry and the just-sautéed vegetables make a pleasant and light sweet and sour taste. Wonderful at a buffet party.

Serves 4 to 6   Ⓜ   *60 minutes & cooling time*

DOUGH

1¼ cups Italian 'OO' flour (see page 16)

1¼ teaspoons salt

6 tablespoons butter, cut into small cubes, at room temperature

1½ tablespoons cold water

———————

Combine the flour and salt in a bowl. Work in the butter with your fingertips until the mixture becomes crumbly. Collect handfuls of dough and gently rub between your palms. Continue this movement to achieve a sandlike texture. Add the water and continue to work with your fingertips until the dough comes together. Gather into a ball and wrap in plastic wrap. Refrigerate for 30 minutes.

Preheat the oven to 350°F. Roll out the dough between two sheets of parchment paper dusted with flour into a large rectangle approximately 17 x 11 inches and ⅛ inch thick. Grease six 3- to 4-inch pie or tart pans with butter. Use a small knife to cut the dough into disks slightly bigger than the pans. Gently line the pans with the dough. Pierce the bottoms with a fork and bake for 10 minutes. Cool completely before gently removing the pastry from the pans.

FILLING

2 tablespoons dark raisins

About 1 cup port wine

¼ cup pitted black olives, coarsely chopped

2 large garlic cloves

5 tablespoons extra virgin olive oil

1 head escarole, cored and coarsely chopped

Salt and black pepper to taste

1 leek, white and light green parts only, cut into thin strips

3 ounces soft sheep's cheese, cut into ¼-inch cubes

———————

In a small saucepan, combine the raisins and enough port wine to cover. Bring to a simmer and turn off the heat. Let stand for 15 minutes to soften. Drain well; discard the port. In a sauté pan, sauté the olives with 1 garlic clove in half of the olive oil for 30 seconds. Add the escarole, season with salt and pepper, and cook slowly over medium heat for 20 minutes, partially covered. Add the raisins and cook uncovered for 2 minutes. Discard the garlic. In a separate sauté pan, cook the leeks with the remaining garlic clove and olive oil over medium heat until tender, approximately 10 minutes. Discard the garlic and gently stir the leeks into the escarole mixture.

ASSEMBLY

Divide half of the cubed cheese between the six pie crusts and spread evenly over the bottom. Spread equal amounts of the filling over the cheese. Top the filling with the remaining cheese cubes and set aside until ready to serve. Reheat on a baking sheet for 5 to 10 minutes at 350°F or until the cheese is melted and bubbly. Serve immediately.

Puff pastry packages filled with spiced couscous. An Italian touch added to a north African dish with an Asian hint!

Serves 8 Ⓜ 45 minutes

COUSCOUS

⅓ cup shelled fresh or frozen peas

Salt and pepper to taste

1½ tablespoons olive oil, plus more for drizzling

1 small garlic clove

1 tablespoon butter

1 teaspoon ground cumin

1 teaspoon curry powder

1 tablespoon grated fresh ginger

½ celery stalk, chopped

1 small carrot, cut into ¼-inch pieces

½ zucchini, cut into ¼-inch pieces

2 ounces cauliflower, broken into small florets (about ¼ cup)

1 small shallot, finely chopped

¼ cup couscous

¼ cup Vegetable Stock (see page 36)

1½ tablespoons pine nuts, lightly toasted

2 tablespoons raisins, soaked in hot water and drained

In a saucepan, combine the peas with enough water to barely cover them, season with salt, and drizzle with olive oil. Cook over medium heat until the peas are just cooked, 5 to 10 minutes. Drain and set the peas aside. In a sauté pan, sauté the garlic in the butter and olive oil. When the garlic browns, add the cumin, curry powder, and ginger. Toss in the remaining vegetables and cook until al dente, seasoning with salt and pepper. Toast the couscous in a nonstick pan until golden brown and set aside in a heat-proof bowl. Bring the stock to a boil and immediately pour over the couscous. Cover and let stand for 10 minutes. Uncover, fluff with a fork, and add to the vegetables. Fold in the pine nuts, drained raisins, and peas. Cool completely.

ASSEMBLY

17½ ounces Puff Pastry (see page 32) or purchased frozen puff pastry, thawed

1 ounce Pecorino di Pienza (see page 20), cut into flat 1-inch squares

1 egg, beaten, for brushing

Preheat the oven to 350°F. Roll out the puff pastry into a large rectangle approximately ⅛ inch thick. Using a pizza cutter, cut the pastry into 4½-inch squares. Place 2 tablespoons of the couscous mixture and one square of cheese in the center of each pastry square. Fold over two opposite corners of each square, sealing one over the other with egg wash. Brush the other two corners with egg wash, fold over, and press gently to seal. Brush the surfaces with more egg wash and set the parcels on a baking sheet lined with parchment paper. Bake for 20 minutes or until puffed and golden. Serve hot.

EMPADINHAS

This savory Brazilian pastry of African origin is traditionally filled with various meats, but the Montali version features delectable hearts of palm and green olives.

Serves 6 (M) *60 minutes*

FILLING

1 shallot, chopped

1 tablespoon extra virgin olive oil

½ cup green olives, pitted and chopped, plus 6 whole olives, pitted, if desired

1 tablespoon chopped parsley

1 (14 ounce) can hearts of palm, drained and chopped

6 tablespoons water

½ quantity Basic Béchamel (see page 26)

Salt and pepper to taste

———

In a sauté pan, sauté the shallot in the oil until translucent. Add the chopped olives, half of the parsley, the hearts of palm, and the water and cook, covered, for 5 minutes. Stir in the Basic Béchamel and cook for an additional minute. Mix in the remaining parsley, season to taste, and remove from the heat. Cool completely.

DOUGH

1 cup all-purpose flour

½ teaspoon salt

6 tablespoons butter, cut into cubes and softened

1 egg

———

In a bowl, combine the flour, salt, and butter and work with your fingertips until the dough resembles coarse crumbs. Gather a handful and gently brush your palms together, allowing the dough to fall back into the bowl. Continue until it reaches a sandlike consistency. Add the egg, incorporating it into the dough. With the help of a dough scraper, continually cut through the dough and work well with your hands until it is even in color and texture. Wrap in plastic wrap and refrigerate for 15 minutes.

ASSEMBLY

1 egg, beaten, for brushing

———

Preheat the oven to 350°F. Between two sheets of parchment paper dusted with flour, roll out two-thirds of the dough (leaving the rest wrapped) into a large disk ¼ inch thick. Using a 4½-inch round cutter or the rim of a drinking glass, cut out six disks. Evenly line six ramekins with the dough so that it comes three-quarters of the way up the sides. Fill each with 1 tablespoon of filling. Place one whole olive in the center and top with 1 more tablespoon of filling. Roll out the remaining dough in the same manner as before, but slightly thinner. Using a round cutter slightly smaller than the diameter of the ramekin, cut six equal disks. Gently press over the filling. Seal the sides to the top with a small knife, working around the edge of the ramekin to create a nice border. With the remaining dough, roll six ¼-inch balls and place on top of the pastry lids for decoration. Brush all over with the egg and bake for 20 minutes or until golden on the outside and heated through. Serve hot.

"We're staying at a what?" Gene asked incredulously as his brother, Joe, pulled in through the entrance gates.

"A vegetarian restaurant and hotel," Joe repeated.

"Oh. That's what I thought you said." Gene and Rob exchanged surprised glances. The month-long trip to Italy was a long time coming and their brother, Joe, the designated itinerary planner, had decided to tell them this now. They laughed at the irony.

The DiSimone brothers from Boston, Massachusetts, were in Umbria for the largest steak festival in the world. La Sagra della Bistecca is held every August in Cortona, and for years the brothers had heard tales of the streets of the medieval city lined with impossibly long grills and smoldering cuts of tender meat brilliantly ablaze at every turn. In 2002, the three devoted meat lovers were looking forward to the festival as one of the major highlights of their trip.

As they pulled up in front of the Country House Montali, none of them knew what to expect. Whether it was the beautiful pictures he had seen online, the convenient distance from Cortona, or plain curiosity about a vegetarian restaurant and hotel, Joe had booked himself and his brothers in for two nights. He, like Gene and Rob, had a preconceived notion of the hotel based on the term *vegetarian*. In Boston, vegetarianism was not so much an eating preference as a campaign to save the world.

Which is what they thought Montali might be like until they saw Alberto chain-smoking Marlboro Reds outside his office. He greeted them warmly, showed them to their room, and informed them that dinner would be at eight in the evening. Joe, Gene, and Rob nodded politely and settled in. They didn't anticipate eating much at dinner, which did not bother them, as they planned to head straight to the festival immediately afterward anyway.

Later, they sat down at dinner, admired the beautiful

setting of the dining room, and discussed the peaceful ambience, but their thoughts were already three hours ahead. However, with each course that Alberto brought and introduced to their table, they grew more and more amazed. The food was incredible.

The completely satiated brothers ended up going to the festival, much to the bemusement of Alberto, but their meal there was not nearly as memorable as the one they had just had. Or the one they had the following night. By the time the three brothers left Montali, they had fallen in love with the food, the surroundings, the quiet, the opportunity to get to know other guests, and the whole relaxing experience. Their emotions had been strained since the passing of their mother nine months earlier, and, after quarreling through the first half of their trip, they were filled with a tremendous sense of calm, which they had not had together in a long time.

The following year, Joe came back to Montali with his brothers and his girlfriend, Sara Concannon. They had met while working on a case together a few years before, he as a sergeant detective for the Boston police and she as an assistant district attorney. Like Joe and his brothers, she was completely charmed by Montali. She loved that there was no menu at all and that dinner was a surprise every night, impeccably presented and delectably prepared. She was introduced to a whole variety of dishes that, out of unfamiliarity, she might have passed over at other restaurants.

Over the next few years, Joe and Sara continued to come back to Montali. They spent late nights talking with Alberto outside on the veranda, quickly developed favorite dishes (which Malu took note of), and became very comfortable and familiar with the property, its surroundings, and each other.

October 23, 2004, was a day that all three brothers remember well for different reasons. After lengthy culinary studies in Italy, chef Rob returned to Boston. On another side of town, Gene was beside himself that evening when the Red Sox won game one of the World Series. And in a quiet restaurant, Joe celebrated his birthday by asking Sara to spend every birthday for the rest of their lives together. It was a good day for everyone.

Neither Joe nor Sara cared for a swanky wedding at the Yacht Club or a ritzy hotel in Boston. They decided very early on that they wanted a small wedding with family and intimate friends in a setting that would be special to both of them. Moreover, Joe had close friends and family in Europe. Montali could provide a warm and personal setting, delicious food, and, particularly, an opportunity to share with those closest to them this treasure of a hotel that they had been raving about.

As dear as Joe and Sara had become, Malu and Alberto took it upon themselves to take care of everything. From the menu to the paperwork to the entertainment and all the minute details in between, everything was taken care of. Alberto ordered flower arrangements, traveled back and forth to Perugia for stacks upon stacks of papers, and set up hair appointments at the best salon in the local town for the morning of the wedding. The salon was not even open on Mondays, the day of the wedding, but Alberto had somehow convinced them to not only open, but also to do so at 7:30 in the morning, two and a half hours before normal opening hours on any other day.

The five-night, five-day holiday for Sara, Joe, and their wedding guests was full of relaxation, succulent foods, and elegant musical entertainment. Filling the restaurant, they chatted and sipped wine late into the evening and spent the days traveling or lounging by the pool. For the staff, it was five seventeen-hour working days, running like mad and functioning on a mixture of caffeine and pure adrenaline. The chefs tried to prepare as many things in advance as they could, but the nature and intricacies of most of the courses demanded that the dishes be prepared fresh and on the day they were served.

Regardless of how intensely anyone worked, Malu worked ten times harder. Somewhere between Sunday night and Monday morning, she had prepared hundreds of assorted delicate Brazilian confections, miniature quiche cups, dozens upon dozens of ricotta-stuffed cannelloni, various sauces, and the wedding cake. When the chefs groggily rolled into the restaurant on Monday morning, they looked at Malu in wonder and amazement as she vigorously smacked a rug against a brick wall while calling out to them, "Ciao, Ragazzi!" The bright eyes and fresh glow of the skin fooled no one; everyone knew that she had barely slept.

The guests began to refer to Alberto as Mr. Rourke from the hit 1970s show *Fantasy Island*, as he made sure everything flowed perfectly. Before they even knew they were warm, Alberto had already opened a window. When they were indecisive about which wine they wanted to drink, Alberto brought out the perfect selection. Whatever need they might have, Alberto anticipated it.

On the day of the wedding, the guests left early to attend a ceremony in a local church. When they returned, they had barely stepped out of the cars before Alberto, Agnes, and Marketa were standing before them with celebratory champagne flutes of chilled Bellini. A harpist and flautist performed under the veranda, and the guests lounged under the shade, enjoying the miniature pizzas and pies that were being passed around. Inside the kitchen, Daniel was in the middle of pouring Cachaça into a punch bowl filled with a fruit juice cocktail when Malu walked by and dipped a cup into the bowl to taste.

"Daniel, it needs something more . . . It needs more tequila!" she said after taking a sip.

"Malu, there's already a whole bottle and a half in there," Daniel replied.

Malu's eyes opened wide and she said, "Basta!" She turned her attention to the miniature Pecorino Romano and walnut breads that had just come out of the oven. "Okay, slice them in half, spread red pepper pâté over them, and give them to the girls to pass around," she instructed, before once more redirecting her attention to the cannelloni in the oven.

Joe, Sara, and the guests had no idea what was on the menu for the day and, assuming that the hors d'oeuvres were the "light lunch," happily devoured them. When the primo of ricotta cheese–stuffed cannelloni and saffron risotto arrived on individual plates, they were pleasantly surprised. Once those plates were replaced by the secondi of coxinhas and puff pastry-encased olives and hearts of palm, they were stuffed. By the time the Brazilian confections, silky-smooth chocolates dipped in chocolate sprinkles or coconut shavings, were passed around, guests were in nirvana. A rest and a few more drinks,

and finally people were ready for the last touch: the wedding cake.

From the kitchen the four usually invisible chefs came out, beautifully and cleanly dressed, carrying the highlight of their working week — a double-layered carrot cake with a layer of apricot marmalade in the middle, covered in chocolate ganache, and decorated with a fresh peony and whipped cream. All the guests greeted them with thanks and joy.

Joe and Sara presented Alberto and Malu with gifts of their appreciation. For Malu, a classy black designer tote bag and, for Alberto, a bottle of Mondavi & Rothschild Opus One, a California specialty. Later, Alberto walked into the kitchen and faced the staff that he knew he had been driving to the ground for days. He saw their bloodshot eyes and bandage-covered fingers. "I know I haven't said this yet, but I wanted to tell you how proud I am of all the work you have done over the last few days. Really proud." And with that, he instructed Marketa to open the bottle of Opus One and distribute it among the staff. He smiled to himself as they clinked their glasses in an "a la salute!" toast before walking outside to the back to enjoy it among themselves for a few precious minutes.

How the wedding party managed to eat dinner only a few short hours after the reception is a mystery. Yet they all showed up and enjoyed every course from the Crudite di Pere e Melone antipasti to the Vulcano di Cioccolato dessert, all while a cello and violin were performing in the dining room. After dinner, they sat outside facing the stone stage that Alberto had illuminated with a single lamp. Two opera singers performed classical Italian pieces like "O Sole Mio" and "Time to Say Goodbye" with the accompaniment of a pianist. The tenor, standing proudly with a colorful scarf wrapped around his neck, captivated the crowd with his deep resonating voice. In a shimmering black dress billowing in the breeze of the late summer night, the soprano sang in a brilliant, crystal-clear tone that carried across the grove. Malu had pulled out chairs for the staff and insisted that they each grab a glass of wine and enjoy the concert outside, an order that they were all happy to obey.

The wedding celebration was, for both the party and the staff, an event to remember. On several late nights the staff would gather around the marble table after everyone had left, cleaning stemware with silk cloths to a spotless shine. Blasting loud dance music past midnight, they would keep their eyes forced open and bob up and down to the beat of the music to stay awake. They would go home, nurse their chapped hands, and completely collapse, only to wake a few hours later to start all over. There were tears of exhaustion, shouting matches, and periods of comatose silence. There were those who needed lively conversation to stay alert, and others who resorted to robot-like behavior as a means to carry on.

More importantly, Joe and Sara's guests were able to experience the beloved Montali they had heard countless stories about for so many years. Above all, they met the legendary Alberto, with his tales and adventures from all over the world, and Malu, his beautiful Brazilian wife and culinary wonder.

Best of all, there were no stressful details to worry over. Joe and Sara simply showed up and enjoyed themselves. As it had since the first time the DiSimone brothers came in 2002, Montali provided them with exactly what they were looking for before they even knew it themselves.

Assortito
SIDES

Fava bean Purée
Serves 6

1/3 cup dried fava beans, rinsed	2 tablespoons extra virgin olive oil
1/2 carrot, halved lengthwise	Salt to taste
2 garlic cloves	1 1/2 cups water
1/2 medium onion, quartered	1 tablespoon lemon juice
1 sprig parsley	1 tablespoon tahini (see page 17)

———

Combine the beans, carrot, 1 garlic clove, onion, parsley, 1 tablespoon olive oil, salt, and water in a large pot and cook over low heat for 40 minutes, or until the beans are tender. Remove the beans and purée them in a blender. Discard the other ingredients. Purée the remaining garlic clove (or crush through a garlic press) and add to the beans, along with the lemon juice, tahini, and remaining olive oil. Season to taste. Cover and set aside.

Carrot Purée
Serves 6

5 carrots, peeled	2 tablespoons grated Parmesan
1 tablespoon butter	1 1/2 teaspoons finely chopped parsley
1 shallot, finely chopped	1 1/2 teaspoons finely chopped chives
Salt and black pepper to taste	

———

Cut the carrots into 2-inch pieces that are equal in size. In a saucepan with a steamer rack, steam with the carrots over simmering water until al dente. In a sauté pan, sauté the carrots in the butter with the chopped shallot and season with salt and pepper. Purée in a blender and set aside in a bowl to cool completely. Fold in the grated cheese, parsley, and chives. Taste for seasoning, adding more salt and pepper, if desired. Serve at room temperature.

Fried Zucchini Flowers
Serves 6

7 tablespoons all-purpose flour	2 ounces Pecorino di Pienza (see page 20)
5 tablespoons cornstarch	12 zucchini flowers
3 pinches of salt	Vegetable oil, for deep-frying
2/3 cup beer	

———

In a bowl, mix the flour, cornstarch, salt, and beer together to make a batter. Cut the cheese into 12 narrow sticks. Remove the centers from the flowers and replace each with a stick of cheese. Working in batches, dip in the batter and deep-fry in oil (see page 20). Transfer to a pan lined with paper towels and season with salt. Serve immediately.

Corn and Apple Salad
Serves 6

1 small ear of corn, steamed until just tender

1 Granny Smith apple

1 shallot, finely chopped

1 tablespoon chopped parsley

3 tablespoons extra virgin olive oil

Red wine vinegar to taste

Balsamic vinegar to taste

Lemon juice to taste

Salt and pepper to taste

1 dash Tabasco

_____

Cut the corn kernels from the ear. Peel, core, and cut the apple into tiny cubes the same size as the corn kernels. Toss all the ingredients together in a bowl. Allow to stand for at least 2 hours before serving to allow all the flavors to blend.

Beet Salad
Serves 8

1 beet (about 10 ounces)

½ cup plain yogurt

2 tablespoons grated Feta

Salt and black pepper to taste

1 tablespoon creamy goat cheese

2 teaspoons finely chopped parsley

2 tablespoons extra virgin olive oil

Lemon juice to taste

_____

In a saucepan, cook the beet in water to cover just until tender. Let cool. Peel and coarsely grate the beet. Place in a bowl and fold in the remaining ingredients. Taste for seasoning. Serve chilled or at room temperature.

Eggplant "alla Siciliana"
Serves 6

Vegetable oil, for deep-frying

1 large eggplant

Salt and black pepper to taste

1 medium celery stalk, coarsely chopped

1 tablespoon extra virgin olive oil

1 tablespoon butter

1 ripe tomato, peeled and seeded

1 tablespoon pine nuts, toasted

1 tablespoon raisins, rinsed with hot water

4 basil leaves, torn into pieces

1½ teaspoons sugar

1 tablespoon red wine vinegar

_____

Heat the oil in a large, heavy-bottomed pot (see page 20). Peel the skin from the eggplant in 1-inch strips so that the eggplant looks striped. Cut into 1-inch cubes and, working in batches, fry in the hot oil until browned. Remove with a slotted spoon and drain on paper towels. Season with salt and pepper and cool to room temperature. Meanwhile, in a sauté pan, sauté the celery in the oil and butter over medium heat until translucent. Add the tomato and cook until most of the liquid released from the tomato has evaporated. Stir in the eggplant, pine nuts, raisins, and basil. Sprinkle with the sugar and vinegar and continue to cook for 3 minutes. Remove from the heat and cool. Let rest for 1 hour to blend the flavors. Reheat before serving.

The relentless heat of late June seeped through the stone walls of the small kitchen where Malu and three chefs were working. A large pot of water was boiling on the six-top, creating a saunalike effect and adding to the moisture in the air that clung to everyone's skin. Earlier, there had been a lovely breeze running through the kitchen from outside but, after it had repeatedly extinguished the flames on the gas stove, it had to be shut out.

Grace stopped grilling slices of zucchini long enough to aerate her long-sleeved chef's jacket and fan her neck. Janko, also melting in the heat, turned to her and asked, "Grace, are you happy?" As if on cue, Grace faced him with a solemn expression and replied, "Yes. Yes, I am happy. But I could be happier." This was their special code for, "Oh, you know what time it is." Without a word, Janko stepped out of the kitchen and returned with four glasses of chilled house white wine with single cubes of ice floating on top. Passing them around, the chefs stood around the large marble table where they were all working, raised their glasses for a quick "a la salute," and clinked glasses. The crisp wine was a welcome relief from the sweltering heat, and Daniel, another chef from the U.S., pressed the cold glass to his forehead before setting it down. Instantaneously, all the chefs returned to work.

With a four-course menu that changes daily, there are two things that remain constant from one day to the next: soft and airy ciabatta served hot and fresh from the oven for the guests and Happy Hour for the kitchen and staff. As the ciabatta should begin baking by 7.30 P.M. to ensure a timely service, Happy Hour must commence by seven o'clock at the very latest. Both are taken very seriously, and absolutely no evening would be complete without them.

A young waiter from California did not know how seriously Happy Hour was taken until he made the mistake of asking Malu, when requested by her to pour wine, if he could use plastic cups instead of wine glasses to avoid washing extra dishes. Without a moment's hesitation, Malu said, "This is our one pleasure! We have to do it the right way. We can't enjoy wine out of a plastic cup!" (It should be noted here that when the Montali staff drink margaritas, the fruits are freshly squeezed and served in salt-rimmed glasses with a lemon wedge.)

Happy Hour of the Montali variety was started by Malu to serve two purposes. The first and most obvious was to provide a daily source of enjoyment for both back and front of the house staff. Every employee works at least twelve hours a day for six days a week, and looking forward to Happy Hour makes each working day that much more agreeable. The second purpose was a clever ploy to ensure that everyone works to his or her maximum capability. There are few other environments as stressful and overwrought with tension as a restaurant kitchen. Starting from the hour before dinner service until the second the last aperitif is served, nervous energies collide among chefs and waiters. A relaxed restaurant staff is both unrealistic and undesirable. The constant sense of urgency pushes individuals to work harder, faster, creating a dynamic, adrenaline-pumping atmosphere that chefs thrive in. On the other hand, an over-anxious person is likely to slip up and make a nervous blunder. Enter Happy Hour, serving to ever so slightly ease the tension before the big push.

One evening earlier in the season, Malu looked up from the lasagne dough that she was diligently kneading on the wooden board and squinted at the clock. "Is it time?" she asked to no one in particular. One of the other chefs laughed, understanding her question perfectly, and Malu called to one of the Slovakian waitresses, "Hey, man! It's time to make Happy Hour!" The waitress grinned and left the room to get the wine glasses from behind the bar. When she came back into the kitchen half a minute later, she was awkwardly holding five glasses in her hands, fingers and stems clumsily intertwined. She tried setting the glasses down on the large marble table where the chefs were working and, unsurprisingly, toppled one glass over another. Shards scattered like dust across the surface of the marble into plates, bowls, and trays holding food that had taken hours to prepare for the evening's dinner.

In any other restaurant kitchen, this kind of mistake would warrant absolute rage and fury from any chef. Meticulously picking through food was out of the question, and everything in the danger zone had to be thrown away. As a result, the chefs would have to work three times as fast for the remainder of the evening to make up for the discarded food.

Malu, clearly distressed, placed her fingertips at her temples and, after a moment, said to the waitress, "Don't make me paranoid, baby! From now on, glass cannot be placed on the table or near the food. It's too dangerous! Please don't stress me." If she was infuriated, she did not let it show. She spoke to the girl in an even, completely nonthreatening tone, like a mother reprimanding her child.

Working quickly, she began reorganizing the pre-dinner preparation time while the other two chefs, keeping their mouths shut, silently swept away the mess. They sadly resigned themselves to the fact that Happy Hour was canceled, until Malu stood straight, put her hands on her hips, and said to the waitress, "At least pour us some wine, baby, or else we can't relax." A few minutes later, the girl returned and distributed wine to the chefs. When she handed Malu her glass, tears sprang to her eyes and she lowered her gaze. Malu lightly pinched her cheek and gave her a quick hug.

In the summertime, cool house white wine is a common choice, as it's light and plentiful from the large jug in the wine fridge. Malu and Alberto also store half-cases of Rapitala solely for the staff to drink, when they prefer a nice red wine or when one of them needs practice opening bottles.

Malu also sees Happy Hour as a time to taste new vintages that are introduced in the local markets and insists that the chefs taste them as well. One can hardly argue with her when she says, "Our chefs must know the good wines!" The beauty of Happy Hour is that it is in no way limited by the quality of the beverage. (Quantity, on the other hand, is at one's own discretion and rarely, if ever, abused.) When Daniel arrived from California, the first thing he did was prepare an ice-cold sour lemon margarita for each person. The very next day, he saw a pile of leftover chopped fruit and immediately put together a pitcher of sangria.

On her day off, Grace wanted nothing more than to eat watermelon all day and drove twenty minutes down the mountain to MaxiSidis, the largest market in the local town. After finishing only half of what she bought, she took the rest into work the next day and kept it chilled in the fridge.

Janko had told her about a slushy watermelon tequila cocktail and she was determined to try it out. At five in the evening, she cut the watermelon into pieces, being careful to reserve all the juice, then seeded it and puréed it in a blender before pushing it through a sieve. Marketa and Agnes helped her with the cocktail, adding not only tequila but also a splash of cranberry liquor and the juice of two lemons. Janko tasted the juice, nodded in approval, and placed it on a rimmed metal baking sheet to freeze quickly.

By seven o'clock, Janko and Grace removed the bowl from the freezer. It was very cold, but still completely liquid. Grace turned to Janko and said, "It's ice cold. Shall I pour?"

"No. The liquid has to have at least a film of ice. Put it back in the freezer. We'll drink it when it's ready."

Grace smiled and obeyed. She turned to Marketa and said, "Quality control. I like his style."

Pane, Focacce & Pizza

BREADS

Tu proverai si come sa di sale
Lo pane altrui e com' è duro calle
Lo scendere e il salir per l'altrui scale
~DANTE, *PARADISO*, 17, 58.60

"Thou shalt prove how salty tastes another's bread, and how hard a path it is to go up and down another's stairs." As a Florentine in exile, Dante speaks of the sadness of adapting to the food far from home and the difficulties of finding work. While saltless bread may taste flavorless to many, the plainness had been adapted by the palates of the Florentine and Umbrian long before Dante's time and has remained so to the present day.

The absence of salt in Tuscan bread-making began in the twelfth century during the vigorous development of Pisa and Florence. Conflict ensued between the two cities, and Pisa blocked salt commerce to Florence, which was forced to import salt from elsewhere at a significantly higher cost. Hundreds of years later, Pope Paul III heavily increased the already high salt tax, affecting Perugia, Umbria, Lazio, Marche, and Romagna. All areas relied heavily on salt for the flavoring and preservation of foods but, in an effort to fight the overbearing system, boycotted the use of salt in breads. Even after the Salt War ended, Tuscan and Umbrian bakers continued to bake their breads without salt.

Not to be confused with popular pressed sandwiches, these miniature breads are a favorite among the Montali guests and staff. While these are a few examples of the freshly baked breads that we serve daily, feel free to improvise with other ingredients to create your own panino.

12 breads Ⓔ *15 minutes & 140 minutes rising & 13 minutes baking*

WALNUT AND PECORINO ROMANO PANINO

1²/₃ cups Manitoba flour (see page 16)

6 tablespoons grated Pecorino Romano

6 tablespoons walnuts, chopped

Black pepper to taste

²/₃ cup warm water (105°–115°F)

1 teaspoon salt

1 teaspoon compressed fresh yeast

PIZZA PANINO

1²/₃ cups Manitoba flour (see page 16)

1 tablespoon dried oregano

4 sun-dried tomatoes, coarsely chopped

½ cup black olives, pitted and chopped

2 teaspoons tomato paste

1 teaspoon minced garlic

1 teaspoon minced capers

²/₃ cup warm water (105°–115°F)

1 teaspoons salt

1 teaspoon compressed fresh yeast

SUNFLOWER AND PINE NUT PANINO

1²/₃ cups Manitoba flour (see page 16)

1 tablespoon sunflower seeds, toasted

1 tablespoon pine nuts, toasted

1 tablespoon pumpkin seeds, toasted

²/₃ cup warm water (105°–115°F)

1 teaspoon salt

1 teaspoon compressed fresh yeast

HERB PANINO

1²/₃ cups Manitoba flour (see page 16)

2 tablespoons mixed herbs (sage, thyme, rosemary, chives, and marjoram), finely chopped

²/₃ cup warm water (105°–115°F)

1 teaspoon salt

1 teaspoon compressed fresh yeast

———

In addition to the quantity of flour in the ingredients, set aside a small bowl of flour for dusting. Combine the flour and flavoring ingredients in a bowl and make a well in the center. In a separate bowl, mix the water, salt, and yeast together. Add the liquid to the well and work with your hands to combine. Work the dough in a wavelike motion to incorporate air. When the texture and color are even (about 1 minute), cover with plastic wrap and rest in a warm, dry place for 35 minutes. Sprinkle the surface of the dough with flour and "turn" it by pulling small portions of the dough from one edge of the bowl toward the opposite side, covering and incorporating the flour. Once one full turn has been made, rest for 35 more minutes. Repeat the procedure two more times, resting for 35 minutes after each turn. While the dough is resting for the final time, preheat the oven to 475°F and heat a baking stone or baking sheet inside. On the bottom rack of the oven, place a small baking pan with a little water in it to produce steam. Hold the bowl at an angle and gently pull out the dough onto a work surface dusted with flour. Sprinkle more flour onto the surface of the dough and gently press with the back of your hands to spread it out. Use a pizza cutter to portion the dough into 12 miniature loaves. Let rest for 10 minutes, covered with a clean towel, then remove the hot stone or sheet from the oven and dust it with flour. Arrange the breads upside down on the stone and bake for 8 minutes. Reduce the heat to 400°F and bake for 5 more minutes or until the breads feel light and golden on the outside and baked through. Remove from the oven and serve warm.

CIABATTA

This well-known Italian bread literally translates to "slipper" because of its long, flat shape. Ciabatta, soft and airy, must be eaten fresh.

1 loaf ⓔ 10 minutes & 140 minutes rising & 20 minutes baking

INGREDIENTS*

3 1/4 cups Manitoba flour (see page 16)

2 teaspoons salt

1 1/4 cups warm water (105°–115°F)

2 teaspoons compressed fresh yeast

———

Place the flour in a large bowl and make a well in the center. In a separate bowl, mix the salt, water, and yeast together. Pour the liquid into the well and work with your hands to combine. Work the dough in a wavelike motion to incorporate air. When the color and texture are smooth, cover with plastic wrap and rest in a warm, dry place for 35 minutes. Sprinkle the surface of the dough with flour and "turn" it by pulling small portions of the dough from one edge of the bowl toward the opposite side, covering and incorporating the flour. Once one full turn has been made, let rest for 35 more minutes. Repeat the procedure two more times, resting for 35 minutes after each turn. While the dough is resting for the final time, preheat the oven to 475°F and heat a baking stone or baking sheet inside. On the bottom rack of the oven, place a small baking pan with a little water in it to produce steam. Hold the bowl at an angle and gently pull out the dough onto a work surface dusted with flour. Sprinkle more flour onto the surface of the dough, gently pressing with the back of your hands to spread it out. Shape into a narrow loaf, cover with a clean towel, and let rest for 10 minutes. Then remove the hot stone or sheet from the oven and dust it with more flour. Gently transfer the loaf, upside down, onto the sheet and bake for 12 minutes. Reduce the heat to 400°F and bake for an additional 8 minutes, or until the bread feels light and is golden on the outside and baked through. Remove from the oven and cool for a few minutes before slicing to serve.

---

*GLUTEN FREE CIABATTA CON FARINA DI CECI (CHICKPEA FLOUR)

2 tablespoons raisins

3/4 cup chickpea flour

3/4 cup rice flour

2 1/2 teaspoons gluten-free yeast

2/3 cup warm water (105°–115°F)

2 tablespoons chopped hazelnuts

Salt to taste

———

In a bowl, soak the raisins in enough hot water to cover for 15 minutes, until plump. Drain. Follow the same procedure as above.

*GLUTEN FREE CIABATTA ALLE NOCI (WALNUTS)

3/4 cup cornstarch

3/4 cup rice flour

2 1/2 teaspoons gluten-free yeast

2/3 cup warm water (105°–115°F)

1/4 cup chopped walnuts

Salt to taste

———

Follow the same procedure as above.

FOCACCIA alle OLIVE

Similar to pizza bread, this soft, flat bread is rich with olives.

---

1 loaf　(E)　*15 minutes & 80 minutes rising & 12 minutes baking*

INGREDIENTS

1 cup Manitoba flour (see page 16)

⅓ cup Grano Duro flour (see page 17)

1 cup green and black olives, pitted and coarsely chopped

1 tablespoon extra virgin olive oil, plus oil for drizzling

½ cup warm water (105°–115°F)

½ teaspoon salt

2 teaspoons compressed fresh yeast

Coarse sea salt

———

Combine the flours and olives in a bowl and make a well in the center. In a separate bowl, mix the 1 tablespoon oil, water, salt, and yeast together. Pour the liquid into the well and work with your hands until the dough comes together. Work the dough in a circular, wavelike motion to incorporate air. When the texture and color are even, drizzle the surface with olive oil and spread gently with your fingers. Cover with plastic wrap and rest in a warm, dry place for 35 minutes. Sprinkle the surface of the dough with flour and "turn" it by pulling small portions of the dough from one edge of the bowl toward the opposite side. Once one full turn has been made, repeat two more times, starting by sprinkling more flour. Drizzle with more olive oil, spread with your fingers, and rest for 35 more minutes.

Preheat the oven to 435°F. Drizzle a baking sheet with 1½ tablespoons olive oil and spread to coat. Gently pull the dough from the bowl onto a work surface dusted with flour. Roll out into a flat disk that is the width of the olive oil coating and transfer, as is, to the prepared sheet. Press down lightly with your fingertips all around the dough, creating indentations, and sprinkle coarse sea salt over the top. Cover with a clean towel and let rest for 10 minutes. Before baking, drizzle the surface with 1½ tablespoons olive oil and spread gently. Bake for 12 minutes. Slice and serve warm.

For a delicious Rosemary Focaccia, replace the olives with 1 level tablespoon of finely chopped rosemary. Before baking in the oven, sprinkle the surface with additional rosemary leaves.

This "white" pizza is an instant hit with children and adults alike. Roasted rosemary and sliced potatoes add a captivating, and addictive, flavor.

One 11-inch pizza　　**F**　　*20 minutes & 70 minutes rising & 12 minutes baking*

DOUGH

1½ cups Manitoba flour (see page 16)

⅓ cup Grano Duro flour (see page 17)

1 tablespoon salt

2 teaspoons compressed fresh yeast

1 tablespoon olive oil

½ teaspoon sugar

½ cup warm water (105°–115°F)

———

Combine the flours in a bowl and form a well in the center. In a separate bowl, mix the remaining ingredients together. Add the liquid to the well and work with your hands to combine. Work the dough in a wavelike motion to incorporate air. Add more water if it is too dry. When the texture is smooth (after about 1 minute of kneading), cover with plastic wrap and let rest in a warm, dry place for 35 minutes. Sprinkle the surface of the dough with flour and "turn" it by pulling small portions of the dough from one edge of the bowl toward the opposite side, covering and incorporating the flour. Once one full turn has been made, repeat two more times, starting by sprinkling more flour. Let the dough rest for 35 more minutes.

TOPPING

1 small potato, peeled and thinly sliced on a mandoline

1 garlic clove, thinly sliced

Salt and black pepper to taste

1 tablespoon extra virgin olive oil, plus more for drizzling

1 teaspoon sea salt

1 sprig rosemary, stemmed

———

In a bowl, toss the potato with the garlic, salt, pepper, and 1 tablespoon oil.

ASSEMBLY

Preheat the oven to 425°F. Drizzle olive oil over a 13-x-9-inch baking sheet. Remove the dough from the bowl and work around your wrists to stretch. Place on a lightly floured work surface and roll out into a rectangle the size of the baking sheet. Transfer gently to the prepared sheet. Overlap the potato slices on the dough, discarding the garlic slices in the process. Drizzle with olive oil and sprinkle coarse sea salt and rosemary over the top. Bake for 12 to 15 minutes or until the bottom of the pizza is brown and crunchy. Remove from the oven, drizzle with additional olive oil, and serve.

PIZZA al POMODORO

Of all the different ways to make the most renowned pizza in the world, this dish will satisfy the most fussy gourmet.

One 11-inch pizza (E) *20 minutes & 70 minutes rising & 12 minutes baking*

DOUGH

1½ cups Manitoba flour (see page 16)

⅓ cup Grano Duro flour (see page 17)

1 tablespoon salt

2 teaspoons compressed fresh yeast

1 tablespoon olive oil

½ teaspoon sugar

½ cup warm water (105°–115°F)

———

Combine the flours in a bowl and form a well in the center. In a separate bowl, mix the remaining ingredients together. Add the liquid to the well and work with your hands to combine. Work the dough in a wavelike motion to incorporate air. Add more water if it is too dry. When the texture is smooth (after about 1 minute of kneading), cover with plastic wrap and let rest in a warm, dry place for 35 minutes. Sprinkle the surface of the dough with flour and "turn" it by pulling small portions of the dough from one edge of the bowl toward the opposite, covering and incorporating the flour. Once one full turn has been made, repeat two times, starting by sprinkling more flour. Let rest for 35 more minutes.

TOPPING

½ quantity Tomato Sauce, at room temperature (see page 36)

1 tablespoon oregano

¼ cup grated Parmesan

5 basil leaves

4 ounces mozzarella, cut into ½-inch cubes

Extra virgin olive oil, for drizzling

ASSEMBLY

Preheat the oven to 425°F. Drizzle olive oil over a 13-x-9-inch baking sheet. Remove the dough from the bowl and work around your wrists to stretch. Place on a lightly floured surface and roll out into a rectangle the size of the baking sheet. Transfer gently to the prepared sheet. Pierce the surface with a fork to avoid air bubbles. Spread the Tomato Sauce over the dough and sprinkle with the oregano, Parmesan, basil leaves, and mozzarella. Drizzle with oil. Bake for 12 to 15 minutes or until the bottom of the pizza is a toasty brown. Remove from the oven, slice, and serve.

TORTA al TESTO

This famous round flatbread from Umbria is crunchy on the outside, soft in the middle, and delicious eaten by itself or stuffed with a variety of foods. Testo is the round pan on which the bread is cooked over the stove and was originally made from stone or terra-cotta and hung over a fire. Today, it is cast iron.

One 10-inch round   Ⓔ   *15 minutes & 70 minutes rising & 5 minutes baking*

DOUGH

1 1/2 cups Manitoba flour (see page 16)

1/3 cup Grano Duro flour (see page 17)

1 1/2 tablespoons salt

2 teaspoons compressed fresh yeast

1 tablespoon olive oil

1/2 teaspoon sugar

1/2 cup warm water (105°–115°F)

———

Combine the flours in a bowl and form a well in the center. In a separate bowl, mix the remaining ingredients together. Add the liquid to the well and work with your hands to combine. Work the dough in a wavelike motion to incorporate air. Add more water if it is too dry. When the texture is smooth (after about 1 minute of kneading), cover with plastic wrap and rest in a warm, dry place for 35 minutes. Sprinkle the surface of the dough with flour and "turn" it by pulling small portions of the dough from one edge of the bowl toward the opposite side, covering and incorporating the flour. Once one full turn has been made, repeat twice, starting by sprinkling more flour. Let rest for 35 more minutes.

TO SERVE

Preheat the oven to 425°F. Gently roll the ball of dough around your wrists to stretch into a rough 10-inch disk and cover with a clean towel. Preheat the testo (torta pan) and sprinkle with flour. When the flour begins to brown, dust off the flour and place the dough on top. Pierce the surface with a fork and cook until the bottom is browned. Carefully flip with a metal spatula and cook on the other side. Transfer the torta, still on the testo, to the hot oven and bake for 5 minutes.

Serve as it is in wedges, or halve horizontally and stuff with fillings, such as buffalo mozzarella, arugula, and Parmesan. Cover with the top half and bake for 3 minutes at 350°F to melt the cheese.

PIZZA RUSTICA al FORMAGGIO

The term rustico is most commonly used in southern Italy and signifies a savory dish made of cheese. This soft bread is perfect by itself or alongside a light lunch of grilled vegetables and soup.

Serves 12　🄴　*20 minutes & 40 minutes rising & 15 minutes baking*

INGREDIENTS*

Extra virgin olive oil, for drizzling

Fine dry bread crumbs

2 cups Italian 'OO' flour (see page 16)

½ cup grated Parmesan

8 ounces Scamorza (see page 20), cut into ¼-inch cubes

1 teaspoon salt

½ cup butter, melted

½ cup warm water (105°–115°F)

2½ tablespoons compressed fresh yeast

1 teaspoon sugar

3 eggs

―――――

Lightly grease a baking sheet with olive oil and dust with the bread crumbs. In a bowl, combine the flour, cheeses, salt, and melted butter. In a separate bowl or cup, mix together the warm water, yeast, and sugar. Add to the flour mixture. Separately beat the eggs with a fork to break the yolks, then add to the flour and liquid mixture. Mix the ingredients together with one hand, using a wide circular motion to incorporate air into the dough. Continue mixing with the circular motion for 30 seconds. Transfer to the prepared baking sheet and level the dough with a spatula, forming a 9-x-5-inch rectangle. Cover with a clean towel and set aside for 40 minutes, or until the dough has doubled in size. Preheat the oven to 350°F. Bake for 15 minutes. Serve hot out of the oven.

*VEGAN ALTERNATIVE

⅔ cup Italian 'OO' flour (see page 16)

3 tablespoons margarine

3 ounces tofu, cut into tiny cubes

1 tablespoon compressed fresh yeast

3 tablespoons soy milk

3 tablespoons warm water (105°–115°F)

Salt to taste

―――――

Follow the same procedure as above.

There exists in this world a precarious, confined space full of razor-sharp edges, blistering fires, and thousands of inflammable objects in close proximity. Those who subject themselves to this environment are machines: highly caffeinated workaholics who operate on auto-pilot. They expertly navigate the system, skillfully avoiding collisions and catastrophe every day. They are the chefs of Montali, and this is their kitchen.

Unfortunately, no amount of culinary training or experience can thwart all accidents, mistakes, and random acts of nature that occur in every restaurant. From minor cuts and burns to complete obliteration of a course minutes before it is to be served, the Country House Montali has had its fair share of debacles. Most incidences are laughable in retrospect, and even if the outcome was not positive, a valuable lesson was always learned.

THE ACCIDENTS

In the life of a chef, cuts and burns are the norm. Especially for a young apprentice, the only way to stop hurting oneself is to learn from many, many stupid mistakes. In some instances, however, the injury is not self-inflicted.

Ten minutes into dinner, all of the guests had been served their wine and were anxiously awaiting their antipasti. In the kitchen, Malu and another chef stood side-by-side frying batches of the mozzarella and tomato-stuffed calzoni. "Be careful when you put the calzoni in the oil!" Malu advised. "It might splash." While she was saying this, the calzoni in her hand slipped out of her fingers and plopped into the oil like a brick. A long splatter of hot oil flew out of the pan and streaked the other chef's hand. Malu gasped and ran to get burn cream from the back, while the stunned chef exhaled through the white-hot pain. Malu reappeared in a matter of seconds. "Excuse me! Oh, I'm so sorry!" she apologized, while applying the cream to the burn. After a second, the other chef burst out laughing, easing Malu's guilt. The irony of the situation was too comical to get upset over a minor burn. In reality, Malu is more likely to be the solution to a dilemma rather than the source.

THE MISTAKES

In dealing with a crisis, the ability to handle problems cooly and effectively separates the professional from the amateur. On occasion, the chefs have had to create brand-new dishes on the fly, minutes before they were set to serve dinner, due to another's colossal mistake.

On a day when Malu was up to her ears with errands, Maria stepped in to save the day. "Malu," she said confidently, "you go and run your errands. I'll take care of the kitchen."

"Are you sure? You can think about today's dishes?" Malu asked her.

"No problem! It's under control. Go ahead," Maria responded. She loved feeling needed. So Malu left, leaving the kitchen in Maria's hands. She went to drop off the laundry, grab a few supplies, buy cases of wine, and pick up her son from school. By the time she came back, it was half past five and she threw on her apron to prepare the evening's dessert.

Maria was working happily when Malu walked in and said, "Maria! I'm back. I'll start on the dolce."

"Don't worry, Malu. I've already done it! You relax!" Maria said proudly.

"Really? Wonderful!" On her command, Malu went back upstairs to work on the following day's menu and spend time with Damiano. At 7:30 P.M., she returned to the kitchen. During dinner, she and Maria were getting ready for the antipasti when Malu casually asked Maria where the secondi was. Maria paused to think for a minute before her eyes bulged and jaw dropped. Without a word, Malu knew exactly what had happened: Maria had completely forgotten to make the secondi.

Leaving Maria to finish serving, Malu threw open the refrigerator and scanned the contents, pulling out various ingredients. Working like a maniac, she chopped zucchini, red peppers, onions, and tomatoes and In a sauté pan, sautéed them over a high fire, finishing them off with chopped parsley and basil. She grilled large seitan patties, originally prepared for the following day's dinner, with mixed vegetables before slicing them very thinly horizontally. She patted each slice with flour, dipped them in an egg wash, and then breaded all sides before frying them to a golden brown in a In a sauté pan, sauté pan. Malu layered the In a sauté pan, sautéed vegetables between three levels of crunchy seitan in a large baking dish, sprinkled assorted grated cheeses on top, cooked it in the oven until the surface was bubbly, and served it to delighted guests right away. A thoroughly embarrassed Maria apologized profusely to Malu who, seeing that Maria was punishing herself enough, chose to console rather than lecture her.

More than other head chefs, Malu has patience for mistakes. She will laugh at the minor things like a

dropped plate here or a river of spilled cream there, putting the guilt-ridden offender at ease. However, if the same person continues to make the same errors in judgment and repeat mistakes, her patience will wear thin.

Several years ago, a young local girl named Marcella was hired to help in the kitchen and dining room. She was proud and arrogant and intensely disliked being told what to do. Because she did not put any thought into her actions, she became notorious for dropping, spilling, burning, and ruining materials around the kitchen. One evening, Malu had her hands full and called Marcella over. "Marcella, can you go to the back fridge to get the chocolate cake? It's on the second shelf, but be very careful when you pull it out."

"Yes, okay," Marcella replied halfheartedly, her gaze elsewhere.

"Marcella, you have to be very careful when you pull the cake out. It's very large and difficult to carry," Malu continued, insisting on eye contact with the girl. Marcella nodded vacantly and went to get the cake. The back room is attached to the main kitchen and only a step away, so when Marcella did not return after three minutes, Malu began to worry. "Luciana," she said, "can you please go check on Marcella?" Luciana stepped out of the kitchen and into the back. When she returned, the shock on her face gave her away.

Malu stormed to the back where Marcella was hovering over a chocolate explosion that was once a rich cake. She had dropped the dolce.

Marcella's mistake was not due to an accidental memory lapse, as was the case with Maria. It was caused by habitual incompetence. Malu absolutely let her have it. For a good five minutes, she ripped into Marcella relentlessly until the young girl was reduced to tears, finally feeling remorseful. After Malu finished projecting her frustrations on Marcella, she ran around the kitchen to prepare some sort of dessert for the guests. She managed to serve them a version of the Fragole con Zabaione e Crema, using mixed chopped fruits instead of strawberries. Marcella spent two more weeks at Montali, until both parties decided the work was not for her.

THE RANDOM ACTS OF NATURE

In the later months of the season, torrential thunderstorms frequent the Umbrian countryside. The Country House Montali has had its fair share of blackouts and floods, the effects of which could have been terrible for the restaurant.

The benefit of having a staff that works, lives, eats, and sleeps at Montali is that their creative minds can run the kitchen like clockwork, even in the dark.

"Alberto, the lights went off again," Sang said to Alberto, as if the fact that the kitchen had gone pitch black was not a clear indication already.

Alberto walked over to the circuit board to flip the switches, which usually turns the lights back on immediately. When that did not work, he tried it another time. Then another time. He waited a few seconds and tried yet again. After the eighth time, he cursed. It was four in the afternoon and the chefs were still in the middle of preparing dinner.

"There's no electricity," he announced as he walked back into the kitchen. "What's the situation on tonight's dinner?"

"We still have to prepare the Strudel di Zucchine! And the bread has to be baked," one chef nervously responded. The oven was completely out and the strudel, a pastry-encased zucchini roulade, had not even been started.

"Va bene," Malu said. "No problem, we'll just change the secondi!" She racked her brain for ideas, but the only secondi that did not require an oven had been served the previous night. Hiding her anxiety from

the other chefs, she breathed deeply and said, "We invent a new one today!" She sat down with Sang and Janko and, collaboratively, they decided to make mixed grilled vegetable and fruit skewers, which later became Spiedini Primavera, a favorite among guests. With the use of the gas stove, they replaced the standard ciabatta with a thin whole wheat *torta al testo* stuffed with arugula and thin slices of Parmigiano Reggiano. Rather than making the Soufflé di Ricotta that required the oven, they made Budino al Cocco, a Brazilian coconut pudding with a rich plum sauce.

Because the water pump was electric, they took turns running to the well in the rain to draw water for cooking.

That evening, guests were served in the romantically lit dining room full of candles.

Without a thought to how the sumptuous dinner had been prepared, the guests raved about it. In the kitchen, the exhausted chefs burst out laughing. The laughter stopped, though, at the thought of the breakfast preparation next morning, as the evening meal had produced dozens of dirty pans and plates that couldn't be washed for lack of water. Great was their relief to see lights popping on again, solving that last problem.

In another storm-induced incident, the guests not only were fully aware of the problem, but were a huge part of the solution. Years before, Malu and Alberto had had electrical wires built underground extending over a half mile past their restaurant so that they would not be visible and unsightly. The installation of the wires created an underground channel through which, Malu and Alberto later found, water could flow.

During the last of four cooking courses with two hilarious English couples, Malu was rolling umbricelli noodles when one of them pointed to the dining room and exclaimed, "The restaurant is flooded!" Malu glanced over and saw that an enormous quantity of water had flowed from the outside into the restaurant. (Later, they discovered that the water had traveled through the electrical channel and through the circuit box attached to the dining room.)

Malu called Alberto, dropped everything, and threw off her apron, and they both ran to the dining room. The four students cheerfully kicked off their shoes and joined in to help them move furniture from the flooded areas. Soaking the water up with towels and draining it into buckets, they managed to get rid of most of the water, wash their hands, and return to their lesson.

At dinner a few hours later, they merrily recounted the story to the other restaurant guests who rolled with laughter. At the end of dinner, all of the guests were sitting in the lounge sipping drinks with Alberto, when one of the chefs in the kitchen noticed that the restaurant floor looked strange. Taking a closer look, he realized that it had flooded yet again, but this time the water was ankle deep. As soon as Malu and Alberto came to look, they ran to call the fire department.

"I'm sorry," said the fireman on the phone, "but we cannot drain your restaurant until the water is at least eight inches deep. Our draining machine will not operate."

"What should I do, then? Flood my restaurant with more water so that you'll come?" Alberto inquired.

"Listen, we can put you on the list and try to come out there tonight, but there is no guarantee when we can come. The entire area is in the same situation you are in, if not worse." The restaurant patrons, when they heard the news, jumped up at the chance to be part of the action. "We'll help!" they exclaimed. For the next two hours, everyone went to work draining the restaurant in the same manner as before, soaking themselves completely in the process.

As the last towel was wrung out, the entrance doors to the restaurant swung open and three burly firemen with their hands on their hips said quite heroically, "We're here!" There was an eruption of laughter as Alberto made his way over to them. Close up, he could see that they were exhausted from following one emergency after another all over northern Umbria. He put his hand on one man's shoulders and invited them in. Alberto distributed glasses to everyone and opened several bottles of wine as the guests and firemen sat in the front lobby and laughed the night away.

Although none of the mishaps over the past twenty years are experiences Malu or Alberto would like to go through again, from them they have countless stories and rich memories. They are imprints of the people that they have shared their lives with and add to the character with which the restaurant and hotel were built. Accidents will happen, mistakes will be made, and fierce storms will pass through for as long as the Country House Montali stands. But as long as Malu, Alberto, and their carefully selected staff are there, they will welcome the challenge.

Dolci

DESSERTS

These chewy, caramel-like Brazilian candies melt in your mouth. For variety, dip the chocolate sweets in coconut flakes, and the coconut sweets in the chocolate sprinkles.

100 of each   E   60 minutes

BRIGADEIROS

1³/4 cups sweetened condensed milk

2 tablespoons butter

2 tablespoons unsweetened cocoa powder

³/4 cup chocolate sprinkles, for coating

———

Combine the condensed milk, butter, and cocoa in a saucepan and mix well. Cook over low heat, stirring continuously, until the mixture begins to pull away from the bottom of the pan. Cook for an additional 5 minutes, then remove from the heat. Transfer to a buttered large heat-proof ceramic plate to cool to room temperature. Roll a teaspoon-sized portion into a ball between your buttered palms. Drop into a bowl filled with chocolate sprinkles and roll until coated. Set aside on a plate and refrigerate, covered. Repeat with the remaining candy mixture.

BEIJINHOS DI COCO

1 medium coconut, grated (about 3 1/2 cups
   unsweetened shredded coconut)

1³/4 cups sweetened condensed milk

2 egg yolks

2 tablespoons butter

1/2 vanilla bean, split lengthwise and tiny
   seeds scraped out with the tip of a knife

³/4 cup sweetened flaked coconut,
   for coating

Cloves for studding (optional)

———

Combine the fresh coconut, condensed milk, egg yolks, butter, and vanilla in a saucepan and mix well. Cook over low heat, stirring continuously, until the mixture begins to pull away from the bottom of the pan. Continue to cook until the bottom starts to color slightly. Transfer to a buttered large heat-proof ceramic plate and cool to room temperature. Roll a teaspoon-sized portion into a ball between your buttered palms. Drop into a bowl filled with flaked coconut and roll until coated. Stud with a clove, if desired. Set aside on a plate and refrigerate, covered. Repeat with the remaining candy mixture.

OLHO DI SOGRA *(Mother-in-law's eye)*

1 medium coconut, grated (about 3½ cups
    unsweetened shredded coconut)

1¾ cups sweetened condensed milk

½ vanilla bean, split lengthwise and tiny seeds
    scraped out with the tip of a knife

2 tablespoons butter

2 egg yolks

About 2½ pounds moist prunes,
    slit lengthwise and pitted

———

Follow the same procedure as the Beijinhos di Coco but, rather than rolling in coconut flakes, press each small ball of candy into a prune so that it is the shape of a big "eye."

Arrange these beautiful sweets on a nice white tray, alternating the black and white colors to bring added elegance to any party.

DELIZIA AL LIMONE

A soft, spongy lemon delight, typical of Campania and the Amalfi coast. Don't forget to keep the Limoncello in the freezer.

Serves 6 Ⓜ *55 minutes & 25 minutes baking*

CAKE

2 eggs, separated

¼ cup sugar

½ teaspoon vanilla extract

Pinch of salt

¼ cup all-purpose flour

1 teaspoon baking powder

Finely grated zest of ½ lemon

———

Butter and flour six ramekins. Line the bottoms with parchment paper. Preheat the oven to 300°F. In a bowl, beat the egg yolks, sugar, and vanilla until pale yellow. In another bowl, beat the egg whites and salt with a mixer until peaks form. Gently fold the whites into the yolks in two batches. Sift in the flour and baking powder and fold in the lemon zest. Divide the batter between the ramekins and place on a baking sheet. Bake for 25 minutes. Remove from the oven and cool.

PASTRY CREAM

¾ cup milk

Peel of ½ lemon

½ vanilla bean, split lengthwise and tiny seeds
  scraped out with the tip of a knife

3 egg yolks

¼ cup sugar

¼ cup all-purpose flour

2 tablespoons lemon juice

———

In a saucepan, heat the milk, lemon peel, and vanilla bean over medium heat. In a separate saucepan, whisk the egg yolks and sugar until pale yellow. Add the flour and continue to whisk well until combined. As soon as the milk comes to a boil, take off the heat and pour into the yolk mixture, whisking all the time. Cook the pastry cream in the top of a double boiler over medium heat, stirring, for 4 minutes or until thickened. Remove from the heat and cool in an ice bath (see page 21). Discard the lemon peel and vanilla bean and add the lemon juice. Mix well. Refrigerate, covered.

BAGNA (SOAKING SAUCE)

½ cup water

2 tablespoons sugar

¼ cup Limoncello

———

Mix the water and sugar in a saucepan and bring to a boil. Remove from the heat and cool. Add the Limoncello.

ASSEMBLY

When the cakes have cooled, run a knife around the edges of the ramekins and remove the cakes. Discard the parchment and cut out a small circle from the bottom of each cake. Set aside. Using a pastry bag, fill each cake with the pastry cream. Replace the cut-out circles and place the cakes, cut-side up, on a plate. Pour the soaking sauce over the cakes, cover with plastic wrap, and refrigerate. Reserve the leftover pastry cream.

TO SERVE

1 cup heavy cream

1 tablespoon confectioners' sugar

⅓ cup Limoncello

Whipped cream, for garnish

Lemon Strings (see page 29)

———

In a bowl, beat the cream with the confectioners' sugar until soft peaks form, then fold two-thirds into the leftover pastry cream. Add the Limoncello and mix. Place the cakes on individual serving plates, cut-side down, and cover with the pastry cream. Top with a dollop of whipped cream, garnish with a few Lemon Strings, and serve immediately.

TIRAMISU

Tiramisu — how it should be! The literal translation for this delectable favorite is "pull me up." The tale of the dessert's origins begin over 300 years ago in Siena with a visit to the medieval city by Grand Duke Cosimo de' Medici III. Bearing in mind his renowned sweet tooth, Sienese chefs created a delectable layer cake they named Zuppa del Duca, or "Duke's Soup." Thoroughly enjoying the dessert, the Grand Duke took the recipe with him to Florence to introduce it to the upper crust of Tuscan society. Over a century later, the dessert became wildly popular among English intellectuals, and, for a short time, it was renamed Zuppa Inglese.

In Italy, the dessert continued in popularity and spread to Treviso, northwest of Venice. Rumor has it that the Venetian courtesans made a point of eating this dessert before business affairs, thus the new name, Tira-mi-su.

Serves 8   Ⓔ   *40 minutes & 2 hours chilling*

INGREDIENTS

⅓ cup brewed espresso, chilled

½ teaspoon each Grand Marnier, Maraschino, and Marsala

4 tablespoons granulated sugar

2 eggs, separated

½ cup mascarpone

Pinch of salt

⅓ cup heavy cream

1 teaspoon confectioners' sugar

3 ounces Pavesini biscuits or other crisp Italian sponge cookies

2 tablespoons grated bittersweet chocolate

1½ teaspoons unsweetened cocoa powder, for dusting

In a bowl, mix the espresso, liqueurs, and 1 tablespoon of the sugar together until the sugar has dissolved. Set aside.

Whisk the remaining 3 tablespoons sugar and the egg yolks in a large bowl until foamy and pale in color. Fold in the mascarpone. In a clean bowl, using a handheld mixer, beat the egg whites with the salt until stiff peaks form.

In another bowl, whip the cream and confectioners' sugar with a handheld mixer until the cream can hold its shape and is no longer liquid. Gently fold into the yolk mixture.

Fold the egg whites into the yolk mixture, using a gentle, wavelike motion to avoid deflating them.

ASSEMBLY

Use a small, rimmed serving dish or glass bowl. Pour a quarter of the egg mixture into the bottom and level with a spoon. Soak a third of the Pavesini biscuits in the coffee mixture, remove, and drain the excess liquid back into the espresso. Lay the biscuits in the serving dish. Repeat the layering process, alternating the egg mixture and biscuits, and finishing with the egg mixture. Sprinkle with the bittersweet chocolate and refrigerate for 2 hours. Immediately before serving, dust the top of the Tiramisu with cocoa powder. Enjoy!

STRUDEL di MELE

Apple strudel. The Austro-Hungarian empire left behind this famous dish, which has been adopted by the northern provinces of Italy bordering Austria. This pastry, the glory of the city of Vienna, has always been a very handy one, as it can be filled with a sweet or savory filling.

Serves 12   **D**   *50 minutes & 55 minutes resting and baking*

FILLING

³/₄ cup raisins

Sherry, for soaking

¹/₄ cup dry bread crumbs

2 tablespoons butter, melted

3 apples, peeled, cored, and sliced into ¹/₈-inch pieces

5 apricots, peeled, pitted, and sliced slightly thicker than the apples

¹/₂ cup almonds, toasted, and chopped

¹/₄ cup pine nuts, toasted

2 tablespoons brown sugar

1 teaspoon ground cinnamon

Finely grated zest of 1 lemon

Finely grated zest of 1 orange

1 teaspoon lemon juice

2 tablespoons apricot jam or marmalade

In a small saucepan, combine the raisins and enough sherry to cover. Bring to a simmer and turn off heat. Let stand 15 minutes to soften. Drain and discard the sherry. In a sauté pan, toast the bread crumbs in the melted butter until golden brown. Cool and set aside. Mix the raisins with the remaining filling ingredients in a large bowl.

DOUGH

1³/₄ cups Italian 'OO' flour (see page 16)

¹/₂ cup water, at room temperature

3 tablespoons butter, cubed and at room temperature

Pinch of salt

Sift the flour onto a work surface. Make a well in the center, add the water, butter, and salt, and work with your fingers until a dough begins to form. Knead for 30 seconds, then forcefully throw the dough down onto the surface 100 times. Cover with a warm glass bowl (the glass bowl can be briefly heated in a warm oven) and let rest for 15 minutes.

ASSEMBLY

3 tablespoons half-and-half, for brushing

Confectioners' sugar for garnish

Whipped cream, for garnish

Preheat the oven to 350°F. Flour a clean towel. Shape the dough into a disk and slowly roll over your wrists to stretch it. When it begins to thin (but not break), place on the towel and gently pull into a rectangle, approximately 18 x 10 inches, maintaining the thickness. The dough should be slightly transparent and as thin as possible. Trim the edges with a pizza cutter. Brush half-and-half over the surface and sprinkle with the toasted bread crumbs. Dot the filling evenly over the crumbs, leaving a ¹/₂-inch margin at one short side uncovered. Using the towel as a guide, fold in the long sides. Pull the towel up from the bottom corners and gently roll up the strudel toward the ¹/₂-inch margin and onto a sheet of parchment paper until the seam side is down. Brush the surface with more half-and-half. Transfer, with the parchment paper, to a baking sheet. Bake for 40 minutes or until golden. Slice and serve warm, dusted with confectioners' sugar and a dollop of whipped cream.

VULCANO di CIOCCOLATO

A chocolate volcano cake served with a licorice ice cream and kiwi sauce. A great way to end an important dinner. The hot and cold contrast is a pleasant surprise.

Serves 8 Ⓜ *30 minutes & 2 hours freezing*

CAKE

5 1/2 ounces 70% bittersweet chocolate, chopped

10 tablespoons butter

1/2 cup sugar

3 whole eggs, at room temperature

1 egg yolk, at room temperature

Pinch of salt

1/4 cup all-purpose flour

Grease and flour eight ramekins and line with parchment paper. Heat the chocolate, butter, and sugar in the top of a double boiler over simmering water until completely melted. Cool to room temperature. In a bowl, beat the whole eggs and yolk and salt until frothy and whisk into the chocolate. (Note: It is important that the chocolate and eggs, when combined, are the same temperature so that the chocolate does not solidify.) Sift in the flour and mix quickly until just combined. Divide the batter among the ramekins, cover with foil, and freeze for at least 2 hours.

LICORICE GELATO

1/2 teaspoon natural licorice candies, finely chopped

2/3 cup heavy cream

1 1/4 cups milk

1/3 cup sugar

Combine all the ingredients in a double boiler over low heat. Stir until the licorice melts completely. Pour through a fine-mesh sieve to catch any remaining solids. Cool in an ice bath (see page 21) and pass through a fine-mesh sieve a second time. Whisk to foam lightly. Pour into an ice-cream or gelato machine and process according to the manufacturer's directions. Store the in an airtight container in the freezer for up to 1 week.

KIWI SAUCE

4 kiwi fruit

Confectioners' sugar to taste

1 teaspoon lemon juice

Purée the ingredients together in a blender. Pour through a sieve and reserve the sauce.

TO SERVE

Confectioners' sugar, for dusting

Chili powder, for dusting

Preheat the oven to 475°F. Place the ramekins on a baking sheet and bake for 7 to 8 minutes, or until the cakes feel crunchy on the outside but are still soft in the center. With a towel in each hand, carefully remove each cake and place, right-side up, on a dessert plate. Dust with confectioners' sugar and a pinch of chili powder. Serve hot with the Kiwi Sauce and Licorice Gelato.

It is crucial that all cake ingredients, when mixed together, are at the same temperature. If not, the chocolate may seize and become brittle. This dessert can stay in the freezer, unbaked, for up to 2 weeks.

TORTA di LIMONE

Lemon pie. The refreshing lemony filling is surrounded by a soft pastry. Ideal for afternoon tea. Great with Carrot Sorbet (see page 279).

Serves 16   Ⓜ   *50 minutes & chilling time*

FILLING

1¼ cups water, at room temperature

1 cup sugar

6 tablespoons cornstarch

Finely grated zest of 3 lemons

1 egg

Juice of 2 lemons

————

Whisk the water, sugar, cornstarch, and lemon zest together in a saucepan. Bring to a boil. Cook for 1 minute, then remove from the heat. Cool completely. Add the egg and lemon juice. Mix well and set aside.

DOUGH

¾ cup sugar

3 cups Italian 'OO' flour (see page 16),

10 tablespoons butter, at room temperature

2 eggs

1 tablespoon Marsala

1 tablespoon lemon juice

2 teaspoons baking powder

————

Preheat an oven to 350°F. On a work surface, combine the sugar with the flour and make a well in the center. Add the remaining ingredients to the well and work with your fingertips until a dough begins to form. Incorporate by cutting through the dough with a dough scraper and rolling back together, three or four times, until the texture and color are even. Wrap in plastic wrap and refrigerate for 15 minutes.

Roll two-thirds of the dough between two sheets of floured parchment paper into a disk about 13 inches in diameter. Remove the top layer of parchment paper and gently invert the dough over a 10- to 11-inch tart pan. Gently press the dough into the bottom, edges, and sides, letting any overhang drape over the sides of the pan. Pour in the lemon filling and spread evenly with a spatula. Roll the remaining dough in the same manner into a disk just big enough to cover the lemon filling. Invert onto the filling and press the edges of the dough together to seal. Cut off the excess dough with a small knife or pizza cutter. Bake for 25 minutes. Cool to room temperature and chill in the refrigerator.

TO SERVE

Confectioners' sugar, for dusting

————

Carefully remove the tart from the pan, slice into wedges, dust with confectioners' sugar, and serve.

TORTA di CIOCCOLATO e NOCI

Chocolate and nut cake. A blend of soft melting flavors that you can enjoy at any time or even use as a base for a birthday cake with a chocolate ganache topping.

Serves 12 **E** *20 minutes & 25 minutes baking*

INGREDIENTS

4 eggs, separated

1 cup granulated sugar

2 drops vanilla extract

Pinch of salt

1 cup walnuts, chopped

1 cup almonds, chopped

7 ounces bittersweet chocolate, chopped

Confectioners' sugar, for garnish

Whipped cream, for garnish

———

Line a 10- to 11-inch springform pan with parchment paper. Butter and flour the paper. Preheat the oven to 350°F. Whisk the egg yolks, granulated sugar, and vanilla together in a bowl until pale yellow and frothy. Using a handheld mixer, whisk the egg whites with the salt until stiff peaks form. Gently fold the two egg mixtures together. Fold in the nuts and chocolate in four batches and immediately pour into the pan. Using a spatula, gently smooth the top. Bake for 25 minutes. Remove from the oven and set aside to cool completely. Serve at room temperature with a dusting of confectioners' sugar and a generous dollop of whipped cream. (For a gluten-free version, do not dust the parchment-lined pan with flour.)

PERE COTTE al VINO BIANCO

Pears cooked in spiced white wine. Present this elegant dish with a drizzle of Cinnamon Pastry Cream and Chocolate Sauce.

Serves 8 ⒠ *40 minutes & cooling time*

PEARS

1 lemon

1 orange

2 cups white wine

½ cup sugar

1 cinnamon stick

5 cloves

8 Bartlett pears, peeled, stems left on

Remove the peel from the lemon and orange in large pieces. Combine with the wine, sugar, cinnamon, and cloves in a large pot and bring to a boil. Reduce to a simmer and add the whole pears. Cover and cook over low heat for 30 minutes or until cooked through. The pears, when pierced with a toothpick, should offer no resistance. Cool completely, strain the liquid, and discard any solids. Set the wine mixture and the pears aside separately.

CINNAMON PASTRY CREAM

1 egg yolk

1 tablespoon butter, chilled

1½ tablespoons sugar

Ground cinnamon to taste

Combine the egg yolk, butter, and sugar in a double boiler and cook over simmering water, stirring continuously, for 3 minutes or until thickened. Add cinnamon to taste and let cool.

CHOCOLATE SAUCE

7 ounces bittersweet chocolate

⅔ cup heavy cream

Grate the chocolate and melt with the cream in a double boiler, mixing well. When smooth, remove from the heat and cool to room temperature. Pour into a squeeze bottle. To reheat, place the bottle in a bowl filled with hot water, being careful not to let the water go inside the tip.

TO SERVE

Reheat the chocolate sauce. Halve the pears lengthwise, then slice each half thinly, starting ¼ inch from the stem (see picture). Press gently so that the slices, fan out. Spoon the pastry cream onto individual plates and place the pears on the cream. Drizzle with the reserved wine mixture and the chocolate sauce and serve.

PESCHE RIPIENE

Stuffed peaches. Amaretti biscuits provide a bitter almond taste that combines with the chocolate and the fresh peaches perfectly. To be made when the best-quality peaches are available. The best are the ones that easily "break" in half.

Serves 6 Ⓔ *10 minutes & 25 minutes baking*

INGREDIENTS

6 firm but ripe peaches

Brown sugar

———

Rinse and split the peaches in half. Remove the pits and scoop out some of the flesh with a melon baller, leaving ¼ inch all round the edge. Reserve the peach flesh. Place the peach halves, cut-side up, on a baking sheet lined with parchment paper. Sprinkle the cavities with brown sugar.

FILLING

6 tablespoons chopped hazelnuts

1½ ounces 60% bittersweet chocolate

12 amaretti cookies, coarsely ground

1 tablespoon Amaretto liqueur (such as di Saronno)

1 teaspoon lemon juice

12 hazelnuts

3 tablespoons brown sugar

Confectioners' sugar, for dusting (optional)

———

Preheat the oven to 350°F. Chop the reserved peach flesh well and place in a bowl. Mix with the chopped hazelnuts, chocolate, ground cookies, liqueur, and lemon juice. Divide the filling among the peach halves. Top each with one hazelnut, sprinkle additional brown sugar on the top, and bake for 25 minutes. Serve at room temperature. Sprinkle with confectioners' sugar, if desired.

CAFFÉ BRULÉE

A soft creamy coffee custard with crunchy caramelized brown sugar on top. An excellent dessert to keep you going. Remember you can also use decaffeinated coffee.

Serves 4 to 6 (E) *25 minutes & 1 hour cooking & 4 hours chilling*

INGREDIENTS

⅓ cup sugar

5 egg yolks

1 tablespoon instant espresso

2 cups heavy cream

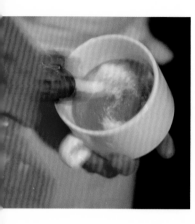

Preheat the oven to 300°F. Whisk the sugar and egg yolks together in a bowl until frothy and well incorporated. In a saucepan, dissolve the espresso in the cream over heat. As soon as it comes to a boil, remove from the heat. Pour into the egg mixture, whisking all the time so as not to scramble the eggs. Pour through a sieve and carefully pour into ramekins or oven-proof coffee cups. Carefully transfer the cups to a baking pan with 2-inch sides. Skim foam and bubbles from the surfaces of the egg mixture with a spoon. Fill the pan halfway up the sides of the ramekins with boiling water and cover with foil. Bake for 1 hour. Remove from the oven, take the ramekins out of the water, and cool to room temperature before refrigerating for at least 4 hours.

COOKIES

2 tablespoons confectioners' sugar

½ egg white

1 tablespoon butter, melted and cooled to room temperature

1 tablespoon all-purpose flour

Preheat the oven to 350°F. In a bowl, beat the sugar with the egg white, then mix in the melted butter. Sift in the flour and whisk well. Line a baking sheet with a silicone mat, grease the mat, and dust with flour. For each cookie, evenly spread 1 tablespoon batter into a 4-inch circle on the prepared sheet. Bake for 2 minutes or until golden brown. Remove from the oven and use a small spatula to transfer the cookies to a tray lined with paper towels. Cool completely.

TO SERVE

6 teaspoons brown sugar

Confectioners' sugar, for dusting

Sprinkle 1 teaspoon brown sugar over the surface of each custard and tap the sides to disperse the sugar evenly. Caramelize the surface with a kitchen blowtorch and serve immediately, topped with a cookie and a sprinkling of confectioners' sugar.

MOUSSE di CIOCCOLATO

This delightful chocolate mousse is airy in texture and rich in taste and goes perfectly with strawberries served at the peak of their season.

Serves 4 to 6   Ⓜ   *50 minutes & 4 hours chilling*

MOUSSE

4 ounces 60% bittersweet chocolate, grated

3 egg yolks, at room temperature

1¼ cups heavy cream, at room temperature

———

Melt the chocolate in a double boiler. Remove from the heat and cool to room temperature. In a bowl, beat the egg yolks and mix thoroughly with the chocolate. In another bowl, whip the cream until soft peaks form with a handheld mixer. Fold into the chocolate until just combined. Cover and refrigerate for at least 4 hours.

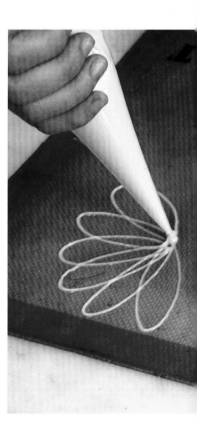

STRAWBERRY SAUCE

20 strawberries, hulled

White wine, for rinsing fruit

¼ cup sugar

2 tablespoons cassis liqueur

———

Gently rinse the strawberries in white wine. Discard the wine. Quarter six strawberries and set aside. Purée the remaining berries in a blender. Press through a fine-mesh sieve into a bowl. Mix in the sugar and cassis. Cover the sauce and set aside.

COOKIES (OPTIONAL)

½ egg white

2 tablespoons confectioners' sugar

1 tablespoon butter, melted and cooled to room temperature

1 tablespoon all-purpose flour

———

Preheat the oven to 350°F. In a bowl, mix all the ingredients together until completely smooth. Pour into a pastry bag with a fine tip. Line a baking sheet with greased parchment paper or a greased silicone mat. Delicately pipe out the batter into the shape of a flower with overlapping petals, approximately 5 inches in diameter or slightly wider than the rim of a martini glass. Bake for 1 to 2 minutes or until golden brown. Remove from the oven and use a small spatula or butter knife to gently remove the delicate cookies while still hot and soft. Lay completely flat on a baking sheet lined with paper towels.

TO SERVE

Scoop the chilled mousse into a pastry bag with a large star tip and pipe out into martini glasses. Arrange four strawberry quarters around the rim of each glass. Drizzle the strawberry sauce around the sides. Serve with a cookie leaning on the side of the martini glass.

SEMIFREDDO DI MELE

A simple apple pudding is heavenly when transformed by the subtle touch of cinnamon, vanilla, and lemon. Enjoy on a cold winter night with a glass of spicy red wine by the fire.

Serves 6   **E**   *20 minutes & 2 hours chilling*

PASTRY CREAM*

2 cups milk

Peel of ½ lemon

½ vanilla bean, split lengthwise and tiny
    seeds scraped out with the tip of a knife

¼ cup sugar

4 egg yolks

¼ cup all-purpose flour

————

In a saucepan, bring the milk, lemon peel, and vanilla bean to a boil, then turn off the heat. Meanwhile, in another saucepan, whisk the sugar with the egg yolks until pale yellow. Sift in the flour and mix well. Discard the lemon peel and vanilla bean from the milk and pour the milk into the egg mixture, whisking all the time. Cook the pastry cream in a double boiler over medium heat for 3 minutes or until thickened. Cool in an ice bath (see page 21). Cover with plastic wrap so that the wrap touches the surface of the cream (to prevent a skin from forming). Set aside.

APPLES

5 Granny Smith apples

Juice of ½ lemon

1 tablespoon sugar

½ cinnamon stick

Peel of ½ lemon

————

Peel and core the apples. Slice thinly on a mandoline or by hand. Squeeze the lemon juice over the apples to prevent browning. In a pot, cook the apples with the sugar, cinnamon stick, and lemon peel over low heat, covered. Stir occasionally. Remove from the heat when the apples begin to caramelize, about 5 minutes. Remove the cinnamon stick and lemon peel, reserving for garnish.

ASSEMBLY

Divide the apple mixture among six martini glasses or small cups. Top with the warm pastry cream. Cool to room temperature and refrigerate for at least 2 hours before serving. Top glasses with a simple decoration using the cinnamon stick and serve.

---

*VEGAN ALTERNATIVE

2 cups soy milk

2½ tablespoons cornstarch

Peel of ½ lemon

¼ cup sugar

½ vanilla bean, split lengthwise and tiny
    seeds scraped out with the tip of a knife

10 saffron threads soaked in 1 tablespoon
    hot water for 1 hour

————

Combine all the ingredients except the saffron and bring to a boil to thicken. When the cream coats the back of a spoon, gently mix in the saffron. Remove from the heat, cover with plastic wrap, and cool to room temperature. Proceed as with the original recipe.

MONTALI AVOCADO SURPRISE

A dessert notorious for keeping the Montali guests guessing until the end of the meal, this Brazilian avocado pudding is as delicious as it is perplexing.

Serves 8 **E** *10 minutes & 25 minutes baking*

INGREDIENTS

5 bananas

6 tablespoons granulated sugar

Brown sugar to taste

Ground cinnamon to taste

2 tablespoons butter

2 ripe avocados

Juice of 2 lemons

1 kiwi fruit

———

Preheat the oven to 350°F. Peel four bananas and halve lengthwise. Place, cut-side up, on a baking sheet covered with buttered parchment paper. Sprinkle with 2 tablespoons of the granulated sugar, then with brown sugar and cinnamon, and dot with the butter. Bake for 25 minutes or until golden brown and caramelized. Let cool.

Using a small knife, peel the avocados. Remove and reserve the pits. Purée in a blender with the remaining 4 tablespoons granulated sugar and the lemon juice. Taste for flavor and add more sugar or lemon if necessary, depending on the quality of the avocado. Place the pits back in the mixture (to keep the avocado from discoloring), cover with plastic wrap, and refrigerate until chilled.

Serve in martini glasses with slices of the remaining banana and kiwi fruit lining the rim and the caramelized bananas on the side.

The avocado must be fully ripe when preparing this dish. To speed the ripening process, wrap fruit in newspaper and store in a warm place until soft.

FRAGOLE allo ZABAIONE e PANNA

Fresh strawberries with zabaglione sauce and heavy cream. The best way to eat fresh strawberries during their season. The sweet zabaglione goes perfectly with the sharp fruit. A small layer of whipped cream tops everything off sublimely.

Serves 6 **E** *15 minutes & chilling time*

STRAWBERRIES

2 cups strawberries, hulled

White wine, for rinsing fruit

Juice of ½ lemon

1 tablespoon cassis liqueur

1 tablespoon sugar

———

Up to 2 hours before serving, rinse the strawberries with the wine and quarter them. Discard the wine. In a bowl, toss the strawberries with the lemon juice, cassis, and sugar. Cover with plastic wrap and refrigerate.

Strawberries are rinsed with white wine to retain the beautiful color of the fruit, as well as to enhance the flavor.

ZABAGLIONE

4 egg yolks

¼ cup sugar

2 tablespoons Grand Marnier or Marsala

2 tablespoons white wine

———

Whisk the egg yolks and sugar together in the top of a double boiler until pale yellow. Mix in the liqueur and wine to combine. Cook in the double boiler, stirring continuously, until thickened, about 5 minutes. Remove from the heat and cool over an ice bath (see page 21). Cover with plastic wrap so that the plastic is just touching the entire surface of the cream (this prevents the cream from forming a skin). Refrigerate.

TO SERVE

1¼ cups heavy cream

1 tablespoon confectioners' sugar

———

Just before serving, in a bowl whip the cream with the sugar until soft peaks form. Beat the zabaglione with a handheld mixer until pale yellow and foamy. Serve in individual wine glasses, with the zabaglione over the strawberries and a dollop of whipped cream on top.

CHARLOTTE dell' ABATE

A fabulous dessert for which the literal translation is "The Charlotte of the Abbot." In the Italian tradition, the abbot was always served the best food as the head of the monastery. A kingly food.

Serves 12 (M) *60 minutes & 4 hours freezing & 1 hour thawing*

ZABAGLIONE

4 egg yolks

¼ cup sugar

¼ cup Marsala

¼ cup white wine

―――――

On the top of a double boiler, whisk the egg yolks with the sugar until pale yellow. Whisk in the Marsala and wine. Cook in the double boiler over medium heat, stirring continuously, for 5 minutes or until thickened. Immediately transfer to a bowl and cool over an ice bath (see page 21), stirring all the time. Cover with plastic wrap and refrigerate until needed.

CHOCOLATE CHIP CREAM

1½ cups heavy cream

3 tablespoons confectioners' sugar

A few drops of vanilla extract

6 ounces bittersweet chocolate, chopped

―――――

In a bowl, whip the cream with the sugar and vanilla until soft peaks form. Fold in the grated chocolate and refrigerate.

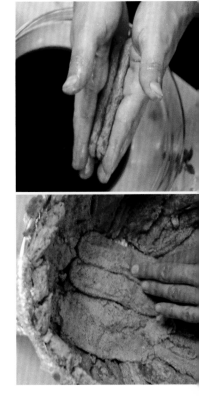

CAKE/ASSEMBLY

7 ounces crisp ladyfingers, such as Pavesini biscuits

3 cups brewed espresso, at room temperature

2 ounces amaretti cookies, coarsely crushed

―――――

Line a medium bowl with plastic wrap, allowing a substantial overhang around the sides. Soak two ladyfingers in the espresso. Place between your palms and gently squeeze out the liquid. If sections of the ladyfingers are still crunchy, soak for a few more seconds. Line the bowl, two ladyfingers at a time, starting with the sides and covering the bottom last.

Pour half of the zabaglione over the bottom and spread evenly with the back of a spoon. In a small bowl, drizzle espresso over half of the crushed amaretti to moisten, then sprinkle over the zabaglione. Add half of the chocolate chip cream over the amaretti and spread evenly. Layer more soaked ladyfingers to cover the cream. Repeat the layering process with the remaining ingredients. Fold the overhanging ladyfingers around the rim, and add one last layer of soaked ladyfingers so the cream is completely enclosed. Cover with plastic wrap and freeze for at least 4 hours.

Thaw for 1 hour before serving. Remove the plastic wrap, invert onto a platter, or remove the remaining plastic wrap, and slice. Serve immediately.

CROCCANTE al PISTACCHIO

Layers of crunchy almond cookies filled with pistachio cream and wild berries. This decorative recipe has a succulent flavor and looks lovely. Great as the grand finale of a upscale meal.

Serves 6 **D** 45 minutes

PASTRY CREAM

2 egg yolks

2 tablespoons sugar

2 tablespoons all-purpose flour

⅔ cup milk

6 tablespoons pistachio nuts, ground

Whisk the egg yolks and sugar together in the top of a double boiler until pale yellow. Add the flour and mix well. In another saucepan, heat the milk. Just before it comes to a boil, add the milk to the yolk mixture, stirring continuously. Continue to whisk the pastry cream for 5 minutes over simmering water in the double boiler, or until thickened to the texture of creamy yogurt. Remove from the heat and cool over an ice bath (see page 21). Set aside 2 tablespoons ground pistachios for garnish and add the remainder to the pastry cream. Cover with plastic wrap and refrigerate.

ALMOND COOKIES

1 tablespoon all-purpose flour

1½ egg whites

1 cup confectioners' sugar

2 tablespoons butter, melted and cooled
to room temperature

½ cup sliced almonds

Preheat the oven to 350°F. In a bowl, whisk all the ingredients together, except the almonds, until smooth. Grease and flour a sheet of parchment paper or a silicone mat and place on a baking sheet. Use a pastry brush to spread 1 tablespoon of batter into a thin 4-inch circle. If the batter is transparent, add more. Fill the sheet with circles, top each with almonds, sprinkle with confectioners' sugar, and bake for 4 minutes or until golden brown. Cool before removing carefully with a spatula. Continue until you have at least 18 nice cookies. Gently layer in an airtight container between paper towels or parchment paper.

MIXED BERRY SAUCE

1 cup mixed berries

1 tablespoon brown sugar

1 teaspoon lemon juice

Mix all the ingredients together in a bowl and refrigerate until needed.

ASSEMBLY

18 strawberries

White wine, for rinsing fruit

6 blackberries

6 sprigs mint

Confectioners' sugar

6 pieces Caramel Lace (see page 27)

Trim the stems from 12 strawberries and gently rinse with white wine. With stems still attached, halve six strawberries lengthwise. Stem and quarter the remaining strawberries. Place a cookie on a plate and, with a pastry bag, pipe out 1 tablespoon pastry cream along one side of the cookie. Top with 1 teaspoon of mixed berry sauce. Arrange four strawberry wedges along the edge of the cookie. Place another cookie on an angle, with one edge against the pastry cream, to resemble an open sea shell. Repeat with more pastry cream, berry sauce, and strawberry wedges, and top with another cookie. Place two strawberry halves, one blackberry, and one mint sprig where the cookies meet (see picture). Sprinkle with confectioners' sugar and the reserved pistachios. Top with one piece of Caramel Lace.

BUDINO al COCCO con SALSA di PRUGNE

A Brazilian coconut pudding served with plum sauce. Requested again and again by guests . . . in a single sitting!

Serves 8 Ⓜ *25 minutes & 40 minutes for sauce*

COCONUT PUDDING*

½ cup coconut milk

½ cup flaked sweetened coconut

½ cup sugar

2 cups milk

2 heaping tablespoons cornstarch

¼ vanilla bean, split lengthwise and tiny seeds
   scraped with the tip of a knife

½ cup half-and-half

Submerge eight decorative ramekins or pudding cups, or one small (5-inch) bundt pan, in a large bowl of water. Combine all the pudding ingredients in a saucepan away from the heat and mix well until the cornstarch dissolves completely. Place over medium-low heat and bring the mixture to a boil, stirring constantly and cooking until the mixture is very thick and bubbling and pulls away from the bottom of the pan. Invert the prepared pudding cups to drain away most of the water (but do not dry) and immediately pour in the hot mixture. The wetness of the cups will keep the pudding from adhering to the sides. Cool to room temperature, then cover and refrigerate until ready to serve.

SAUCE

⅔ cup water

⅓ cup sugar

Peel of ½ lemon, removed in large strips

2 tablespoons lemon juice

Combine all the sauce ingredients, except the lemon juice, in a small saucepan and simmer for 40 minutes or until the liquid is reduced by half. Remove from the heat and cool completely. Remove the peel and add the lemon juice. Refrigerate.

TO SERVE

8 prunes, pitted

Carefully invert the puddings, running a knife around the edges if necessary. Top each pudding with one prune and drizzle 2 tablespoons of sauce over the top. Serve immediately.

*VEGAN ALTERNATIVE

Change the milk to soy milk and the half-and-half to soy cream. Follow the same procedure.

CROSTATINE di MANDORLE

Crostata is surely one of the most popular cakes in Italy. This fanciful variation is filled with sweet almonds instead of jam. Excellent for afternoon tea.

Serves 6 Ⓜ *35 minutes & 30 minutes chilling*

DOUGH

3 cups Italian '00' flour (see page 16)

½ cup sugar

2 teaspoons baking powder

14 tablespoons butter, at room temperature

1 egg

1 tablespoon Limoncello

Finely grated zest of 1 lemon

Pinch of salt

3 tablespoons water

———

On a work surface, combine the flour, sugar, and baking powder and make a well in the center. Add the remaining ingredients to the well and work with your fingertips until a dough begins to form. Incorporate by cutting through the dough with a dough scraper and rolling back together, three or four times, until the texture and color are even, adding a little water if the dough is too dry. Wrap in plastic wrap and refrigerate for 30 minutes.

FILLING

2¾ cups ground almonds

1 cup sugar

2 eggs, lightly beaten

Finely grated zest of 1 lemon

¼ cup water

———

In a bowl, combine all the ingredients and mix well to blend. Set aside.

ASSEMBLY

Confectioners' sugar, for dusting

———

Preheat the oven to 350°F. Roll out two-thirds of the dough between two sheets of parchment paper into a 13-inch disk. Remove the top sheet and carefully invert the dough onto a 10- to 11-inch tart or pie pan. Gently press the dough into the edges and rim. Run a rolling pin over the rim to cut off excess dough and add the trimmings to the remaining third of the dough. Fill the tart with the almond mixture and spread smoothly with a spatula. Roll out the remaining dough between two sheets of parchment paper into 12-inch disk. Use a pastry cutter to cut into ½-inch-wide strips. Layer half the strips horizontally ½ inch apart. Layer the remaining strips ½ inch apart diagonally over the top. Gently press to seal where the strips meet the tart edge. Bake for 20 minutes or until the pastry is golden and cooked through and the filling is set. Cool completely. Slice and serve at room temperature with a sprinkling of confectioners' sugar.

This same recipe can make 12 miniature tarts or pies, following the same method. Lower the temperature to 325°F and bake for 15 minutes.

BISCOTTO alla PANNA

A chocolate and whipped cream roulade that is this delicate and light can only be achieved with the highest-quality cocoa powder. Very quick to make, it's a fabulous dessert.

Serves 10 Ⓔ *20 minutes & 1 hour chilling*

CAKE

4 eggs, separated

5 tablespoons sugar

Pinch of salt

¼ cup unsweetened cocoa powder

————

Preheat the oven to 350°F. Butter a 14-x-14-inch sheet of parchment paper and place on a baking sheet.

In a bowl, whisk the egg yolks and sugar together until they are pale yellow. In a clean bowl, whisk the egg whites with the salt until stiff peaks form. Fold into the yolks in three batches, fully incorporating each time. Sift in the cocoa powder and fold to incorporate, being careful not to overwork the mixture. Pour the egg mixture over the parchment paper and, working quickly, spread it evenly with a spatula, covering the surface of the parchment. Bake for 7 minutes, or until it springs back to the touch. Avoid overcooking, as the cake will become too hard and crack. Remove and let cool completely.

FILLING

1½ cups heavy cream

2 tablespoons confectioners' sugar

1 teaspoon vanilla extract

————

In a bowl, whisk all the ingredients together until soft peaks form.

ASSEMBLY

Transfer the cake, still on the parchment sheet, to a work surface. With a spatula, spread the whipped cream evenly over the cake, leaving a 1½-inch margin uncovered on one side at the top. Using the parchment paper as a guide and beginning at the side opposite the uncovered margin, roll the cake until the seam is facing down. Carefully pull the cake off the paper and place on a long serving plate. Fill the ends with any remaining whipped cream and refrigerate, loosely covered, for at least 1 hour before serving. Slice with a sharp knife so that the roulade holds its shape.

SOUFFLÉ di RICOTTA

A chocolate and ricotta cheese soufflé served with a Grand Marnier and basil cream. This is one of the most sophisticated desserts at the Country House Montali and always receives praise from guests.

Serves 8 **D** *55 minutes & 1 hour freezing*

CHOCOLATE HEARTS

2 ounces 60% bittersweet chocolate, grated

2½ tablespoons heavy cream

Warm the chocolate and heavy cream together in a double boiler over low heat until melted and smooth. Cool to room temperature. Line a small plate with plastic wrap and scoop out teaspoon-sized portions. Freeze for at least 1 hour.

BASIL ZABAGLIONE

3 egg yolks

3 tablespoons sugar

6 tablespoons Grand Marnier

⅔ cup heavy cream

5 basil leaves, finely chopped

Whisk the egg yolks and sugar together in the top of a double boiler until pale yellow. Add the Grand Marnier and cook in the double boiler, stirring, for 5 minutes or until thickened. Remove from the heat and cool over an ice bath (see page 21). Cover and refrigerate. Thirty minutes before serving, beat the zabaglione with a handheld mixer until foamy. In a bowl, whip the cream until soft peaks form. Fold the cream and basil into the zabaglione and refrigerate.

SOUFFLÉ

1 cup ricotta

2½ tablespoons honey

1½ quantities Lemon Strings (see page 29), finely chopped

1 tablespoon lemon juice

1 egg yolk

3 tablespoons sugar

2 tablespoons cornstarch

4 egg whites

Pinch of salt

Preheat the oven to 400°F. Butter eight ramekins and dust with sugar. Bring a pot of water to a boil. In a bowl, beat the ricotta with a fork until very creamy. Mix in the honey, two-thirds of the Lemon Strings, lemon juice, and egg yolk, mixing well after each addition. Sift in the sugar and cornstarch and mix. In a clean bowl, beat the egg whites and salt with a mixer to form stiff peaks. Fold gently into the ricotta mixture. Spoon 1 tablespoon of the mixture into each ramekin. Remove the chocolate hearts from the freezer. Place a chocolate heart in the center of each cup and top with another tablespoon of the mixture. Place the ramekins in a baking pan with 2-inch sides. Pour in boiling water to reach halfway up the sides of the ramekins and bake for 17 minutes.

TO SERVE

Lift the ramekins out of the water. Gently invert each soufflé onto a wide spatula, place on a plate, and serve with the Basil Zabaglione. Top with the remaining Lemon Strings.

TORTA SACHER

The story of this famous dessert comes from Vienna in 1832 when the city was the capital of the Austro-Hungarian empire. For many years there has been a dispute over the real creator of the recipe. On the one hand was Franz Sacher, the young pastry chef of Prince Von Metternich Winnesburg, and on the other was Edward Demel, manager of the most famous pastry shop in the town, at that time owned by the Hotel Sacher.

Serves 16 Ⓜ *50 minutes & 15 minutes chilling*

CAKE

5 eggs, at room temperature, separated

Pinch of salt

3/4 cup sugar

A few drops vanilla extract

2/3 cup sunflower oil

1/2 cup all-purpose flour

1/4 cup unsweetened cocoa powder

2 teaspoons baking powder

1/4 cup almond flour (almond meal)

———

Line the bottom of a 10- to 11-inch nonstick springform pan with parchment paper. Preheat the oven to 350°F. In a bowl, beat the egg yolks, the salt, 1/4 cup of the sugar, and the vanilla together with a handheld mixer until pale yellow. Pour in the oil in a steady stream, mixing constantly. In a separate bowl, sift the flour, cocoa, and baking powder together, then add the almond flour. In a clean bowl, whip the egg whites with the handheld mixer until stiff peaks form, adding the remaining 1/2 cup sugar halfway through. Add half to the yolk mixture. Sift the dry ingredients into the egg mixture in four batches, gently incorporating after each addition. Mix in the remaining egg whites. Pour the batter into the pan and bake for 35 minutes. Cool completely.

ASSEMBLY

2 cups apricot jam

———

Carefully even the top layer of the cake with a serrated knife. Slice the cake horizontally into three equal layers. Remove the top two layers and spread a third of the apricot jam over the bottom layer. Top with a layer of cake and spread with half of the remaining jam. Add the final layer of cake. Pass the remaining jam through a fine-mesh sieve, discard any solids, and coat the top and sides of the cake with a thin layer of the smooth jam. Transfer the cake to a cake stand.

GLAZE

10 ounces 70% bittersweet chocolate

1 tablespoon water

2 tablespoons sugar

1/3 cup heavy cream

———

Melt the chocolate in a double boiler over low heat. In a small saucepan, heat the water and sugar together until the sugar dissolves. Transfer the sugar syrup to a bowl. Heat the cream to a boil and immediately pour into the syrup, whisking continuously. Add the melted chocolate to the syrup and whisk quickly to incorporate well. The mixture will be bubbly. Let stand for a few minutes until the glaze is completely smooth and bubble-free (test by coating the back of a spoon for a shiny and smooth texture). Pour the warm glaze evenly over the cake, covering the surface. With a spatula, spread the glaze over the top and sides and refrigerate for 15 minutes to set the glaze. Slice and serve.

Note: For a very traditional cake, reserve a small amount of the glaze in a pastry bag fitted with a very fine tip. After the cake has chilled briefly, write "Sacher" on top of the cake with the reserved glaze.

VEGAN SACHER

This vegan version of the traditional dessert loses nothing in texture or flavor.

Serves 8 Ⓜ *50 minutes & 15 minutes chilling*

CAKE

1 cup unsweetened cocoa powder

1½ cups Italian 'OO' flour (see page 16)

1 cup sugar

½ teaspoon salt

1¼ teaspoons baking powder

1 teaspoon vanilla extract

5 tablespoons brewed espresso, cooled

6 tablespoons sunflower oil

2 tablespoons distilled white vinegar

1 cup soy milk

1 cup apricot jam, for assembly

———

Preheat the oven to 350°F. Line an 8-inch square baking pan with parchment paper with a 2-inch overhang on all sides and grease lightly. Sift the dry ingredients together into a medium bowl. In a larger bowl, stir the vanilla, espresso, oil, and vinegar together. In three batches, sift the dry ingredients into the liquid, whisking well after each addition. Mix in the soy milk. Pour the batter into the baking pan, spread evenly, and bake for 35 minutes, or until a toothpick comes out clean when inserted in the middle. Cool completely in the pan.

The assembly is the same as for the traditional Sacher.

GANACHE

2 tablespoons unsweetened cocoa powder

3 tablespoons confectioners' sugar

2 tablespoons warm espresso

2 tablespoons margarine, at room temperature

———

In a double boiler, combine all the ingredients and mix over low heat until melted and smooth. Remove from the heat. While still warm, pour evenly over the cake and spread with a spatula or knife. Cool completely and refrigerate for 15 minutes before serving.

Literally "colds." Classic Italian ice creams. What better way to spend a hot summer afternoon with your friends than tasting a variety of these? Always a favorite with children. While these recipes call for the use of an ice-cream maker, they can be made efficiently without it. Follow the procedure as given, freeze the ice cream for 20 minutes in a large bowl, whisk vigorously for 1 minute until creamy, refreeze, and repeat twice.

Chocolate Ginger
Serves 8

½ cup milk

½ cup heavy cream

1 teaspoon grated fresh ginger

2½ ounces milk chocolate, grated

2 egg yolks

¼ cup sugar

———

Combine the milk, cream, and ginger in a saucepan over medium-high heat. Bring to a boil, turn off the heat, and add the chocolate, stirring occasionally until melted. Meanwhile, in a second saucepan, whisk the egg yolks and sugar together until pale yellow. Pass the chocolate cream through a fine-mesh sieve directly into the egg mixture and whisk until well combined. Continue to whisk in a double boiler for three more minutes. Remove from the heat, cool over an ice bath (see page 21), and pass through the sieve once more. Process in an ice-cream or gelato machine for 30 to 40 minutes or according to the manufacturer's instructions. Freeze in an airtight container for up to 1 week. (Note: For a basic Chocolate Gelato, leave out the ginger.)

Licorice
Serves 8

½ teaspoon natural licorice candies, chopped

¾ cup heavy cream

1¼ cups milk

⅓ cup sugar

———

Combine all the ingredients in a double boiler over low heat. Stir until the licorice melts completely. Pour through a fine-mesh sieve to strain out any remaining solids. Cool over an ice bath (see page 21), pass through the sieve another time, and whisk to foam lightly. Process in an ice-cream or gelato machine according to the manufacturer's instructions. Freeze in an airtight container for up to 1 week.

Strawberry
Serves 8

2 cups strawberries, hulled

White wine, for rinsing fruit

Juice of 1 lemon

½ cup sugar

⅔ cup heavy cream

½ cup milk

———

Rinse the strawberries gently in white wine and discard the wine. Purée in a blender. Press through a fine-mesh sieve and discard any solids. Pour into a bowl and add the lemon juice and sugar. Mix until well incorporated. Add the cream and milk and whisk until the mixture is creamy. Process in a gelato or ice-cream machine for 30 to 40 minutes or according to the manufacturer's instructions. Freeze in an airtight container for up to 1 week.

Amaretto and Apricot

Serves 8

5 dried apricots, finely chopped
Grand Marnier, for plumping
1/2 cup heavy cream
3/4 cup milk

1/4 cup sugar
1/2 cup fresh apricot purée
2 teaspoons lemon juice
8 amaretti cookies, crushed

———

Combine the dried apricots and enough Grand Marnier to cover them in a small saucepan. Heat for 2 minutes, drain, and set the apricots aside. In a bowl, beat the cream and milk with the sugar, apricot purée, and lemon juice. Process in a gelato or ice-cream machine for 30 to 40 minutes or according to the manufacturer's instructions. When the gelato is nearly done, fold in the liqueur-infused apricots and the crushed amaretti. Finish processing. Freeze in an airtight container for up to 1 week.

The apricots can be replaced by the same quantity of peaches.

Lemon

Serves 8

3/4 cup milk
3/4 cup heavy cream
Juice of 3 lemons

2/3 cup sugar
1/4 cup Limoncello

———

In a bowl, whisk all ingredients together until airy. Process in an ice-cream or gelato machine according to the manufacturer's instructions. Freeze in an airtight container for up to 1 week.

Avocado

Serves 8

2 ripe avocados, peeled and pits removed
Juice of 1 lemon
5 tablespoons sugar

1/2 cup heavy cream
1/2 cup milk
1/3 cup sweetened condensed milk

———

Purée the avocados in a blender with the lemon juice and sugar. Add the remaining ingredients and blend for an additional minute. Process in an ice-cream or gelato machine for 30 to 40 minutes or according to the manufacturer's instructions. Freeze in an airtight container for up to 1 week.

Coconut
Serves 8

1 cup coconut milk
2/3 cup heavy cream
2/3 cup milk

1/4 cup sugar
1 vanilla bean, split lengthwise and tiny seeds
   scraped out with the tip of a knife

———

In a bowl, beat all the ingredients together. Pour through a fine-mesh sieve and process in an ice-cream or gelato machine for 30 to 40 minutes or according to the manufacturer's instructions. Freeze in an airtight container for up to 1 week.

Mango
Serves 8

2 ripe mangoes, peeled and pits removed
1/2 cup heavy cream

1/2 cup milk
2/3 cup sweetened condensed milk

———

Purée the mangoes in a blender and pour through a fine-mesh sieve to strain out the solids. In a bowl, whip the pureé with the remaining ingredients. Process in an ice-cream or gelato machine for 30 to 40 minutes or according to the manufacturer's instructions. Freeze in an airtight container for up to 1 week.

Mint and Basil
Serves 8

12 mint leaves, rinsed and dried
10 basil leaves, rinsed and dried
1 1/2 cups milk

1 1/2 cups heavy cream
5 egg yolks
1/2 cup sugar

———

Freeze the mint and basil leaves for 10 minutes. Chop and freeze again until needed. In a saucepan, bring the milk and cream to a boil, then remove from the heat. In the top of a double boiler, whisk the egg yolks with the sugar until pale yellow. Pour the milk into the eggs while whisking constantly. Cook the mixture in the double boiler until thickened to the point of coating a wooden spoon, approximately 5 minutes. Cool completely over an ice bath (see page 21) and strain through a fine-mesh sieve. Mix in the frozen herbs. Process in an ice-cream or gelato machine for 30 to 40 minutes or according to the manufacturer's instructions. Freeze in an airtight container for up to 1 week.

Carrot, Orange, and Limoncello Sorbet
Serves 8

2 carrots, peeled and grated
1 cup orange juice
1 cup water
3 tablespoons lemon juice

Finely grated zest of 1 lemon
3 tablespoons Limoncello
1/2 cup sugar

———

Purée all the ingredients together in a blender. Process in a gelato or ice-cream machine for 30 to 40 minutes or according to the manufacturer's instructions. Transfer to an airtight container and freeze for up to 1 week.

This sorbet is wonderful to clean and refresh the palate between courses.

Rum Raisin
Serves 8

2 egg yolks

½ cup sugar

1 cup milk

⅔ cup heavy cream

5 tablespoons raisins

1 tablespoon rum, plus more for rehydrating

———

Beat the egg yolks and sugar together in the top of a double boiler until pale yellow. Combine the milk and cream in a saucepan over medium-high heat. Bring to a boil, turn off the heat, and pass through a fine-mesh sieve into the egg mixture. Cook in the double boiler for 3 minutes, whisking continuously. Remove from the heat, cool over an ice bath (see page 21), and process in a gelato or ice-cream machine for 30 to 40 minutes or according to the manufacturer's instructions. Meanwhile, rinse the raisins, place in a saucepan with enough rum to cover, and simmer. Drain and cool completely. When the ice cream is almost done, add the raisins and the 1 tablespoon rum. Freeze in an airtight container for up to 1 week.

Hazelnut – Vegan
Serves 4

1¼ cups soy milk

¼ cup soy cream

½ cup chopped hazelnuts

1 tablespoon hazelnut butter

2 tablespoons brown sugar

———

Mix all the ingredients together in a double boiler and cook over low heat until the sugar has completely dissolved. Cool over an ice bath (see page 21), then pour through a fine-mesh sieve. Whip lightly for 30 seconds, then process in a gelato or ice-cream machine for 30 to 40 minutes or according to the manufacturer's instructions. Transfer to an airtight container and freeze for up to 1 week.

Chocolate – Vegan
Serves 4

1 cup soy milk

½ cup soy cream

2 ounces fine-quality bittersweet chocolate

3 tablespoons sugar

———

Mix all the ingredients together in a double boiler and cook over low heat until the sugar has completely dissolved. Cool over an ice bath (see page 21). Pour through a fine-mesh sieve. Whip lightly for 30 seconds, then process in a gelato or ice-cream machine for 30 to 40 minutes or according to the manufacturer's instructions. Transfer to an airtight container and freeze for up to 1 week.

When the telephone rang that day, I thought it was someone trying to sell me something. The person on the phone was a bit too kind, calling from overseas, and it sounded a bit like when someone calls you to ask you to advertise in the daily paper. It took me a little while to realize the man was instead phoning from London and looking for a company capable of doing "live" cooking courses at an upcoming Earls Court event. He told me a little about the new, innovative entertaining plan his company had just developed. I immediately found the idea very interesting and thought it was an absolutely new concept.

The idea of a big open cooking school at a big open event in one of the oldest English exhibition centers in central London was fun, and it hadn't been done before. Many cooking schools were on television or in hotels but not at a big city event.

Coincidentally, I had already planned to be in London on business, so I said, "OK. Let's talk in Earls Court on Wednesday." And that's what we did. I met the lovely Silvia, show manager of Brandevent. She was not the actual person who had called on the phone, but she was just as pleasant.

Brandevent is a major UK company for public events. Among the different programs offered within the exhibition itself was a cooking school, and the possibility of being part of it looked like a lot of fun. People doing the cooking courses would be learning some great recipes from some highly qualified chefs and would be seen by thousands of other people passing by. A bit like being on a television show. Quite exciting! You could be in the show yourself, as well.

So we decided to participate, and we also offered to bring quite a big team: one executive chef, two sous-chefs, one apprentice chef, two waitresses, myself, and also my little boy of eleven, who, it was decided, was not going to miss such an event.

We realized it could very quickly turn into a lot of work, with a lot of very stressful moments, but we were on board.

I am usually considered a bit of a pain because of my pedantic perfectionism, but this means I simply love to work with real professionals — and I love to work with such a good team as the one in Earls Court for those days. I arrived a few days before the official opening, as I wanted to enjoy all of the processes on the spot, and also because I was expecting that a big cooking school would have many technical problems as well.

I was frightened when, on my arrival at the enormous Earls Court ground just two days before the event, I found that they were just ready to start. I thought they were very late! The first person who was very helpful to me in that crowd was Peter, a very nice Welshman working for many years at these kinds of events. From his long experience, he told me immediately, "Don't worry, everybody thinks the same when they come to such a vast event for the first time. They always think everything is late." And it was true.

But a crowd of builders, plumbers, electricians, and painters arrived, and the funniest and most exciting part of the show started. In my life, I have had to build different stone houses, which not only has helped to give me chronic backache but also has created an interest in *doing*, or watching, any good artisan attending his craft. It was so impressive to see such a number of people and all with great skill. And all working eighteen hours a day! I simply loved the feeling.

Only once before in my life had I assisted on something similar, but on a much bigger scale: building a city in two days during a Kumbha Mela in Allahabad, India. There, on the banks of the River Ganges, they literally established a complete temporary city out of nothing, as the monsoons washed away everything a few months later, and all for fifteen million people. But that's another story.

Still, it had been an exciting experience that my son loved seeing as well, watching an enormous ground, almost deserted, turn so quickly into an Italian piazza with its bars and restaurants and hundreds of the most sophisticated shops and boutiques selling goods from a Castle in Apulia to homemade Sicilian gelato or perfectly tailored leather gloves, among other things.

Naturally, the stands were made of plastic or the lightest material, as they were supposed to last only three days. Our stand was one of the most complicated from a technical standpoint, because, of course, one can easily sell cashmere scarves in a plastic shop, but not make food.

To have an open kitchen in an open place, and with unknown people with unknown health backgrounds, is a real challenge in modern times, considering all the British and international health rules! Luckily, the overall location was great, and Brandevent spared no expense, creating a really big space with an metal table for every single person in the school. The best of hygiene was provided at all times. Still, in the final confrontation with the health inspector of Olympia and Earls Court, we had to face a problem that had never arisen before.

"What are you going to do with the food that will be produced by the participants of your cooking classes?" was the question that a very elegant and educated gentleman asked me while I was watching the school being built. I hadn't thought about it yet, so I said, "Well, if they have made it, I think they can eat it." Then I added that I would have never allowed them to give the food to another, thinking of the millions of laws.

I learned instead that we could teach cooking to members of the public who asked for the lessons, but we were responsible (and had to sign a document) for prohibiting the participants from eating their own food. I was already thinking that someone who has just spent forty-five frantic minutes, with hundreds of people watching, working hard to try to do something not particularly simple, was going to have his food not only taken away from him but thrown away . . . well, no way! Fortunately, after hearing differing opinions, the health inspector finally decided that we could allow the people to eat what they prepared.

God bless the guy. It was so funny when, at the end of the show, a German woman watching the food show armed herself with a plastic spoon, went up to a participant of the school who was enjoying her just finished tiramisu, and simply took a big spoonful of her dessert uninvited. I was scared. I could have gone to jail for that! When I said to the woman that she was breaking 154 different rules, she told me, smiling, she was scared that instead she could get some illness from the other woman! Well those are, of course, things that happen when you have fifteen thousand people around.

It was so much fun. We have done cooking courses for ten years at our resort, but it is one thing to run a course in your own kitchen where you know everything and every place. It is another to do it in a place that did not even exist two hours before . . . and having EXACTLY forty-five minutes to do it! Of course, the first time we did it, we took sixty minutes, and we had to fly to do the cleaning, to be ready for the next course in time! But the second one was 100 percent precise, and from that moment on, we knew how to do it.

There was so much pleasure to be found in such an international environment, with so many things going on at the same time. The Earls Court event will remain one of the best memories of our working life. The whole event was a big success, and I also hope that people learned to cook something.

—Alberto Musacchio

LA DOLCE VITA

Italy. The simple name carries with it an air of elegance and delicious charm. It boasts the birthplace of unparalleled artists, architectural wonders, and gastronomic delights. It is the land of pleasure, style, and fashion. It is Audrey Hepburn and Cary Grant on a *Roman Holiday*, enjoying gelato and cappuccino, taking motorbike rides to faraway villas.

La Dolce Vita, the most commonly used and profoundly accurate term to describe Italy, was also the title of a three-day expo in Earls Court, London.

Exhibiting the most splendid elements of Italian living from property ownership to Venetian glass jewelry to freshly cut aged Parmigiano Reggiano, the event attracted thousands of potential buyers, gourmands, and curious locals who read the morning paper.

The Country House Montali had been invited by La Dolce Vita's organizers to teach three cooking courses for each day of the event. As there were only two other chefs and six total cooking classes per day, this was clearly an honor for Alberto and Malu. They planned every detail, shopped for materials, and worked on recipes. They bought plane tickets for six of their best former staff from all over the world. They packed the truck with as many nonperishable goods as possible, and Alberto and Janko left three days in advance to make the drive to London. Even when the brake pedal in the car stopped functioning properly during his two-day drive, Alberto wouldn't let something small like that slow him down. "Well, Janko," he said as he sped through France, "it looks like we won't be able to use the brakes for a while!" By chance, Malu had heard from a friend the night before she was to leave that all flights in and out of Rome had been canceled. Beloved Pope John Paul II had passed away just the day before, and great security measures were being taken to prepare the Vatican City for the arrival and gathering of world leaders for the pope's funeral. Rather than departing from Rome Ciampino, Malu was now redirected to fly from Pescara, adding hours of driving to her itinerary. After leaving early the next morning, Malu checked in at Pescara Airport with Damiano and Grace. She then made her way to the information counter to secure their return flight back to the same airport. Fortunately, she was at the front of the line when an announcement was made over the intercom: "Attention, all travelers," it began, "all inbound and outbound flights from Pescara Airport have been canceled. Please direct all questions to the information counter. I repeat…" For three seconds there was a lull throughout the small airport before a massive stampede toward the tiny information counter, where sat two poor administrators with eyes as big as dinner plates. Malu, with three hundred angry, frustrated, and bickering travelers lining up behind her, somehow managed to convince the supervising administrator that she was his top priority. "I am expected at a manifestation of Italian culture of the highest importance! You must get me and my team to London tonight!" While others had told her that there were no outbound flights whatsoever until the next morning, the manager searched frantically and landed her a flight departing in three hours from Bologna-Forli, a two-hour minimum drive from Pescara.

After profusely thanking the kind gentleman, she grabbed Damiano, Grace, and all their belongings and raced them out of the automatic doors and into the car, and she sped back onto the autostrada.

Meanwhile, in London, Alberto was busy setting up and making moves of his own. He had been informed weeks earlier that cooking course participants would not be permitted to actually eat what they made during the course and had accidentally voiced his opinion on the matter to the health and safety director of the event. "How can these people be forbidden to eat what they make themselves? They paid for this event. I would hate to be forbidden to taste my own food in a cooking class."

The director responded, "Quite right. Okay, we'll change that rule." Alberto was stunned for a few minutes, and then walked back to his team to let them know of the changes.

Afterward, they went to a classy new Turkish restaurant where Alberto had made reservations long before. He had heard from his wife that there were problems leaving Italy, but he assured his team that she would be there.

"Don't worry," he said. "My wife is the type of person to throw herself in front of a moving plane and yell, 'You get me to London right now!' Whatever the problems, she'll find a way to get here tonight."

After numerous cappuccino and restroom stops along the Autostrada, Malu made it to Bologna-Forli, but it wasn't until their plane had actually lifted off that Malu's nerves lessened. When the plane landed in London and began taxiing for an abnormal period of time, Malu began nervously checking her watch again.

"This is ridiculous. Why won't they let us off the plane? We have to catch the last train to central London! We have to get there tonight!" Her anxiety built and, as soon as everyone unloaded, she cried, "Run, baby, run!" The three raced through the terminal toward the shuttle service that would take them to baggage claim and customs.

In customs, the three of them waited in the short line under the sign, "Origin: European Union." The young airport agent took one look at Grace's American passport and said, "I'm sorry, but you have to go through the non-EU line." Grace turned and looked to her right where all non-EU people were waiting in the longest, windiest line she had ever seen that didn't appear to be moving at all. She glanced from panic-stricken Malu to the ticket agent and stammered, "But I flew from Italy!" "It doesn't matter," he responded flatly.

"Listen, we're in a rush. Is there any way I can do this quickly?" "You'll have to go through the line like everyone else." She ran to the middle of the line and said, "Excuse me, but how long have you been waiting for?" "Forty-five minutes" was the reply.

She ran back to Malu and said, "Malu, this line is going to take forever. At least an hour!" "No, you make it to the front. Do what you have to do, but go to the front of the line!" Grace glanced toward the front and, making no effort to hide her emotion, went to the third person in line and said, "I'm very sorry to have to ask you this, but I'm in such a hurry, and I have to be on a train in ten minutes. Would you mind letting me in?" While the person kindly obliged, a string of travelers cursed her from behind.

After a few minutes, the three made their way past baggage claim and hurried to the mass-transit area.

Due to construction there were no trains, but buses in their place, and they managed to catch one just as it was leaving for central London. They arrived by taxi at the hotel on Bedford Avenue at two o'clock in the morning to the sight of Alberto, Janko, Agnes, Marketa, and Matthew. Despite being exhausted, they had all waited up for Malu in the lobby and greeted her with drowsy eyes and drooping postures.

Malu, on the other hand, looked like she had woken up from a deep, energizing sleep.

Sitting down, they chatted for a few minutes, agreed on a time to meet the next morning and went to their hotel rooms. Lying on her bed, Grace folded her hands behind her head and thought to herself, "Okay. We're here. The hard part is over!" The following morning, it wasn't the noise of loud morning commuters and blaring car horns outside the Bedford Hotel that woke the three girls. It was the piercing sound of the telephone at 6:30 in the morning that jolted them out of bed.

"Mmmm… Hello?" Marketa groggily answered.

"Good morning! Its time to run!" Alberto was calling from the lobby, his unmistakable voice awfully cheery so early in the morning.

Fifteen minutes later, bathed and dressed, Agnes, Marketa, and Grace made their way down to the lobby to meet the rest of the Montali team. After a quick breakfast, they sat down together to delegate the work for the rest of the day. "Now, I want us all to be there by nine in the morning, so we need to run to the nearest Tesco to pick up a few things and then hurry to Earls Court! Everybody, grab your things!" Malu, Alberto, and their entourage raced out the door into the early morning fog of central London.

At a large Tesco near King's Cross, they raced through the aisles picking up perishables like dairy, herbs, and vegetables, paid at the counter, and raced to the nearest tube. Damiano's arms were laden with chef jackets and uniforms in garment bags as he strode alongside Marketa, who was holding three trays of eggs in one hand. Alberto, walking behind her, shouted, "Nobody bump Marketa! She cannot drop those eggs!" A hair's breadth before nine, the team made it to Earls Court in time to see a long queue forming outside awaiting the opening. After flashing their exhibitor cards, they ran inside and weaved through the various booths and displays packed inside the hall toward one of the storage rooms. There was no time for separation of gender. Everyone piled into one room and changed from street clothes into their Montali uniforms. Wrapping bandannas around their heads, they chased after Alberto, who was headed for the cooking school area.

There they had the pleasure of meeting the two other Italian chefs with whom they would share the cooking school. The two had been living and working in the UK for a long time, gaining national respect.

Alberto and Malu decided months earlier that they were going to have interactive, unique dishes, and that each lesson would focus on a different thing. This was their chance to shine. In the afternoon they were scheduled for three forty-five-minute slots with fifteen minutes of resting and cleaning time in between.

Everyone mistakenly believed that minimal prep work would be needed. They would be at Earls Court for six hours, maximum.

"What is wrong with this plastic wrap?" Matthew cried out as he struggled to tear the plastic. The perforator had detached and he did not have the time to look for it. Grunting, he tore the plastic with his hands and attempted to wrap it around a bowl of chopped nuts. The cheap plastic refused to adhere to the bowl and clumped loosely. "Argh!" he shouted.

Janko looked over at Matthew from the metal cart where he was chopping tomatoes for the calzoni stuffing. With each move of his knife, the unsteady metal cart shook loudly. He bit his lip in annoyance and carried on.

Malu, trying to keep her thoughts organized while simultaneously greeting various event organizers who came to introduce themselves, found herself scanning the floor for her husband. She turned to Agnes by the dish station and asked, "Do you know where Alberto is?" Agnes pointed to the other side of the cooking school area where Alberto was discussing logistical issues with one of the coordinators. She started walking over to him when Grace approached her. "Malu! I don't know what's wrong with the oven, but the cake is not baking!" "What?" The Torta di Cioccolato e Noci was scheduled to be the third lesson of the day, and they needed to have a few cakes cooked and cooled in advance to serve at the end of the lesson.

She ran to the oven and stuck her hand inside to get a feel for the temperature. The temperature gauge was set correctly and the oven was hot, but not hot enough. "Damn!" Grace stuck her hand inside as well. Shaking her head, she looked up at Malu and started pulling her hand out, when she suddenly felt a searing jolt of pain. In her distracted state, she had burned her hand on the inside of the oven. She bit her lip, cursing. Malu grabbed her hand to look at it and said, "Go and put some cream on it right away!" As Grace ran off, Malu attempted to track down a maintenance officer to see about the oven temperature.

The first five hours of preparation flew by as everyone, Damiano included, was consumed by their own set of responsibilities while trying to stay out of one another's way. A little after one in the afternoon, Malu pulled Marketa outside and put a few bills in her hand. "Go and find us some lunch, and grab a few beers!" Finding a filling lunch shouldn't be too much of a problem. They were at La Dolce Vita where gastronomic delights were aplenty.

Unfortunately, as Marketa and Agnes searched through the maze, they discovered that food stands did not accept cash, only tickets issued for La Dolce Vita participants. Instead, they had to purchase premade sandwiches from the Earls Court café. They stocked up on brie and arugula sandwiches for everyone and brought them back to their station. Everyone was shaking from hunger, but there just was not enough time to eat! Putting her foot down, Malu demanded that they at least eat in shifts. The girls were the first to eat, and they sat in a confined storage space and rapidly ate their lunch in silence. Halfway through her sandwich, Grace looked up at the other two and asked, "Do your jaws hurt from chewing so hard? Ouch." Marketa and Agnes nodded and laughed.

As insane as the preparatory work had been, nothing could have prepared them for the actual cooking classes. In between the sessions, Damiano raced around madly, wiping down all the work tables and setting out portioned quantities of various ingredients. The chefs were called to walk around the tables during the sessions to help the participants, while running behind the scene to finish preparing for the following courses.

"Why is it we have nothing here we need, but too much of what we don't?" Janko speculated while look-ing at the cluttered dumbwaiter in search of a whisk. Finding none and no decent alternative, he grabbed a plastic fork and went to work beating eggs.

"Chef?" Malu called out during session two. She ran to the back and asked one of the chefs, "Where is the fourth demonstration dough for the calzoni?" "What? I thought I only had to do three!" Seeing Malu's panic-stricken face, she grabbed the second demonstration dough, portioned off half and said, "Use this!" Without a word, Malu grabbed the soft, sticky dough and raced back to the front stage.

The rest of the day continued on in the same fanatical manner until nine in the evening when the last of the event participants walked out of the door.

The cooking school area and the backstage were piled with partially used ingredients and materials everywhere. Stacks of bowls, pots, and cutting boards caked with dough sat in the sink, while half-empty boxes were strewn across the floor, hastily ripped open in a desperate moment of need. Malu, ignoring the mess for the time being, brought out two bottles of wine and a large wedge of cheese and distributed glasses among her staff. "Va bene, ragazzi. You did a great job today." Everyone droopily raised their glasses in appreciation, drank, and went back to cleaning for the next hour.

As they walked out of Earls Court, Alberto was all smiles. "Everyone was so happy today! Good job. Tomorrow morning we meet at the same time."

The next two days continued on in the same frantic manner. Without the comforts of the Montali kitchen, everyone was forced to invent makeshift solutions to their problems. Ciabattas were made in soup pots, pints of espresso were brewed two ounces at a time, and kilos of mushrooms were In a sauté pan, sautéed in three-minute windows. Along with never having enough cooking supplies and utensils, there was one severely flawed oven for the entire cooking school, two outlets, one stove, and never enough space. The same brie and arugula sandwiches were hastily eaten in shifts in the tiny storage closet, but later Marketa and Agnes bartered with a nearby espresso stand, exchanging pizza for coffee.

By the third day, a natural rhythm had been found. The staff, having a clearer idea of the structure of the day as well as what materials were available, worked more smoothly and were able to anticipate Malu's needs in advance. The major source of anxiety was the La Dolce Vita birthday cake that Alberto had insisted on for the closing celebration. "I want an enormous chocolate cake, covered in rich chocolate ganache, decorated with whipped cream and with fireworks on top.

"Wow, fireworks . . . that sounds new!" was the staff's immediate answer.

With the limited use of one poor oven and the lack of baking pans, the chefs baked a total of twelve flourless chocolate nut cakes over a period of eight hours while managing the prep work and helping during the cooking classes. With the exhibition hall closing earlier that evening, Alberto wanted the cake to be presented at six o'clock. By 6:15, there was an explosion of cocoa powder, the cream still needed to be whipped, and Janko and Malu were busy assembling the delicate twelve cakes on a large wooden board.

"Go, baby, go! We need this cake right now!" said Alberto, anxious to respect the time schedule and seeing they were late.

"Don't stress me!" she half-joked as she focused her attention on smoothing the crumbling edges.

In five minutes, she was finished with the assembly and she and her husband cautiously placed the candles around the edge while writing "La Dolce Vita Year One" across the cake.

Alberto passed out matches to four of his staff and said, "When we get there, light all the candles at once and let's do it all together. Last will be the fireworks!" They rolled the cake across the exhibition floor to the main office where everyone had gathered.

The candles were lit and crackling lights crowned the cake. The director of the event was beside himself and broke out champagne bottles while everyone hurried to grab a slice.

In that joyful final moment, both the organizer and the workers reunited to spend a very emotional moment together. "No one has ever done a good wishes cake for us," said the chief executive of the main organization. Hard work had been done, and it

all had been a big triumph. La Dolce Vita 2005 could definitely be filed as a big success! After having all enjoyed a nice piece of cake, chefs and waitress came back to the stall.

There, Malu had lovingly set up more slices of cheese and bread and glasses of wine for her staff.

"It's all over now, we can collapse indeed!" she laughed with them.

Of the four chefs and two waitresses, only a few of them had met each other prior to the event, having worked different seasons. They had little time to interact socially or get to know each other during the event, but later that night, as they sat together at an Indian restaurant, they laughed as old friends and shared hilarious knee-slapping stories of their own Montali experiences. Spending so many months with Malu and Alberto in the lifestyle of the Country House had formed a unique bond among them, despite their diverse backgrounds. While the prospect of going to London had been exciting, they all knew they were not there on holiday. After years apart, they still felt a strong commitment to Malu and Alberto, two people they had come to know and love as family. It was their devotion to them and Montali for which they put forth so much of their time and energy. It was stressful, frustrating, and exhausting to the point of hilarity. But to them, it was just like old times.

Henry Togna once said, "A hotelier must be a diplomat, a democrat, an autocrat, an acrobat, and a doormat. He must have the facility to entertain prime ministers, princes of industry, pickpockets, gamblers, bookmakers, pirates, philanthropists, popsies, and prudes." He meant, of course, that it is a necessity in this kind of profession to always be ready with an appropriate answer under any circumstance.

As I started running restaurants and entertaining people at a very young age, I have been trying to learn this all my life, even if not always successful. Still, I would hope I have developed quick-thinking reactions while conversing with others, because this is often required in hotel life. There are always many people around and many conversations going on.

Nevertheless, the day in which two California women checked into my hotel, I ended up, for the first time of my working life, absolutely tongue-tied. As one of the two women was quite a bit older than the other, I politely asked if they were sisters. A good hotelier would never make the mistake of asking if they were mother and daughter, because if they were actually sisters, he would be in trouble. As I was trying to be charming, I did ask them, but, to my major surprise, I received an honest and unexpected answer from the oldest lady, "Oh, no. We are lesbians!" I said, "Wow, congratulations . . . no, oops." What can you answer to someone, absolutely unknown to you, who tells you about her private life on first meeting? But now I have learned my lesson. Now when I see two women with an age difference, I don't ask, "Are you sisters?" I just directly ask, "Are you lesbians?" and I have seen it work! Well, hotel life. "How many stories behind those walls!" Ours is a small country resort thankfully, with a very good clientele.

People don't "pass by" our place, as it is five miles in the middle of nowhere. All our guests have really made an effort to book, fly, drive, and come all the way up to Montali. All this creates a very friendly and elegant crowd, quite happy to have a nice relaxing time, conversing with other people and enjoying the best food. People are generally not here for a single night in a marathon of "touring Europe in 15 days." The attraction of the food, moreover, tends to bring people from many different countries and with many different views, as well as those with a spe-

cific diet. We work, for example, with many Jewish people, both from Israel and the U.S., and I find the kosher approach to vegetarianism interesting.

We cater to specific tailormade diets for many other groups: vegan, people with gluten problems, dairy allergies, egg-free diets, and many new modern allergies and food intolerances, as well.

We had a case of a client intolerant to 90 percent of the possible products in the world, being allergic to a very common element present in nearly everything. We could only use six ingredients in total to make all her food. Of course, my wife, every day for a week, wanted to create the usual four full gourmet courses especially for her! But to keep varying four courses for seven nights, with only six ingredients both for sweet and for savory dishes was definitely not easy!

That was a real culinary challenge that later became a big lesson for us. I remember the emotions when, at the end of her stay, the nice woman came to thank my wife and the kitchen staff for the effort of making such varied food, in such quantities, and with that level of difficulty.

All this just for her! Sadly she added how she had not been able to go to any restaurants for a good 13 years because of her illness. The chefs felt immediately proud of their job, and no one felt tired that night, despite the amount of hard work that been done.

I still remember my wife telling me months later how interesting she had found that specific culinary experience. To have been forced, for a full week, to cook with only a limited number of products had gotten her involved in a kind of molecularly different food dimension. Any taste she wanted to create had to be produced with only those few ingredients. This was highly unusual considering that we usually use at least 26 different kinds of cheese in our kitchen. Yes, only cheese! You can imagine that the number of entire ingredients in a professional kitchen can go up to hundreds. She found she really had to enter the molecular inner world of those six materials to try to develop as many new tastes as possible if she wanted to succeed in the challenge. Of course, you have to develop to always keep changing the taste of the same product.

But she discovered some new, interesting means of doing it.

She generally started by using one single ingredient of the six. Then she would try to modify it by heating the ingredient, by shaking it, by roasting it, by stirring it, by shaking and heating it, then by mixing it with another product and then again heating or shaking or . . .

No longer was it the usual recipe, such as 2 pounds tomato and 4 pounds potato, which you just cook and mix together. Rather, it was more like, "three warm molecules of corn oil heated to 115°F, mixed with other two molecules that have been grilled at 350°F, and then mixed with half the sugar already steamed at 250°F."

Pure alchemy! As a professional chef you would never tend to cook like this, as you can achieve the same taste much more quickly using more ingredients. But not having the ingredients, this was the only way. For a good chef like Malu, it was a real "taste sublimation test." It was a real journey through palate, brain, and stomach to check how the brain could fool the palate with the help of the stomach! This was a real goal in culinary life. If that gentle lady has been thankful to my wife for such food, my wife was surely even more grateful for having had the chance to undergo such a journey in the culinary sciences.

Some satisfaction, some hard times — that's how life goes. I am just happy that we never had to face any terrible customers in our little resort. Just try to imagine, for example, how difficult times can be working in top-quality hotels. So often, the aim of big-spending guests is to give the people working there a hard time, as a kind of personal gratification and justification for spending so much. The manager of the Mandarin Hotel once wrote that the most demanding customer of his working life had been a pop star who didn't like . . . the wallpaper of the room. The problem came when she wanted it to be changed before the end of the day. You can imagine.

Our guests are so varied; none, luckily, so demanding. A lot of musicians, artist, intellectuals, gourmets.

Many nationalities, as well. In the kitchen last year spoke English, Polish, American, Korean, Slovakian, Spanish, Portuguese, Swedish, and eventually Italian, too. My son was driven mad.

Some customers have definitely left us with nice memories. Some have left us with a good laugh. I remember a couple from the UK coming to dinner with a big bottle of Moet et Chandon for us and the staff, as they had just heard that Montali had been chosen for a BBC holiday program.

A California woman once made my day when I went to announce that food was ready. She called me to a corner to tell me privately that she was . . . a vegetarian, but she would have been happy to eat even a simple salad, as she didn't want to create any inconvenience to my staff. She had booked three nights in our resort and didn't notice the place is fully vegetarian. This was a happy accident, considering how she ended up loving the food. She made my day full of fun and the chefs made her three days worthwhile with their food.

Of course, we sometimes get the opposite case, where people book without noticing the place is exclusively vegetarian. I recall an elderly couple from Belgium, speaking very little English (and, of course, no Italian). The husband started to shout at his wife in front of me when I told them that the food was only vegetarian. She had chosen the hotel from a tour operator's catalog, but she thought it was only an option to the regular food, and so the gentleman got really mad at her (and me) for having booked here. The funny part was that he started to enjoy the food so much, he literally licked every plate. I was almost saying, "Hey, weren't you the person who didn't want to eat here at all?" When you work with people, you don't always get only the good ones.

But you must always try to please everyone. That is your only goal.

That is why you are there. The important thing at the end, is that, when someone leaves your door, he will take something with him: hopefully some good energy, perhaps some nice food, definitely a pleasant relaxing memory. I always teach my wait staff that the most important thing to leave a client with is a beautiful warm smile. Arm yourself with a good sense of humor and you will manage to succeed, smiling through your life.

There is no better sentence to conclude the book than what Daniel said once in the kitchen, "My favorite vegetable is bacon!!" That's the philosophy of how to work in a vegetarian hotel.

—Alberto Musacchio

INDEX

Q